W9-ANO-348

TO

_____

FROM

_____

YOU CAN'T SCHEDULE STUPIDITY

A DILBERT® BOOK
BY
SCOTT ADAMS

Andrews McMeel
Publishing

Kansas City

ISBN: 0-8362-5632-8

YOU CAN'T
SCHEDULE STUPIDITY

THIS HELPS A LOT.
I'M STILL WORKING ON THE LIST OF "MUST DO" "B" PRIORITIES.

WELL, WHEN YOU FACTOR IN HOW YOU'RE SAVING THE PLANET BY NOT DRIVING, YOU ONLY OWE ONE HOUR.
AND THIS MEETING COUNTS.

THE RESULT...

DID YOU JUST SEND AN OBSCENE MESSAGE TO YOUR BOSS?
NO... I THINK I HIT THE GROUP CODE.

WE'RE HAVING AN ISO 9000 AUDIT THIS WEEK.

TAKE A LOOK AT YOUR DOCUMENTED JOB DESCRIPTIONS AND MAKE SURE THAT IT'S WHAT YOU'RE DOING IF THE AUDITOR ASKS.

ACCORDING TO THIS I'M SOME SORT OF ENGINEER.
AS IF WE'D HAVE TIME FOR THAT...

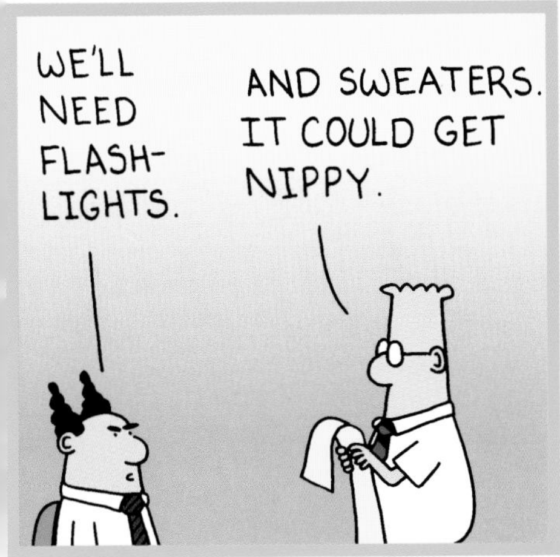
WE'LL NEED FLASH-LIGHTS.
AND SWEATERS. IT COULD GET NIPPY.

ALICE, YOU'VE BEEN WORKING EIGHTEEN HOURS A DAY. I REALIZED I MUST ADD A PERSON TO THE EFFORT.

SO I HIRED A NIGHT SHIFT MANAGER. AFTER I GO HOME AT FIVE O'CLOCK HE'LL TAKE OVER AND ASK WHY YOU'RE BEHIND SCHEDULE.

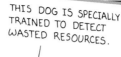

HERE'S MY TIME SHEET, INCLUDING GUESSES FOR THE NEXT TWO DAYS SO I CAN MEET YOUR ARBITRARY CLERICAL DEADLINE.

IF ANYTHING IMPORTANT COMES UP, I'LL IGNORE IT TO PRESERVE THE INTEGRITY OF THE TIME-REPORTING SYSTEM.

ARE YOU FINISHED ANNOYING ME YET?
ACCORDING TO MY TIME SHEET I'LL BE HERE FOR ANOTHER 14 MINUTES.

LET'S HAVE A LITTLE PREMEETING TO PREPARE FOR THE MEETING TOMORROW.

WHOA! DO YOU THINK IT'S SAFE TO JUMP RIGHT INTO THE PREMEETING WITHOUT PLANNING IT?

OKAY, LET'S GET THIS PRELIMINARY PREMEETING MEETING GOING.
YOU THINK YOU'RE FUNNY, BUT YOU'RE NOT.

JUST GIVE ME A THOUSAND MOCK-UPS. THE FIRST ONE WAS TERRIFIC!
THE MOCK-UP WAS OUR COMPETITOR'S PRODUCT WITH DUCT TAPE OVER THE LOGO.

AND THEN YOU'LL HAVE ENOUGH TIME?
NO, THEN I'LL GIVE YOUR PARENTS THIS PAMPHLET ON CONTRACEPTION.

AND I NEED IT YESTERDAY.
I USED TO THINK THAT WAS JUST A FIGURE OF SPEECH.

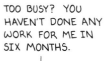

THE CONVERSATION WENT
DOWNHILL FROM THERE.

Their eyes met and Trent felt a quick pitch of his heart. One word filled his mind. *Innocent.*

Unexpected guilt passed through him in a painful ripple of unease. *Get hold of yourself, Mueller. This woman is nothing more than a means to an end.*

He hardened his heart as he had too many times in the past six months.

"You are an expert dancer, Mrs. Elliott." He put only a hint of his usual charm in his voice, just enough to avoid increasing the woman's suspicion of him. "I always enjoy a partner who knows—"

"Please, Mr. Mueller," Savannah cut him off midsentence, her eyes filled with distress. "I would prefer you not call me Mrs. Elliott."

Interesting, but not surprising, especially considering the way her husband had died. "What name would you prefer?"

She lowered her lashes, sighed softly, and then lifted her gaze back to his. "Savannah will do."

"All right, Savannah. Since we're dispensing of formalities…" He swept her across the dance floor with smooth, graceful steps. "Call me Trent."

Her unexpected smile hit him like a sucker punch.

Books by Renee Ryan

Love Inspired Historical

The Marshal Takes a Bride
Hannah's Beau
Heartland Wedding
Loving Bella
Dangerous Allies
The Lawman Claims His Bride
Courting the Enemy

*Charity House

Love Inspired

Homecoming Hero

RENEE RYAN

grew up in a small Florida beach town. To entertain herself during countless hours of "lying out" she read all the classics. It wasn't until the summer between her sophomore and junior years at Florida State University that she read her first romance novel. Hooked from page one, she spent hours consuming one book after another while working on the best (and last!) tan of her life.

Two years later, armed with a degree in economics and religion, she explored various career opportunities, including stints at a Florida theme park, a modeling agency and a cosmetics conglomerate. She moved on to teach high school economics, American government and Latin while coaching award-winning cheerleading teams. Several years later, with an eclectic cast of characters swimming around in her head, she began seriously pursuing a writing career.

She lives an action-packed life in Georgia, with her supportive husband, lovely teenage daughter and two ornery cats who hate each other.

RENEE RYAN
Courting the Enemy

Love Inspired

Recycling programs
for this product may
not exist in your area.

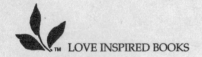

LOVE INSPIRED BOOKS

ISBN-13: 978-0-373-82883-8

COURTING THE ENEMY

www.LoveInspiredBooks.com

Printed in U.S.A.

Be strong and courageous. Do not be terrified, do not be discouraged, for the Lord your God will be with you wherever you go.
—*Joshua* 1:9

To my father, Dr. Augustus Emmett Anderson, Jr.
Thank you, Daddy. Your insight into life
during the war was invaluable. I love you!

Chapter One

~~

The Florida Yacht Club,
Jacksonville, Florida, June 1943
2130 Hours

The betrayal came at too high a cost. That was the thought that tormented Savannah Elliott as she stood on the fringes of her own party. After all these months, she still couldn't wrap her brain around what Johnny had done. What he'd taken from her. From them both.

If only she could forgive him. Or at least forget. For this one night Savannah wanted to be free of the sadness, the pain. The guilt.

Yet, no matter how hard she focused, she barely noticed the music, the dancers, the conversations playing around her. Her mind kept racing back to that terrible moment when her world had changed forever. When *she* had changed forever.

Savannah tried to keep her expression neutral, tried to clear her mind of all thought. The memories came anyway. In hard, brutal snatches that shot through her like well-aimed bullets. Dinner with friends. Johnny unexpectedly arriving at the same restaurant. Another woman on his arm. The car crash. The ensuing scandal. The—

Savannah shut off the rest of her thoughts. She only had herself to blame. Friends had warned her about Johnny's lack of character. Her father had tried to make her see reason, first by cajoling and then by threatening to cut her off financially. Nothing had swayed her. Even her mother, her sweet, docile mother, had expressed suspicion.

Savannah didn't want to admit they'd been right. But the truth could no longer be ignored. Johnny hadn't been what he'd seemed.

What did it matter now? Her husband was dead. And no amount of anger, tears or bargaining with the Lord would bring him back. Why couldn't everyone leave it at that?

Because of the way he died.

A small gasp, nearly a sob, slipped out of her while memories of that fateful night slithered through her mind. Had her husband died in the war, perhaps tonight would have been easier. Perhaps the whispers would have been less painful to endure.

Squeezing her eyes shut, Savannah took a deep breath. The pleasant scent of magnolias and fresh river water did nothing to dispel the anger clawing for release.

She would not give in to the emotion. She would not.

She would learn from her mistakes. *Be ye therefore wise as serpents and harmless as doves,* wasn't that what the Lord commanded?

Never again. She promised herself that she would *never again* fail to look below the surface.

Focusing on the scene in front of her, Savannah forced herself to catalog every detail, as though she were listing them in neat columns in her ledgers. Numbers, equations, order, those were the things she understood.

She counted a total of twenty band members. They played an old-fashioned waltz rather than a more popular swing number. *One, two, three.* The perfect order found in the beats below the waltz's haunting melody soothed her far more than words from well-meaning friends. *One, two, three.*

One.

Two.

Three.

Savannah swayed slowly, counting every beat in her head. Comforted by the precision of the music, she continued her inspection. The women, save for a few matrons, were dressed in long, shimmery gowns. Matching jewels glittered around their necks. The explosion of color hurt Savannah's eyes, but was a perfect foil to the red-red lips and loosely rolled hairstyles. At least the men wore more serious clothing. The black tuxedos and stark-white shirts better fit Savannah's dark mood.

Unfortunately, their laughter rang too loud, too bright, too... false.

Needing order once again, she resumed counting the precise beats below the music. *One, two, three.* No one seemed to care that the world was at war. Or maybe they did care. Maybe this was their way of coping. Maybe—

"You're frowning, Savannah."

She swallowed a sigh at the gentle admonishment. Not wanting to worry her father—this party had been his idea, after all—she pasted a smile on her face and turned to face him. "Am I? I didn't realize."

He gave her arm an affectionate pat. The gesture calmed her, enough that she found it in her to smile again. This time the effort came easier.

She adored her father. They'd always had a special bond. William Klein was everything a father should be. Savannah knew that now. Not only was he tall, with broad shoulders large enough to carry his loved ones' burdens, he was also trustworthy.

The handsome face had few lines, even though he would turn fifty next month. His full head of blond hair had very little gray and, best of all, his pale blue eyes held nothing but fatherly concern. No judgment. No condemnation. No reminder that she'd let him down by marrying a man like Johnny.

She'd been right to come home.

"Savannah, my dear." He lowered his voice so only she could hear his words. "You're supposed to be enjoying yourself. This party is for you."

Yes, the party was being held in her honor, but Savannah knew this night was important to her father as well. A time for him to express his joy over her return. A time to celebrate the wayward daughter's homecoming after her season of rebellion.

But how could Savannah pretend all was well? Even without the loss of her husband in that car crash, and the subsequent scandal that had followed, the world was at war. Young men—American men—were dying. *Dying.* In record numbers. She'd already lost too many friends.

Smiling, laughing, waltzing, it all seemed so…so…inappropriate.

"Come, Savannah, I'll not have you cower in the corner at your own party."

The genuine worry in her father's tone brought a sting to her eyes. Still, she couldn't make herself pretend she wanted to be here, no matter how hard she tried.

"I have to be at work early in the morning," she said, hoping she didn't sound as disagreeable as she felt.

Surely her father would accept her excuse. After all, he'd insisted she take the job at Pembroke Shipyard, one of his bank's best clients and in desperate need of a replacement bookkeeper now that the other man had enlisted.

A chance for her to get her mind off her problems—that had been her father's reasoning. Hers as well, at least at first. But within days of her becoming the shipyard's sole bookkeeper matters had changed.

An ever-increasing sense of purpose had settled over her.

She was doing her part for the war effort, ensuring the shipyard ran smoothly and efficiently. Their overall production of Liberty ships had already improved since she'd joined the operation. Her contribution mattered. And perhaps, for the first time in her life, *she* mattered. Not as someone's daughter. Not as someone's wife. But as herself.

It was a heady feeling, knowing that she was headed in a new, even noble direction with her life. For God and country.

"One dance, my dear." Her father persisted. "That's all I ask. Then, if you are still inclined, you may leave."

She opened her mouth to argue, but he preempted her with a dismissive wave of his hand. "If you continue lurking in the shadows, people will begin to talk."

Savannah blinked up at her father. He meant well. He always meant well. And she loved him for it, loved the way he worried about her even when it wasn't necessary.

But didn't he know people were already talking? They hadn't bothered hiding their curiosity, were openly staring at her, whispering as soon as she passed by. She knew what they were thinking, what they were saying about her, about Johnny and that other woman.

In truth, she'd rather be anywhere but here at the country club, but Savannah knew her father would continue to push her—gently, of course—until she ultimately agreed to his request.

"All right," she said. "One dance."

Hooking her arm through his, she stepped forward.

He pulled her back to his side. "Not with me." He nodded toward his assistant, who was winding his way through the sea of dancers. "With Peter."

Peter.

A chill ran down her spine, ending in a cold shiver. Savannah quickly averted her gaze so her father wouldn't see her reaction to his suggestion. Ever since coming home, their only source of conflict had been over Peter. She certainly didn't want to continue the argument here tonight.

If only she could figure out why the man made her so uncomfortable, why he put her on edge. Her aversion made little sense. On the surface, there was nothing wrong with Peter. Blond hair, chiseled features, aristocratic bearing—he was beautiful, if a man could be called such.

Oh, but his eyes. Pale blue, icy, they made her uneasy, especially when he was looking straight at her. Like he was now.

Another shiver coursed through her.

Something wasn't right about the way he watched her with that stony expression, as if Savannah was somehow a threat to her own father.

Ridiculous, of course. Peter was the real problem. Ever since hiring the man three years ago, her father had changed. Not in things that mattered—such as his love for her and her mother—but in other, more subtle ways. His choice in music. The artwork he purchased. Even his preferred reading material.

Perhaps Savannah's perceptions were colored by her recent disillusionments. Perhaps she was more cynical than she should be. Yet, she couldn't shake the notion that Peter was dangerous to her father.

It would do well for her to keep an eye on him, to uncover what made her question his very motives.

She would start tonight.

"Yes, Father." She lifted her chin a fraction higher. "If it pleases you, I'll dance with him."

Satisfaction flickered in his eyes. "That's my girl."

Trent Mueller entered the ballroom as he did every party—with a beautiful woman on his arm. It had been his trademark since his college days. But unlike the carefree life he'd led back then, there would be no time for amusement this evening. No chance to partake in the laughter.

And absolutely no room for error.

The stakes were too high to forget why he was here and what he had to do in less than seven days. The woman by his side had her own role to play. Like Trent, Katherine Gallagher was a highly trained OSS agent. Despite her flawless features, coal-black hair and startling green eyes, Kate knew her duty down to the letter. Her slight personal connection with Trent, though indirect, wouldn't interfere with her performance tonight. *Or* his. In truth, their mutual bond through Kate's brother only enhanced Trent's cover story.

Stopping at the edge of the dance floor, he took in the room with a single glance. He gauged the players, memorized the exit points and determined his next course of action. Dance. He needed to get Kate out on the dance floor as soon as possible.

With the ease of a man used to leading, Trent guided his "date" forward, his hand at the small of her back. In unspoken agreement, they settled into each other's arms and then fell in step with the other dancers.

The music was spectacular, world-class. For a moment, *just one,* Trent allowed the sound to wash over him, to remind him of better times, when his biggest concern had been which party to attend first. So caught up in nostalgia, he nearly lost his bearings. The glitter, the music, the carefree laughter, it was as if he'd been transported to a world where there was no war, no pain. And no death.

A dangerous illusion.

Didn't these people, these fortunate *Americans,* realize what was happening across the Pond? Hadn't they heard about the terror? The courageous sacrifices made by those who laid down their lives daily? Hourly? Not just men, but women and children as well. Children like little Heinrich. The ten-year-old boy who'd saved Trent's life, only to be shot down by a standard-issue Gestapo firearm because Trent hadn't been quick enough.

Senseless death. Mindless killing. A hardened heart. All were the legacies of his life as a spy. What would become of his soul?

Rolling his shoulders, Trent shoved aside the disturbing question, reset his frame and then steered Kate through a series of complicated turns. She matched him step for step, her eyes casually scanning the room for one person in particular.

Trent waited, keeping his mind sharp, his instincts on alert. The music was forgotten. Or rather, ignored. If he failed, if the mission didn't go exactly as planned, the Nazis would succeed in bringing the war to American soil.

Unacceptable.

"There she is," Kate said, her voice just above a whisper. "On your left. The self-possessed blonde in the ice-blue dress."

Another smooth turn and Trent caught sight of the woman. The air in his lungs expanded then clogged in his throat. He blinked, swallowed several times, repeating the process until he had his breathing back under control.

He simply hadn't been prepared for his first glimpse of Savannah Elliott, recent widow and daughter of a suspected traitor. She was beyond beautiful, stunning even, the type of woman he'd once found impossible to resist. But Trent was no longer the carefree second son of an important, well-connected family. And Savannah—*Mrs. Elliott*—was only a means to an end, a way into her father's world.

Knowing his duty, Trent glided Kate through another turn, all the while keeping his gaze locked on their quarry. He shifted his attention to her dance partner. They made a striking pair. "Who's the man with her?"

"Peter Sorensen."

Peter Sorensen. William Klein's assistant. Trent fought to keep his expression bland. The Norwegian was a shameless social climber, one who'd made a name for himself riding on his boss's coattails over the past three years. Trent didn't like the man on principle, but there were other, darker reasons for his disdain. Enough suspicion surrounded Sorensen to make him a threat in his own right.

"And there's the man of the hour, Savannah's father, on your left." Kate hitched her chin over her right shoulder. "Conversing with his wife by the banquet table."

Sweeping them in that direction, Trent eyed the older couple. The wife was a more mature, equally striking version of her daughter. A cool, regal blonde, she was the perfect accessory for a prominent banker and businessman known for his philanthropic contributions.

The Kleins seemed so carefree. So normal. So…*American*.

A surge of derision bolted through Trent. Despite appearances, despite popular opinion among locals, William Klein was not what he seemed. The OSS had undeniable proof he was a Nazi sympathizer. Worse than that, Klein was a possible traitor, one suspected of plotting with the Germans to sabotage the U.S. war effort in the next seven days.

He returned his attention to the woman in his arms. A local girl, Kate had grown up with Savannah Klein Elliott. They'd been friends since they were young girls, which was the key to Kate's involvement in this mission. "Does Savannah know who, or rather *what*, her father is?"

Still in character, Kate gave him a dazzling smile, and then let out a tinkling laugh. "That's one of the things you're here to find out."

Trent returned her smile, even as his mind disconnected and worked through the potential hazards ahead. He'd prefer not to involve the daughter, especially if she was unaware of her father's activities with the Germans.

Dear God, if she's innocent—

He cut off his silent plea. Better to sacrifice one than forfeit a multitude. The mission was all that mattered. There was no room for guilt in espionage, and absolutely no opportunity for heroics. His superiors believed Savannah was the most expedient route to her father. With the time line they'd given Trent, he had little choice other than to proceed with the plan.

The waltz ended.

Savannah and her partner moved off the dance floor. Trent followed suit, keeping Kate close. "It's time," he whispered. "You know what to do."

She nodded.

They shared a grim look before she lifted her voice and said, "Come, Trent, darling. Come meet one of my dearest friends in the world."

"With pleasure." He put on his most charming smile, the one that had won him countless female hearts in the past. A slow swivel of his head and his gaze settled onto Savannah Elliott's exquisite face.

She was alone once again, her dance partner no longer by her side. She was watching him in return. Boldly, candidly. As Trent continued holding her gaze, moving slowly toward her, like a train on a collision course, something in him shifted, softened, resettled in the kind of way that made a man want to take stock of his life.

He broke eye contact, swallowed back an uncomfortable sensation of guilt and prepared to follow the plan as laid out by General Donovan himself. *For God and country.*

Even as he considered the stakes, Trent wondered if the Lord would forgive him for what he was about to do, and he realized the answer didn't matter. This was war.

He captured Savannah Elliott in his gaze once again.

The mission was underway.

Chapter Two

Once Peter had left her alone, under the guise of searching out her father, Savannah had expected to feel less tense. Instead, she stood frozen inside a stranger's stare. An aura of mystery and danger emanated off the man, trapping her in place as if she were a small woodland creature caught in a cobra's trance.

Air tightened in her lungs.

Who was he? And why couldn't she look away from all that intensity? She wasn't uneasy, exactly. Nor was she alarmed, not really, not like she was when Peter held her in his gaze. No, Savannah was simply...mesmerized.

It had been a long time since she'd experienced such a reaction to a man. It was as if she was awaking from a dream and her mind hadn't quite caught up with the rest of her body.

Seconds ticked by, pounding in perfect rhythm with her heartbeats, and still she remained where she was, actually captivated into immobility.

She slowly became aware of people moving around her. Dancing. Laughing. Enjoying themselves immensely. Savannah should be a part of the festivities, or at least pretend to be a part of them. She took another raspy breath.

The man started toward her.

Her hand instinctively flew to her throat. She took several

more swallows of air and tried to look away. But the stranger's hooded gaze—that remarkable, compelling gaze—continued holding her rooted to the spot. The logical part of her brain noted his spectacular good looks. Tall, masculine, he had thick, dark blond hair, a broad chest and movie-star features.

Who *was* he?

The question gave way to a more disturbing thought. He wasn't alone. He was with her friend Kate.

Savannah's heart took a dive to her stomach, while her brain raced through a myriad of questions.

Why was Kate in the company of such a man? And why hadn't she mentioned him this afternoon when they'd shared a cup of tea in her mother's parlor?

Swallowing back her confusion, Savannah tried to discern the emotion in Kate's eyes as she looked at her escort. Affection, perhaps? Admiration? No, something far more complicated than either of those.

A year ago Savannah wouldn't have noticed the subtle undercurrents between Kate and her escort. But now…

The two moved as a unit, like a well-oiled machine rather than a couple. They looked beautiful together. Kate's dark hair to his light, her fair skin to his tanned. And yet, they didn't appear fully together.

This was why Savannah preferred numbers, this confusing mix of contradictory messages. Numbers were always constant. Even if they didn't add up the way she would like, they never gave false impressions.

A soft, humorless laugh bubbled in Savannah's throat. *Look at what I've become.*

Johnny and his lies had done this to her. One night—one impromptu dinner at the wrong place, wrong time—and now Savannah questioned everyone's motives. First Peter's, now Kate's. But where Peter gave her pause, Kate was her oldest and dearest friend. There was no reason to doubt her.

Before Savannah could contemplate why she found no comfort in that thought, Kate closed the distance and pulled her into a warm hug.

"Savannah, darling." She spoke in her trademark breathy voice. "You look perfectly stunning in that dress."

The compliment was the most sincere Savannah had heard all evening. She suddenly had to resist the urge to cling to her friend. How she hated this sudden, inexplicable need to be comforted by someone she'd known and trusted before Johnny had entered her life.

Releasing her hold on Savannah, Kate stepped back. Her brows drew together in a slight frown. Savannah knew that look. Kate was worried about her.

Savannah opened her mouth to field the questions that were sure to come, but she was interrupted when Kate's escort cleared his throat.

Savannah blinked up at the man. He was standing too close. So close, in fact, that she could smell his spicy aftershave, a pleasant mixture of cedar and lime. The scent made her head spin.

"Kate," he said without taking his eyes off Savannah. "Aren't you going to introduce me to your friend?"

The rich baritone washed over Savannah like liquid silver, sending a severe sensation through her, one that had her tugging for air in her already tight lungs.

Kate gave the stranger an odd look, almost a warning, before she let out a soft laugh. "Well, honestly, where are my manners? Savannah, this is Trent." She swept a graceful hand toward her escort. "Trent Mueller."

Trent Mueller. The name meant nothing to Savannah, but she found herself intrigued nonetheless.

He really was quite handsome, tawny and golden, with a strong jaw and sculpted cheekbones. He might look like a suave, sophisticated man about town, but Savannah sensed there was more to him. Something dark and dangerous and unmistakably male.

"Trent," Kate continued, breaking the silence that had fallen over them. "This is my dear friend Savannah Klein, I mean, Elliott. Savannah *Elliott*."

"A pleasure, Mrs. Elliott." The response came quickly and smoothly, a little too smoothly. Although Trent's manner appeared relaxed, the cool indifference was at odds with the rigid angle of his shoulders.

Savannah suddenly felt one step behind. It was as if she were missing some vital piece of information, moving through the scene like an actress who had forgotten her lines.

Something felt…wrong about this whole situation. About Trent Mueller himself.

Then why was she so drawn to the man?

As if he could read her thoughts, a faint smile spread across his lips.

"Mrs. Elliott." He bent his head close to her ear. "Would you do me the honor of the next waltz?"

A shiver of anticipation spread through her.

Be wise as serpents and harmless as doves…

Was she supposed to be a serpent or a dove in this situation?

"Thank you, but I…" Her words trailed off as a movement on her right caught her attention. Her father was speaking with his assistant. They were both watching her.

Savannah's mouth went dry. Peter had been polite enough during their foxtrot. But his eyes had been those of a predator, his conversation bordering on intrusive. After one dance, Savannah was all the more convinced that Peter Sorensen was not a man to be trusted.

Although she had nothing of substance to go on *yet,* her father's association with the man was a bad thing. Very bad. Somehow, someway, she would find the evidence necessary to prove her theory as fact.

As if sensing he'd lost her attention, Trent shifted into her line of vision and held out his hand in silent invitation.

With that far-too-pleasant smile on his face and that intense look in his eyes, he seemed marginally less dangerous than Peter. But, at the moment, the lesser of two evils.

"I think, Mr. Mueller—" she placed her hand in his "—I would like nothing more than to waltz with you."

Trent guided his quarry toward the dance floor, allowing nothing to break his concentration, not even the ripple of shock tracking through him. The OSS had completely miscalculated the situation. Consequently, so had Trent.

Savannah Elliot wasn't cold, as reported. Nor was she distant and callous. She was merely wary, skittish—wounded, even. The undisguised vulnerability he'd caught in her eyes tugged at the very heart of him. He'd recognized her grief and distrust below the cool blond exterior, as well as a refusal to buckle under the emotions.

Trent was intrigued. Utterly captivated. By the one woman he needed to suspect most.

He had to remember she was the daughter of a Nazi sympathizer and suspected traitor to the United States. She could be a traitor herself. His gut rolled at the thought.

He drew her into his arms and a sense of utter calm took hold of him. He immediately shook himself free of the sensation and guided them into the first steps of a Viennese waltz.

Avoiding the woman's remarkable, silvery-blue eyes, Trent glanced around the perimeter of the room. Peter Sorensen was no longer in sight. His sudden disappearance presented a number of concerns, all of which Trent would deal with later. For now, he sought out Kate's statuesque form.

As expected, his partner carried out her portion of the mission with the clean, sophisticated movements of a fox. She wound her way through the tangle of humanity, stopping to speak with individual guests in a seemingly random fashion. Trent knew better.

He left Kate to her task and focused on the woman wrapped in his arms. Their eyes met and he felt a quick pitch of his heart. One word filled his mind. *Innocent.*

Unexpected guilt passed through him in a painful ripple of unease.

Get hold of yourself, Mueller. This woman is nothing more than a means to an end.

He hardened his heart as he had done too many times in the past six months.

Six months. That's all it had taken to turn him into a completely different, harder man than the carefree one he'd been before the war.

"You are an expert dancer, Mrs. Elliott." He put only a hint of his usual charm in his voice, just enough to avoid increasing the woman's suspicion of him. "I always enjoy a partner who knows—"

"Please, Mr. Mueller." She cut him off midsentence, her eyes filled with distress. "I would prefer you not call me Mrs. Elliott."

Interesting, but not surprising, especially considering the way her husband had died. "What name *would* you prefer?"

She lowered her lashes, sighed softly, and then lifted her gaze back to his. "Savannah will do."

"All right, Savannah. Since we're dispensing with formalities…" He swept her across the dance floor with smooth, graceful steps. "Call me Trent."

Her unexpected smile hit him like a sucker punch. "Trent." She repeated his name in an elegant tone that rolled off her tongue. "The name suits you."

For several heartbeats he simply stared at her. Reminding himself of his duty, he took in a deep breath and executed another turn.

"So, Trent. Tell me. How do you know Kate?"

Direct and to the point. No games. No dancing around the issue. Once again the woman surprised him.

His trained, calculating mind reassessed the situation, compartmentalizing the pertinent details into two, distinct categories. The mission and the woman.

Only the mission mattered.

"I met Kate through her brother."

"You were a friend of Bobby's?" It was Savannah's turn to sound surprised.

"We served together." Trent swallowed past a dangerous need to say more than he could. Savannah was someone who'd known Bobby. The real Bobby. Not the OSS spy who'd died inside enemy lines because the countless intelligence agencies had been unwilling to share information with each other.

"His death was a blow," Trent admitted.

Her fingers tightened over his hand. "Yes. Oh, yes it was. Bobby was one of a kind."

"That he was."

Their gazes melded together, and for a brief instant they shared a moment of solidarity through their common sorrow over the loss of a good man.

"I was with him when he died," Trent said in a hoarse whisper. He didn't expand further. He couldn't. The details surrounding Bobby's death were classified. Even Kate, the man's own sister, didn't know all the facts.

Savannah's quick intake of air was the only sign of her shock, while everything else in her softened. Her eyes, her stance, even her grip communicated her sympathy.

"I'm sorry," she said at last. "I…" She shook her head and sighed. "There aren't words, are there?"

"No, there aren't."

How many times had people tried to comfort Trent, not only over Bobby's death but his brother's as well? As with all the people who'd tried before her, Savannah's sympathy should have fallen flat. But this woman clearly understood grief mixed with anger. Trent wanted to rest in her sincere compassion. Maybe he'd even find forgiveness there, if only—

No. He'd already done unspeakable things in his role as a spy. Forgiveness was not his to ask, not from anyone. Not even God. And certainly not from this woman. She was his potential enemy, at worst; unnecessary fallout, at best. Neither optimal.

As he wrestled with the reality of what might come of his actions, Trent could practically hear Savannah's mind working through everything he'd said. He saw the exact moment when she fit a few of the missing pieces together. "But...if you were with Bobby when he died—" she stopped and frowned at his formal dinner jacket "—why aren't you in uniform now?"

"I'm no longer in the Army. I had a career-ending injury." He didn't expand. Again, because he couldn't.

Savannah would never know that Trent had been handpicked by General "Wild Bill" Donovan to work in the OSS only days after Bobby's death. The new, overarching intelligence community was still young, but it was addressing the main problem that had caused countless, unnecessary deaths like Bobby's. One agency now gathered all the intelligence information needed to execute unconventional warfare against the enemy. It—

"What do you do now?" Savannah's voice cut through his thoughts. "If you're not in the Army anymore?"

Trent didn't miss a beat. "I'm a professor of philosophy and theology at Princeton University."

It was a complicated, layered lie concocted expressly to lure William Klein into Trent's confidence. The Nazi sympathizer was something of an intellectual snob, especially when it came to the writings of notable German thinkers of the previous century. Prophecy was his favorite subject. And, consequently, *Professor* Mueller's expertise.

"I would have never guessed you for a professor." Savannah's suspicious tone matched the doubt in her eyes. Trent needed to tread carefully.

"Academia wasn't my initial choice." It was the truth. He'd have preferred a more direct route into Klein's world, banking perhaps. But the OSS had decided to go after the suspected traitor from a different, less obvious angle. Had they made a mistake? Did the man's daughter see through the subterfuge already?

"Then why become a professor at all?" Her entire body had grown tense in his arms.

Trent was about to lose her trust completely.

He gave her an elegant, nonchalant shrug, then idly rubbed the small of her back until she relaxed. "Academia might not have been my first choice, but I like exploring the human psyche. From a purely intellectual standpoint, of course."

He paused, taking the time to draw on the information he'd read in the briefing this afternoon. "I like exploring why we're such contradictory creatures," he continued. "Why do we love so completely, yet wage war so ruthlessly?"

Her eyes took on a faraway look as she considered his words. "I'd say it's not something we're supposed to understand. God's ways aren't our ways. We live in a fallen world."

He had no ready response, primarily because the man Trent had been before the war agreed with her assessment. However, the college professor was supposed to be an agnostic. The paradox left him without words once again.

For the next few moments, they danced in silence, each lost in their own thoughts.

Trent breathed in Savannah's clean, fresh scent. He liked the way she felt in his arms. At five seven, she was the perfect height for his six-two frame. The top of her head reached to just below his chin. "And you, Savannah. What do you do besides attend parties at the country club?"

He already knew the answer, of course. But he needed to hear her response. Often what people revealed, or rather what they *didn't* reveal, told of their true loyalties.

After a short pause, she answered his question. "I work at Pembroke Shipyard." Unmistakable pride filled her voice. "I'm the bookkeeper."

Trent waited for her to reveal the rest, specifically the part about her father securing the job for her at the shipyard through a business associate of his. When she failed to give that vital piece of information, he eyed the woman with growing suspicion.

Pembroke was one of the reported targets of the Nazis' sabotage plans. Bombing the shipyard would only be the first of several deliberate acts of war. And William Klein was the suspected mastermind behind the plot.

Trent's jaw tightened. He no longer had to remind himself why he was here.

What role, if any, did Savannah play in her father's treason? Was she feeding him information? Giving him the employees' work schedules? Copying blueprints of the shipyard's layout?

Searching for clues, Trent stared into her startling gaze. The eyes that looked back at him were wide and clear. Guileless, even. There was no doubt Savannah Elliott was a beautiful woman.

But was she a traitor?

Chapter Three

Savannah knew she was in trouble when the waltz came to a close and she remained locked in Trent's arms. She should have felt awkward. Or at the very least foolish, especially now that the music had stopped and silence had fallen over them. But all she could do was blink up at her dance partner. And wait.

A feeling of expectation curled in her throat, as if she was teetering on the verge of something...important.

Swallowing past the strange emotion, Savannah made herself look at Trent in the same brash way he stared at her. His eyes had turned a pure blue but his gaze was deadly serious, almost fierce.

A shiver slid up her spine.

This was no ordinary man.

Yes, Trent Mueller was outwardly cultured and sophisticated, but there was also a heightened readiness in him, a physical alertness that spoke of his military background. Savannah couldn't shake the notion that he still had a dangerous side, one he hid well.

Why wasn't she more afraid of him?

Because he'd served with Bobby, a man Savannah considered a brother in all ways but blood. She hadn't expected to bond with this stranger so quickly over their mutual loss. After all, the world was at war. *Everyone* had suffered loss on some level.

And yet, for a moment, when she'd recognized the sorrow in Trent's eyes, Savannah had forgotten about her own troubles and had tried to offer what comfort she could. Their shared pain had broken through the normal barriers. War had a way of accelerating relationships.

There were so many things Savannah wanted to ask Trent, questions she hadn't had the courage to ask Kate. How had Bobby died? Had he been in pain? Had the end come quickly?

Just as she opened her mouth, Trent broke eye contact and pulled away from her. A swirl of hot June heat snaked through the distance he'd put between them.

"Thank you for the dance, Savannah." His words came out so very polite, as if they'd never shared that moment of grief.

A pang of regret swept through her. The opportunity for questions was lost, as was the bond she'd felt with this man.

"You dance exceptionally well," she said, unable to think of a better way to fill the moment.

He nodded once in silent acknowledgment of her compliment, then placed his hand at the small of her back and led her off the dance floor.

Out of the corner of her eye, Savannah slid a covert glance in Trent's direction. His strides were confident, each step light, quick, methodical. Nothing like the way he'd danced. Just as she puzzled over yet another contradiction in him, he turned his head and smiled down at her.

The boyish tilt of his lips wiped away years from his face, making him look so…very…approachable.

Savannah sighed.

Oh, he was a smooth one. *Just like Johnny.*

Frowning at the thought, she veered away from Trent. At the

same moment, he drew to a stop. She looked ahead of her and nearly gasped. She hadn't realized where he'd led her.

"Ah, there you two are. I was just telling Savannah's parents about you, Trent, and how we know each other through Bobby."

Smiling broadly, Kate hooked her arm through his and began the formal introductions. "Trent, darling, I'd like you to meet William and Alma Klein. Mr. and Mrs. Klein, this is Trent Mueller, an old friend of Bobby's."

As would be expected of a gentleman, Trent acknowledged Savannah's mother first.

"Mrs. Klein, it's an honor to meet you." He took her hand and touched his lips to her knuckles. The artful gesture was one that couldn't be learned overnight, a sure sign the man had moved in elite social circles all his life. "I now see where your daughter gets her extraordinary beauty."

Her mother blushed like a schoolgirl at the outrageous compliment. "Well, isn't that a kind thing to say?"

"It's the simple truth. In fact—" he leaned in a shade too close "—you are one of the loveliest women here tonight."

Her mother giggled in response. The prim and proper Alma Klein actually giggled.

Who *was* this man? And why wasn't Savannah more outraged by his practiced charm?

Wondering what her father thought of the newcomer's boldness, Savannah glanced to her left. He was staring at Trent with equal parts suspicion and caution. The longer Trent flirted with Savannah's mother, the darker her father's mood became.

Just what sort of game was Trent playing?

He had to know he wasn't winning points with a very powerful man, a man who could make his life difficult. And yet, Trent continued flirting outrageously with Savannah's mother.

Did that make him a charming rogue? Unbelievably arrogant?

Or just plain oblivious?

Of all the possible scenarios, Savannah dismissed the latter. Trent Mueller was completely in control of the moment.

The question, of course, was why? *Why* was he intentionally alienating her father?

Trent was well aware all eyes were on him, including Kate's, even though she wasn't officially a part of their group anymore. She'd melted into another conversation several feet away. Her transition had been flawless, the kind seen at hundreds of parties all over the world. Nevertheless, her timing had been impeccable, changing the dynamics of the situation without any of the Kleins realizing what she'd done.

For the next few minutes, Mrs. Klein carried most of the conversation. Trent gave her his rapt attention, responding when necessary and in the most charming way possible. The OSS report hadn't been clear as to whether or not she was party to her husband's nefarious activities. Trent chose to reserve judgment until he had more information.

He took note of the other two in their little circle. Neither William nor his daughter interrupted the ongoing conversation, although both looked unhappy with the events unfolding in front of them.

Perfect. Their growing distrust was the exact reaction Trent had set out to gain.

The evening was progressing as planned.

Not wishing to overplay his hand, Trent waited for Mrs. Klein to wind down, then shifted his gaze to the patriarch of the family.

One step at a time, he reminded himself. Patience was the key. "Mr. Klein," he said. "Let me take this opportunity to thank you for allowing me to join your celebration this evening, especially on such short notice."

William nodded, eyeing Trent with open skepticism now. Trent held steady under the man's inspection.

There was superiority in the way Klein held his shoulders and an unmistakable arrogance in his gaze. Trent had met similar men in Germany, high-ranking SS officers who thought the rules didn't apply to them.

In Trent's estimation, William Klein was little better than a street thug. The man would definitely fight dirty. Good. Trent understood—and welcomed—that particular type of warfare.

"Mueller." William repeated Trent's last name slowly, drawing out the first syllable longer than necessary. "From what part of Germany does your family hail, exactly?"

Straight to the point. Like father, like daughter.

"We come from Hamburg." Trent put a considerable amount of pride in the name of his ancestral city. The emphasis came at a price. For a split second, sorrow threatened to break through his rigid control.

There'd been a time when Trent had considered his German heritage with a sense of dignity. Germany had produced some of the world's greatest thinkers, scientists and technological advances. But now, Hitler—with the help of his SS henchmen—used those innovations for his own dark purposes.

How could a country come back from an evil that gripped the very soul of its people? Too many good Germans had fallen into line without a fight. Too many had ignored their faith in a just God and had put their hope in the promises of prosperity and a better life. Promises that were nothing more than lies used to cover genocide and other monstrosities.

Americans like William Klein, men who supported the monster regime with their money and resources, had to be stopped.

"Tell me, Mueller." William's clipped words brought Trent back to the matter at hand. "How long has your family been in this country?"

The thinly veiled interrogation was precisely what Trent had expected from the man. He held back a cynical smile. "My mother is a Powell." He cleared his voice of all emotion, save one. *Arrogance.* "Of the Connecticut Powells. Her family came to this country before the Revolution."

Trent's answer wasn't what William had wanted to know. Ah, but Trent was in control of this game. The Nazi sympathizer would have to work to get the information he wanted.

"And your father?"

"He came over from Germany as a boy."

Eyes gleaming with interest, William rubbed his chin between his thumb and forefinger. He was fully engaged now, playing his own game with what he thought were his own set of rules.

Trent was one step ahead.

"Do you still have family in Germany?" William asked.

Trent's pulse soared through his veins. He hadn't expected the question so soon. Right here, right now, what he said next could determine the fate of the mission. Anticipation shimmered along his skin.

Patience, he reminded himself. He couldn't rush this process. Trent needed to gain William's confidence slowly. Step by step.

He offered up a silent prayer for wisdom then gave Savannah a brief glance. She looked uncomfortable with the direction of the conversation, but she didn't try to interrupt. Neither did her mother.

Unless they were directly embroiled in the sabotage plot, perhaps Trent wouldn't have to involve either woman after tonight. Perhaps the truth would be all he needed to enter into William's world.

"My father has several family members still living and—" he held the pause for effect "—working in Germany."

"I...see."

Yes, Trent thought, the man saw the situation exactly as he

was supposed to see it. The game was about control now. Trent allowed William to think he had all the power.

"And you, Mueller." He gave Trent a thin smile. "What do you do with yourself besides attend other people's parties at the last minute?"

Savannah made a sound deep in her throat then shifted to a spot directly in front of Trent. "Please, Father. That's enough questions for one night. Mr. Mueller is a friend of Kate's." She tossed Trent a quick smile from over her shoulder then turned back to face her father again. "That's all that matters here tonight."

William looked down at his daughter. "Savannah." He let out a slow, hissing breath. "You know I'm only trying to—"

She held up her hand to keep him from continuing. "I know, Father. I..." Her shoulders drooped slightly forward. "*Know.* But you and Mother mustn't ignore your other guests. I'll entertain Mr. Mueller until Kate returns." Her tone brooked no argument.

Scowling, William started to say something more, but his wife chose that moment to intervene. "William, Savannah wishes to be alone with Mr. Mueller." She smiled at her daughter. "Isn't that right, dear?"

Savannah gave one firm nod. If only Trent could see her face he would know what she was thinking.

"Yes, Mother. That's exactly what I want. Please," she appealed directly to her father, "I'll be perfectly fine in Mr. Mueller's company."

William stared at his daughter for an endless moment, eyes sweeping across her face with an unreadable expression in his gaze.

Savannah held firm, actually shifting a bit closer to Trent as if to shield him. Was the woman trying to protect him?

How...utterly...enchanting.

"All right, Savannah, we'll leave you two alone. For the time being." To emphasize his point, Klein lifted his gaze over his daughter's head and glared an unspoken warning at Trent.

Trent nodded.

"Enjoy the moment, Savannah." Alma Klein patted her daughter's cheek then tugged on her husband's arm. "Come along, William. There's Andy and Joy by the punch bowl. We haven't spoken with them all evening."

Eyeing Trent a moment longer, William eventually allowed his wife to pull him away.

A tense silence fell in their wake.

Only after her parents were out of earshot did Savannah spin around to face Trent. "I'm sorry about that. My father, he…" Her lips twisted into a grimace. "Means well."

"I'm sure he does."

"It's just…" She sighed. "He's a bit overprotective after what happened with…that is, since…" She lowered her lashes and sighed a second time.

Oddly moved by her inability to continue, and knowing what lay behind it, Trent reached out to touch her cheek. He dropped his hand before he made contact. "You don't have to explain anything to me."

"I…thank you." She smiled up at him.

That smile. It slaughtered him. Hit him right at the core of the man he'd once been, a man with nothing more on his mind than romancing a beautiful woman.

Had he ever been that carefree? That self-centered?

Trent's heart pitched in his chest. What would he have thought of Savannah had they met at another time, under different circumstances?

It was a question he had no right to ask.

There was, however, a request he needed to make of her. Regardless of what Trent Mueller wanted, the OSS spy wasn't through with this woman. He told himself it wasn't personal, it was *never* personal, but a jolt of guilt curled the fingers of his right hand into a tight fist.

"Savannah, I'm only in Jacksonville a few weeks." He relaxed his hand, along with his tone. "Would you allow me to take you to lunch tomorrow?"

"I…" She drew her bottom lip between her teeth. "…Don't know."

"It's just lunch." He touched her hand, surprised at the swift roll in his gut when their fingers met. "*Lunch*, Savannah, nothing more."

She hesitated several endless seconds. When her shoulders finally relaxed, Trent knew he had her right where he wanted her.

"Well," she began. "I suppose there's no harm in having a meal with you."

Yes, there was considerable harm, to her, anyway, but the stakes were too high for Trent to gain a conscience at this juncture.

"Splendid." He took her hand in his and rolled his thumb across her knuckles. "You won't regret this."

She blinked up at him, looking as though she already had a few second thoughts. "Shall I meet you here at the club?"

"No." He raised her hand to his lips then released her slowly. Very, *very* slowly. "I'll pick you up at the shipyard."

"Oh." She cocked her head as if that thought hadn't occurred to her. "Do you know where it is?"

He knew where all three of the Nazis' targets were located. But he simply said, "No."

She rattled off the address then gave a few simple directions to help him avoid the noon-hour traffic.

Having all he needed from the woman tonight, he touched his left ear. On cue, Kate rejoined them and soon had Savannah engaged in a discussion about an upcoming shopping trip to Atlanta.

Trent only half-listened to their conversation. Now that he'd secured the lunch date with Savannah, his mind began working out phase two of the operation. He caught sight of William Klein on the other side of the room. The man looked entirely too confident for someone the U.S. government had in its sights.

Trent allowed a slow smile to spread across his lips. There was nothing he liked better than a mission proceeding exactly as planned.

Chapter Four

SS Sturmbannfuehrer Hans-Peter von Heinberg, alias Peter Sorensen, surveyed the ballroom with the cold, calculating mind he'd developed in the Hitler Youth. Befitting his rank of major, he stood erect, head held high. But he was careful to hide his thoughts behind a blank mask.

No one looking at him now would realize he was ready to strike if the need arose. Herr Klein gave a slight, imperceptible nod as he passed by with his wife on his arm. Like Peter, the older man watched the activities around him with a bored expression on his face. Peter knew better. Herr Klein was on high alert as always.

Peter waited until the Kleins joined another couple near the buffet table before he took a moment to review the upcoming mission in his mind.

The next few days were the most important. Coordinates had to be calculated then relayed accurately to Germany. Schedules had to be carefully aligned. Supplies gathered. Maps drawn. There could be no mistakes. Nothing left unchecked.

Watching the activity around him, Peter pressed his lips into a thin line. The arrogant Americans thought the war was across the ocean. *Over there,* as they so often said to one another. They would soon discover their error. When it was too late to change the tide of war.

Of course, Peter would rather face the enemy with more conventional means, but his current mission was equally important to the Fuehrer's master plan. Clandestine warfare used unconventional weapons, but the goal was still the same. Bring down the enemy. Swiftly, cleanly. Decisively.

Peter's heart lurched in his chest. Sabotaging the American war machine was only the beginning. Soon, German pride and power would be felt throughout the world. At last, the Master Race would rule a thousand years, as prophesied.

Smiling slightly, Peter melted deeper into the shadows, pivoted, and then leaned one shoulder against the wall behind him.

The thick Florida heat floated through the opened doorways. Maintaining his casual air of boredom, Peter checked his wristwatch: 2130. The evening was proving long and tedious, like most of these pointless social affairs.

He lowered his hand and took a closer look at the people milling around the room. As true of most parties, the dynamics were in a constant state of change. Knots of small groups morphed into larger ones then dissipated altogether. Laughter rang out, grating like nails to a slate chalkboard.

Peter ignored the people who made no difference to him, and kept a close eye on the only one who mattered.

Savannah Elliott.

An unexpected, black emotion tried to creep through his control. Peter shoved it aside and continued surveying the room. It was much too soon to make a judgment about Herr Klein's daughter.

Physically, Savannah was the ideal Aryan. Tall, blonde, with the requisite blue eyes, she would make a proper breeder of future Nazis. But it was her independent streak that made Peter's gut churn with dark emotion. If her father didn't ensure she fell into line soon, Peter would do so himself. Not even Herr Klein's daughter would be allowed to threaten their mission.

Blood, soil and struggle, Peter recited the founding principles of the SS under his breath and touched the small badge hidden inside the lining of his lapel. The button was nothing more than a black swastika against a red background on an inexpensive piece of metal. Ah, but the symbol represented eternal hope to the true elite. Blood and soil were the heart and soul of the new religion and the only things worth worshipping.

Peter's gaze landed on Savannah once again. She'd turned slightly, enough that he could better see the man next to her. Peter didn't like the stranger's looks. He was tall and broad-shouldered, and his hair was cut short and neat in a style that denoted American military. Even more suspect, the man kept himself balanced on the balls of his feet while his eyes tracked everywhere. Right to left, left to right.

Time for an introduction.

Peter shoved away from the wall. Herr Klein stopped him halfway to his destination and motioned him in the opposite direction.

Hesitating only a moment, Peter shot one last glance in Savannah's direction then followed the other man out the French doors. They walked in silence along the marble portico, their heels striking the polished stone like hammers to nails.

He noted the clouds peppering the sky above. The accompanying breeze turned the Yacht Club's lawn into a slew of moving shadows. The outdoor lighting warred with those shadows, losing in some places, winning in others.

They cleared the upper deck and moved to the docks, where a myriad of sailboats bobbed in the water.

Herr Klein stopped walking abruptly and turned to face Peter. "A matter has arisen, one which I need you to address immediately."

Peter offered the mere suggestion of a nod. Whatever Herr Klein asked of him he would do without question.

"The man Kate brought with her tonight, the one speaking with Savannah now. His name is Trent Mueller."

A German-American. Peter hadn't expected that. But when he chewed on the notion a bit longer he realized he wasn't surprised by the news. There had been something in Mueller's bearing—a keen sense of entitlement—that Peter had recognized. The man clearly had a superiority of breeding that could come only from the Nordic races.

But what of his loyalties?

As though sensing the direction of Peter's thoughts, Herr Klein continued. "Mueller is supposed to be a former friend of Bobby Gallagher, Kate's brother. But I wonder. I need you to find out who the man really is."

Peter relished the task. "You don't think he's who he claims to be?"

"I have my doubts." Herr Klein drew in a breath, held it a beat, then blew out a slow hiss. "Despite the fact that he came with another woman, Mueller is showing obvious interest in my daughter."

Knowing he was treading on dangerous ground, Peter spoke his next words carefully, with no inflection in his voice. "Savannah is a very beautiful woman."

"Yes, she is." Herr Klein frowned. "But she's also a poor judge of character."

The worry in the man's tone said more than his words. Considering Savannah's choice in husbands, Herr Klein was right to be concerned. The selfish woman had already caused enough problems. Peter would not allow her to become a further distraction to her father.

"You don't believe Mueller's interest is…" Peter searched for the proper word in English. "…sincere?"

"Hard to say." Herr Klein placed both hands behind his back

and began to pace. "Mueller says all the right words. He's full of charm and sophistication, but his eyes reveal nothing of his motives. That sort of discipline doesn't come naturally. He's had training."

A chill of anticipation iced across Peter's skin.

"I need you to find out what sort of training Mueller's had, where he got it from and why he's sniffing around my daughter."

Peter nodded, knowing exactly who to contact, but he needed to know where to start. "Tell me what you've already discovered about the man."

A long pause followed, broken only by the breeze sweeping through the trees. Peter knew better than to break Herr Klein's concentration. The man was a brilliant strategist. His mind could work through a web of seemingly unrelated threads until he found the proper connection.

"Mueller claims to be from a prominent New England family, with relatives still living in Germany. However..." Herr Klein stopped pacing. Hands still behind his back, he stared out across the river. "The timing of his arrival is disturbing."

Disturbing? No, Peter thought, the man's timing was wholly suspect. After a full year of preparations, the strike against the U.S. war machine was finally underway. In five short days, U-boat 117 would deposit six saboteurs on the coast of Florida near Herr Klein's beach house. If the landing went as planned, the men would hit their first target an hour later.

Peter's primary role was to guarantee that nothing hindered the mission. Nothing and no one. "I'll begin making inquiries at once."

"Excellent."

With their business complete, Peter turned to go.

"Peter." Herr Klein clasped him on the shoulder. "I'll want your report in two days. No later."

Peter glanced briefly at the hand holding him in place, then allowed a slow smile to spread across his lips. "You'll have it in one."

Trent slipped back into the ballroom several minutes behind William Klein and his lackey, Sorensen. Neither man had noticed Trent following them, nor did they realize he'd heard their entire conversation.

Their words had been brief, and they had confirmed what Trent already knew. Klein was clearly the leader of the organization, but Sorensen was the more brutal of the two. Formidable foes, both of them, for very different reasons. Each man was equally dangerous. Trent would have to figure out a way to keep an eye on both of them.

With more than enough information to take the next step, Trent searched the ballroom. He caught Kate's eye and angled his head toward the foyer leading out into the parking lot.

She gave her friend a quick kiss on the cheek then extricated herself from their tiny group. Without breaking stride, she nodded to several people, stopped only once to speak with the hosts of the party and then joined Trent in the lobby.

"Well?" she asked.

He started to respond but stopped himself. Not only was this not the place for a briefing, Trent could feel someone watching him.

His gaze landed squarely on Savannah Elliott. Their eyes locked and held.

For a stunning moment, Trent's brain simply stopped working. He couldn't organize a single coherent thought. Just as quickly, his mind revved up with a thousand, complicated images colliding into one another. A lone thought rose through the mist. *It's never too soon to prepare for unexpected contingencies.*

General Donovan's motto was the very thing Trent needed

to keep in mind, especially after tonight. Savannah Elliott was proving to be an unforeseen complication, one that needed addressing quickly. Purposefully.

Before matters got out of hand.

"Trent?" Kate's voice reverberated through his head, calling him back to reason.

He continued staring at Savannah.

"Trent."

Surprised at his own reluctance, he slowly broke eye contact and returned his attention to Kate.

"Is there something you want to discuss with me?" she asked.

"Not at the moment, no."

"Don't pretend you don't know what I mean." Her voice held a large dose of agitation. "Just now, I saw the way you were looking at—"

"Not here, Kate." He thrust his hand between them. *"Not. Here."*

Her scowl digging deeper, she shot a quick glance over her shoulder and sighed. "You're right. This isn't the time or place."

Without looking at Savannah again, Trent escorted Kate out of the building. Neither spoke as they walked across the parking lot to his car. Despite the tension that had fallen between them, they were still on duty. Consequently they smiled and laughed at each other, creating the perfect picture of old friends happy to be in each other's company.

Kate, professional as always, waited until they were both settled in the car before she allowed her true feelings to show. Lips pursed, one lone eyebrow lifted, she wasted no time getting straight to the point. "Do we have a problem?"

"Not from my perspective." He looked out over the hood of the car. "We're right on schedule. Klein took the bait. Sorensen is checking into my background as we speak."

"Good. *Good.*" She let out a slow, relieved breath of air. "But that's not what I meant."

"Yes, Kate, I'm well aware of that." Still looking straight ahead, Trent started the ignition. But instead of putting the car in gear, he placed both hands on the steering wheel in a loose ten-and-two hold.

"Savannah got to you, didn't she?"

Trent didn't answer immediately. He might never be a godly man again, not after the past year, but he wasn't enough of a hypocrite to outright lie to his partner. Besides, Kate would see right through his attempt to hide the truth. "She wasn't what I expected, if that's what you're asking."

"No. She wasn't. And I'm as surprised as you are." Kate lifted a slim hand to brush her hair off her face. "She's much more vulnerable than I realized, and yet, strong as well. Take tonight, for instance. She was even less guarded than usual. More like the woman I used to know."

Trent's grip tightened on the steering wheel. Already struggling to maintain his own perspective, he didn't want to hear Kate's doubts spoken with that hint of shock in her voice. He couldn't allow anything to undermine his resolve. Or his detachment. "That doesn't make her innocent."

Kate sighed. "No, it doesn't. It's just... Oh, Trent." She threw her head back against the seat and squeezed her eyes tightly shut. "What if Savannah *is* innocent? What if she has no idea what her father is up to?"

Trent had already had this conversation with himself. Several times, to be exact. He wasn't having it again. Not with Kate. Not with anyone.

"Listen to me, Kate. We're at war. If Savannah Elliott is guilty of treason it's our job to ensure she's stopped. By any means necessary." His gut rolled at the burst of images that spread through his mind. "*Don't* make this personal."

"But it is personal. That's why I'm involved, because of my *personal* connection." She spoke calmly enough, but her hands shook as she fiddled with the latch on her purse. "I just never thought my best friend would be under suspicion. Her father, yes. But not Savannah."

Nevertheless, she was under suspicion. They both needed to get that straight in their minds.

"Harden your heart, Kate." Advice he'd given himself earlier. Advice he needed to take now. "There's no room for a conscience in our line of business."

"You think I don't know that?" She swung around to face him. The moonlight shone like fire in her eyes. "You think I haven't watched people die because of my choices, my interference? You think I'm not struggling to hold on to my own morality? My very soul?"

"It's too late for second thoughts."

"I know." She lowered her head and ground her teeth together. *"I know."*

Even with the emphasis on each word, Kate's voice lacked conviction.

Trent would have to keep an eye on her now. Kate had an important role to play in this particular intrigue. Her involvement was key but not essential. If she couldn't handle the personal components of the situation, Trent would work around her. "Do you want to review the plan for tomorrow?"

She accepted the change of subject with a swift shake of her head. "No. I'm ready."

"That's what I wanted to hear." With cool precision, he put the car in gear and steered out of the parking lot. "In the meantime, we need to put additional surveillance on Peter Sorensen. He's proving to be a bigger part of the operation than we first expected."

"I could always…" Kate visibly shuddered. "Cozy up to him."

"Not a bad idea, except for one problem." Trent took his eyes off the road and placed his attention directly on her hair. The deep, rich color was darkened to a coal black in the confines of the car. "You're not his type."

She threw her head back and laughed. "Trent, darling, I'm every man's type."

Under normal circumstances, Trent would agree. Kate's remarkable beauty was an effective weapon in the game of espionage, hence her original recruitment in the OSS.

However, in the case of Peter Sorensen, not only would Kate's particular brand of beauty be ineffective, it could become a hindrance.

When she didn't come to the same conclusion right away, Trent helped her along. "Kate, *darling.*" He used her same tone as he returned his gaze to the road. "You aren't a blond-haired, blue-eyed Aryan."

After a brief moment of silence, one where he could practically hear her arguing with herself, she conceded the point with a short nod.

"No, I'm not." She sighed quietly. "We'll just have to figure out some other way to monitor Sorensen's activities."

"Agreed." Trent would work on the problem once he was alone in his hotel room.

Another moment of silence passed before Kate spoke again. "Trent?"

Knowing by her tone alone he wasn't going to like what she had to say, he braced himself. "Yes?"

"If you knew Savannah was innocent, I mean, knew it for certain, what would you have thought of her tonight?"

The question brought an unexpected, yet profound sadness. On that fateful day General Donovan had insisted Trent join the OSS his life had taken a dramatic turn, one that made individual opinions irrelevant.

"It doesn't matter." It *couldn't* matter.

"Just answer the question."

He swallowed back an oath, paused, then forced the truth past tight lips. "I would have thought she was the most remarkable woman I ever met."

Chapter Five

A sense of safety.

Time to heal.

Escape from scandal.

Whatever her original reasons had been for coming home, Savannah was no longer certain she'd made the right decision. Especially now, as she stood in her parents' kitchen, attempting to defend her actions as if she were a naughty child caught misbehaving. All she'd done was tell her father about her upcoming date with Trent.

"I only agreed to have lunch with the man," she said a second time in so many minutes. "Nothing spectacular or unusual, just lunch."

The more she spoke the more he scowled. "Why him?"

She lifted a shoulder. "I find him…amusing." It was true enough, if not the full truth.

Her father set his briefcase on the floor near the back door, then straightened. "Perhaps this date seems innocuous to you, Savannah, but you must be careful. Amusing or not, you don't know anything about the man."

Ignoring her father's glare, Savannah paced through the kitchen and stopped at the sink. She looked out the window.

Her mind raced as fast as the pair of birds chasing one another across the dew-covered lawn.

What did it matter if she didn't know much about Trent? Wasn't that the point of a casual lunch, to get to know one another better?

Despite her father's displeasure, Trent Mueller intrigued her in a way she couldn't quite define. Or understand. She was inexplicably drawn to him, as if she were the tide and he the moon. Adhering to his strong pull seemed...inevitable.

"Savannah, are you listening to me?"

Realizing her father had continued talking—arguing, actually—she spun back around and cut him off with a swipe of her hand. "I've heard what you had to say and find it rather insulting. Regardless of what you might think, I am capable of choosing my own lunch companions."

Bold words. Yet, as she stared into her father's worried gaze, she admitted he had a point. A very small one, but valid all the same. She really didn't know much about Trent. A year ago, that small factoid wouldn't have mattered to either her or her father. But now they had the benefit of hindsight. For what it was worth.

Sighing, she picked her way around the breakfast nook and dropped into a chair with a soft whoosh. "If I hadn't married Johnny, if he hadn't...died the way he did, would you still be warning me away from Trent?"

"Yes." The answer came too quickly.

Savannah whipped her gaze back to her father, only to find him hovering over her. He'd moved without a sound, and was standing so close she felt the tension pulsing through him.

Still scowling, he ran a hand down her hair in a familiar gesture from her childhood. The one he'd used when she'd needed comforting. "Try to understand my point of view. I don't want to see you hurt."

Savannah sighed again. Her father meant well, he always meant well. But he was refusing to accept that she was a grown woman, one who'd run her own household for over a year. She didn't need his advice on such a simple matter as a date.

"It's just lunch," she repeated more forcefully than before. "Nothing earth-shattering, Father, and certainly nothing to concern yourself with."

Pressing his lips into a hard line, he dropped his hand and stepped back. "Under normal circumstances I might agree. But you're still in a vulnerable state, my child, easy prey for a man like Trent Mueller."

Easy prey. As if she was incapable of seeing past a man's outer façade to the true person underneath. Insulted more than before, Savannah fought for calm. She wasn't ignorant, or an idle socialite, or a weak woman who couldn't think for herself. She was an educated woman finding her way in the world, doing her part for the war effort as the sole bookkeeper for a large shipyard.

"This discussion is over," she declared.

The look on her father's face told her he had more to say on the matter. "Not until you admit that your judgment isn't as sound as it should be."

Her judgment not sound? Now Savannah was angry. Really angry. "*My* judgment?" She rose from her chair so quickly it teetered on one leg before settling back on all four with a bang. "What of yours?"

He straightened to his full height. "Mine is quite intact, I assure you."

"Is it?" She held his stare. "I wonder."

"I know where this is heading," her father said. "Do not try to redirect this discussion. I'm not the one having lunch with a strange man."

"No." She swallowed back an unladylike snort. "Yet, you hired one you knew equally little about."

Owl-eyed, her father blinked at her as though he had no idea who she meant.

They both knew that wasn't remotely true. This wasn't the first time she'd spoken against his assistant.

Nevertheless, she clarified, "I'm talking about Peter. He's… that is, I don't…" She let her words trail off, unsure how to proceed. Like all the other times she'd raised her suspicions, she didn't have anything concrete to hold against the man. Her dislike of Peter Sorensen was based on mere impressions.

Soon, she promised herself, she would have her proof very soon.

"You don't…what, Savannah? What is it you want to say against Peter?"

"He…" She lifted her chin. "I don't trust him." There. She'd spoken her piece of mind.

But rather than showing anger over her declaration, her father laughed at her. He actually laughed. "I can assure you, as I have done ever since you arrived home, Peter is a good man and quite trustworthy."

With that bold tone, her father sounded rather convincing. Savannah was almost willing to give Peter a second chance. But she'd spent enough time in his company to know he was not the man he pretended to be around her father.

Peter Sorensen was hiding something, something…criminal. Or perhaps something far worse.

Her father's blind faith in him concerned Savannah. She would find out what the man was hiding, if for no other reason than to protect her father from harm, as he'd tried to do for her with Johnny.

She only prayed he would be more receptive to the truth than she had been.

"Savannah, as much as we need to continue this conversation, I have an early meeting this morning." He still didn't look her in the eye. "And you should be on your way as well."

Now he was hustling her along? When he'd been so adamant about talking before they both left for work?

It was Savannah's turn to blink at her father in surprise.

He leaned down and kissed her on the cheek. "Promise me you'll keep what I said in mind. You don't know anything about Trent Mueller." He headed toward the door. "I'll see you later tonight."

Without another word, her father picked up his briefcase and walked out of the house, effectively ending the conversation.

That, she realized, was the first time her father had ever run from a difficult conversation. The thought left her apprehensive. And determined to prove her suspicions were real.

Savannah thought over the disturbing run-in she'd had with her father back at the house. Although offensive at first, she had to admit that his worries about Trent Mueller made a strange sort of sense, given her recent history. However, his reaction to her responding qualms about Peter did *not* make sense.

Her father might have laughed at her concerns, but her judgment couldn't be that far off. Her doubts about Peter were too strong not to be founded on some basis of truth. Unfortunately, without concrete evidence, her father would never listen to what she had to say.

Unsure how to prove her suspicions were real, she pushed her glasses in place, opened one of her ledgers and concentrated on the first batch of numbers running in neat, precise rows down the page.

This was where she was supposed to be. Making a difference for the U.S. war effort, small as it might seem to the outside world. Just last week she'd found a discrepancy that had resulted in the firing of a shady manager. The company's production had already increased under the new manager's leadership.

Smiling, Savannah silently checked off each column. The sounds of the shipyard wafted through the seams of her closed door. The familiar high-pitched grinding of drills and the pounding of hammers to metal soothed her, as did the scents of oil, melted tar and charred wood. They were doing important work at Pembroke. Everyone's contribution mattered.

Blowing a loose strand of hair off her forehead, Savannah ran her gaze down the next column of numbers. Even as she found satisfaction in her work, this wasn't where she thought her life would lead.

Hadn't she been obedient all her life, following the Lord's commands since her youth, dutifully memorizing Scriptures every week as a child? Yet, here she sat, starting over at the age of twenty-five.

Savannah leaned back in her chair and closed her eyes. This bout of self-pity wasn't like her. Life was messy. Life was unfair. Life was…life. She had to believe God was with her, regardless of her current circumstances. She was on the right path now, that's what mattered most.

A quick, hard knock on her door jolted her upright. She opened her eyes and took note of the clock on the far wall. Twelve noon on the dot.

Trent Mueller was a punctual man. Yet another fine quality to recommend him.

Rising from her chair, Savannah smoothed a surprisingly shaky hand down her hair, picked up a portion of her skirt and flicked out the wrinkles. Only just remembering her glasses, and oddly embarrassed that vanity got the best of her, she stuffed them in a drawer and then rubbed the bridge of her nose.

Satisfied she was presentable at last, and that Trent wouldn't find out she needed glasses to read fine print, she called out, "Come in."

The door creaked open and Trent entered the room in two long, confident strides. The moment his gaze found hers he stopped dead in his tracks and simply stared at her. His eyes filled with masculine appreciation.

Savannah's heart did a quick dip in her chest. And then another. She knew she was staring in return. But, oh, the man made quite a sight. Not only was he taller than she remembered, he was broader, too. And he looked incredibly handsome with his hair illuminated to a polished gold in the sunlight streaming through her window.

Dressed in a perfectly tailored dark blue suit and complementary gray silk tie, he shouldn't look this appealing. This... approachable. But the unspoken pull was back between them, stronger than before, calling to her.

She took a step forward. Just one tiny step. Air hitched in her throat.

But then he blinked, and thankfully—*regrettably?*—the moment was gone and she could breathe normally again.

Trent's lips lifted into a carefree grin.

"Savannah." He drawled her name in that rich baritone of his. "You're more beautiful than I remember." He took her hand and rubbed his thumb along her knuckles in a slow, rhythmic motion. "Utterly captivating."

"I..." Words escaped her. What could she possibly say in response to such a blatant attempt to charm her? He might not be evil, but he was proving dangerous.

She carefully drew her hand free.

Still smiling, he took a respectful step back and shifted his attention to her office.

"So." He looked around him in interest. "This is where you work."

Unable to decipher what she heard in his voice—something more complicated than mere curiosity—Savannah tried to view her office from a stranger's perspective.

Three filing cabinets of exact style and height stood shoulder to shoulder along the wall opposite the window. Two wooden chairs faced her large, mahogany desk. A threadbare rug sat perfectly square in the exact middle of the room. There was no other furniture. No paintings on the walls. No frills. Nothing that spoke of her personality, or her femininity, or the fact that she'd had this job for nearly a month.

"Your décor is very…" He appeared to search for the proper word. "…serviceable."

"I like order."

She knew she sounded defensive. But she doubted a man as sophisticated as Trent would understand her need to keep her work space free of clutter. Besides, how did she put into words her abhorrence of chaos when she didn't have the explanation quite right in her own mind? Anything she said now would come out sounding petty or trite or maybe a little foolish.

As if reading her thoughts, Trent gently touched her hand. "I find there can be exceptional beauty in order." There was such understanding in his eyes. And something else as well, something that fell just short of pity. Compassion, perhaps? Empathy?

Feeling that pull again, she took a step closer.

"What is it the Apostle Paul said?" He lifted his gaze to the ceiling. "Ah yes, 'God is not a God of disorder but of peace.'"

Caught slightly off guard, Savannah blinked up at the ceiling as well. Why was the man quoting Scripture, at such an odd time as this? Then she remembered he was a professor of theology. Or course he would apply Scripture to any occasion. It was probably as much a professional hazard as a way of life.

He lowered his head to look at her again. "Are you ready for lunch?"

"Almost. Give me a moment to gather my belongings."

The request earned her a dry chuckle. "Take all the time you need."

While she tidied her desk he strolled through the room with the same ease he'd demonstrated on the dance floor last evening. He was very graceful, like a large jungle cat on the prowl.

Shuddering at the image, Savannah watched Trent make his way around the perimeter of her office. He ran a finger along the top of the file cabinets, paused, cocked his head slightly, then began moving once again.

He was clearly inspecting her work area.

But why? Surely he was just killing time while he waited for her.

Or was he?

Her father's words popped into her mind. *Be careful, Savannah. You don't know anything about Trent Mueller.*

A shiver of alarm raced through her.

Then she remembered once again that Trent was a college professor. It made sense that he would be inquisitive about his surroundings. Wasn't that the nature of someone who chose a profession such as his?

She was still pondering the question when he moved to the window overlooking the St. Johns River. He stuffed his hands in his pockets and rocked back on his heels. His stance was casual, loose. Relaxed.

He glanced over his shoulder and caught her watching him.

He smiled. "I didn't realize Pembroke had operations farther down the river as well as here."

Something in his tone gave her pause. "We don't."

He looked down at her desk, hesitated a fraction of a second, then turned back to glance out the window. "Then what is that down there?"

Something in the way he posed the question made her wonder if he was testing her, which made no sense at all. She wasn't one of his students, and this wasn't a classroom.

Puzzling a moment longer, she pulled on one glove, then the other, wiggling her fingers until both fit snugly on her hands.

"You're looking at Anderson Shipyard," she said at last.

"Ah. So it's a separate operation from this one."

"Completely separate." She picked up her hat and began pinning it in place. "Anderson makes minesweepers and subchasers for the Navy, while we make Liberty ships."

"That seems like a lot of shipbuilding for one area." His tone came out mildly perplexed.

Then why did she get a feeling he was interrogating her, as though setting her up to slip somehow?

Utterly ridiculous. She had nothing to hide.

Nevertheless, she proceeded with caution and answered his leading statement with a bland one of her own. "It isn't so surprising when you consider where Jacksonville is located."

His shoulders stiffened ever-so-slightly. "I don't catch your meaning."

Somehow, she thought he did.

Wondering why he needed her to spell out the obvious, she said, "Well, for one thing, we have several naval bases nearby. Add in our mild climate, the reality that we are at war and the fact that the St. Johns River empties into the Atlantic Ocean only a few miles north of here, and it's a wonder there are only two shipyards in the area."

"Yes. I see."

What, precisely, did he see? Not sure she wanted to know the answer, Savannah picked up her purse and walked around her desk. "I'm ready to go now."

He spun around to face her, his face devoid of all emotion. "Splendid."

Trent guided Savannah through the shipyard. The noise and general commotion made speaking impossible, which was just as well. He needed a moment to sort through his thoughts, to remind himself he was here to gather information.

Now that he'd had a good look around Savannah's private office, he understood why William Klein had set up his daughter at Pembroke. Although the room was small and sparse, even by military standards, her desk was situated at an angle that gave her a direct line of vision to Anderson Shipyard. It would be easy enough to record comings and goings from such a vantage point.

Was Savannah a part of the Nazi plot, after all? Or was she merely a pawn in her father's game? Trent was no closer to an answer than the night before.

Holding to his silence, he steered Savannah in the direction of the parking lot. He kept his eyes straight ahead, his stride relaxed, ensuring he didn't call attention to himself. Not that it mattered. Unlike German shipyards, security was practically nonexistent at Pembroke. With or without the identification badge he'd taken off the work floor on his way in, it would be easy enough to sneak in at night for a better look around.

Trent glanced at Savannah out of the corner of his eye. A surge of emotion flashed through him, a feeling that was almost primitive—an unwelcome sensation that whispered: *Mine.*

What was he thinking? Allowing her to get to him so quickly and profoundly? Just last night he'd warned Kate not to let this get personal. He was a hypocrite.

What he couldn't understand was why. *Why* was Savannah Elliott different from the others? Yes, she was young and chic and beautiful, but he'd met many women with all those same qualities. His attraction to her went beyond the physical. A first for him.

Maybe it was that faint air of hope under her pain that captured him, a sense that no matter how bad things got for her she would survive. Maybe he simply wanted to rest in that hope. Just for a moment.

Impossible. And potentially deadly. The woman could very well be his enemy. Getting close to her could be a death sentence, not only for him but for others.

He turned his focus to the shipyard. In a swift glance, he counted six docking bays along the river, one central work area, two large cranes to the east and various scaffolding built at different heights on the west end of the building. He saw too much vulnerability to calculate an exact target for sabotage.

He would definitely have to come back at night. Alone.

Savannah stumbled over a piece of stray tubing. Breaking stride, Trent caught her before she fell.

"I…" She looked at his hand, frowned, then glanced back up at him. "Thank you. I'm fine now."

He dropped his hand and breathed in her soft, floral scent, which wafted over the shipyard's stench. He ordered himself to remember who she was, *who her father was,* but Trent couldn't quite make his brain accept the reality of the situation, or the danger. Savannah seemed so…innocent.

He shrugged off the thought. "Where would you like to eat this afternoon?"

She stared at him a moment. "There's a department store downtown that has a lovely restaurant on the top floor. I can easily recommend the food. I eat there several times a week."

All of which Trent already knew. In fact, not only did Savannah eat at the restaurant she just mentioned, so did other prominent citizens of the city. Trent couldn't have planned a better place for their lunch. "Sounds perfect."

In silent agreement, they resumed walking.

Once they stepped into the parking lot, he directed her to his car, opened the passenger door and offered her his hand.

Accepting his assistance, her gloved fingers curled over his. He swallowed hard and forced himself to ignore the way his pulse jumped as he continued holding her hand until she was settled in her seat.

Frowning, he shut the door and then strode around to his side of the car. With each step, he realigned his priorities in his mind. He might not look like a soldier on the outside, but he was fighting this war with every weapon at his disposal.

His reaction to Savannah Elliott—personal, profound or otherwise—was irrelevant. The woman was the quickest and easiest avenue into her father's world.

One of Trent's other objectives was to ferret out Savannah's loyalties, but in order to do that he had to gain her trust first. As quickly as possible. With no bouts of conscience getting in the way.

Nothing personal.

No hard feelings.

One step at a time.

Chapter Six

The Carmen Café was more crowded than usual, with only one empty table left along the column of windows overlooking Hemming Park. Savannah took Trent's arm as he guided her through the maze of other diners. She kept her eyes focused straight ahead, refusing to acknowledge the interest thrown their way.

Nevertheless, a hush filled the restaurant. Conversations halted. Heads turned. Disapproval floated on the air.

Savannah clutched Trent's arm a little tighter and kept walking. Perhaps it was the man by her side, perhaps it was her own frustration, whatever the reason, for the first time since arriving home she felt ready to face the curious stares. *And* the speculation that came with them.

It was time to quit feeling sorry for herself.

Johnny was dead. There was no rewriting the story's end. Perhaps if he'd suffered a more noble demise, say on the front lines of the war, there might be less gossip surrounding his death. Perhaps the rumors would be kinder.

Or…perhaps not. People were, after all, people. It was basic human nature to think the worst of others and then share those thoughts with anyone willing to listen.

Lord, when did I become so cynical?

Was the next step bitterness?

Not if she could help it.

Trent's gaze met hers. The look in his eyes proclaimed he was fully in the moment. With her. Savannah's mood immediately lifted. It would appear she had an ally in this particular drama.

Adding to the picture of the two of them against the world, he made a grand display of pulling out her chair and waiting until she was settled before rounding the table. Savannah removed her gloves and made eye contact with the people staring back at her.

She belonged here as much as anyone else.

She smiled at her father's friend Dr. Klinger and his wife, Cora. They returned her smile without a hint of judgment in their eyes.

Such a kind couple, Savannah thought.

The ladies from her mother's bridge club were a different matter. Each woman sent her the *look,* as Savannah thought of it, the same unconcealed censure she'd endured at the club last night.

Savannah sighed.

"Ignore them," Trent said, his voice filled with such compassion she could have wept.

He wasn't unaware of the whispers. He just didn't care what others thought of him. Or rather, he didn't care what others thought of them being together.

In that moment, Savannah decided to enjoy this lunch date. *Really* enjoy it.

"What do you recommend?" Trent asked, running his gaze down the menu in slow perusal.

"Everything." She smiled at him as she spoke. And, oh, it felt good to smile. "But I'm partial to the catfish. It's always fresh."

He looked over the top of the menu at her. "Is that what you're having?"

"It's what I always order."

"Then I'll try it, too." He lifted his hand in the air.

A waiter instantly appeared.

While Trent recited their orders, Savannah took the opportunity to study him. There was something very male about him, an aura that exuded masculine confidence. He was clearly a man in charge of his own destiny.

He must have been an officer in the Army, she thought, and a good one at that. She'd caught the way he'd surveyed the restaurant when they'd first arrived.

Surely he'd behaved out of habit.

Her stomach fluttered with a wave of panic. Not because she was afraid of Trent, but because she *wasn't*. Although she knew virtually nothing about him, Savannah couldn't help feeling secure when she was in his company. Maybe even safe.

Absurd. And yet...

What if Trent was different from other men? What if he was worthy of her trust?

Savannah swallowed, suddenly remembering a Bible verse she'd learned during the dark days after Johnny's death. She couldn't remember the exact words now, but the Scripture had something to do with putting her trust in the Lord rather than man. But, she'd always wondered, how could she learn to trust an invisible God if she couldn't first trust a living, breathing human being?

"I must say, Savannah." Trent's voice broke through her thoughts. "Your choice in restaurants is commendable. The view is lovely."

His eyes never left her face.

Was he talking about the scenery outside their window? Or her? She shifted uncomfortably in her seat and glanced at the scene below. Hemming Park was pretty, with the flowers in bloom and the sun glinting off the Civil War monument.

The people in the park seemed so carefree, so picture-perfect, going about their business as though it was just another day in sunny Florida. There were no signs of war here today, no real hardships to endure. Life went on as usual.

An illusion, of course, but one that made Savannah want to sigh with contentment. If only for a moment.

"The flowers are gorgeous this time of year." She turned back to face Trent. He'd relaxed in his chair and was watching her with lazy, half-lowered lids. Casual. Comfortable. Completely approachable.

She let down her guard a little more. Enough to add, "I like watching the people from way up here on the fifth floor."

"Is that right?" Something in his nonthreatening posture instilled a further sense of confidence. Another portion of the wall she'd constructed around her heart fell away.

"It's easier to watch them than get involved in their lives."

Mortified at what she'd just revealed, she clamped her lips tightly shut. Why had she said so much? What must he think of her? She wasn't really afraid to live in the world among people. Not anymore.

Maybe she'd never been afraid. She'd simply been grieving. Grief could make even the strongest person buckle for a time.

Trent reached out and placed his hand over hers. "Savannah. Who hurt you?"

Mesmerized by his warm touch and the look of genuine concern in his eyes, she rotated her wrist until their palms met.

Safe.

Even with that intriguing aura of mystery that surrounded him, or perhaps because of it, the man made her feel so...incredibly...safe. After all, he was a stranger she might never see again. What did it matter what he thought of her? He would be gone in a few days' time. The knowledge made her feel free. She wanted to tell him everything.

Shocked at the direction of her thoughts, she pulled her hand back and placed it in her lap. "I didn't say anyone hurt me."

Strong words, *bold* words, but her voice came out raspy. The kind of sound that preceded tears.

"You didn't have to say it." He smiled that lazy, attractive smile of his. A mask? Or a natural part of the attractive, appealing man he seemed to be.

"I…" He'd left her speechless again, just as he had back in her office.

Why was he being so kind? And so…persistent? What did he really want from her?

"Savannah, you don't strike me as a woman afraid to live in the world." His voice dropped an octave. "You're too vibrant to lurk behind a wall of windows watching other people go about their lives without you."

Something clutched around her throat, something wonderful. With a few well-chosen words Trent Mueller had penetrated the rest of her defenses and touched her heart.

She leaned toward him then snapped back, *finally* remembering this could all be a game to him. And she just another woman in a long line of others.

"Are you trying to gain my trust through false flattery?"

"It's not false when it's the truth."

His earnestness sent her pulse scrambling. It would be so easy to trust this man, to believe he meant well.

But what was really behind that handsome façade of his? She had to know, had to take command of this conversation. "What are *you* hiding, Trent?" She angled her head to study him better. "What's your secret?"

Except for a slight narrowing of his eyes, her question seemed to amuse him. He leaned back in his chair and steepled his fingers beneath his chin. "I have no secrets, beautiful." His eyes crinkled along the edges. "I'm exactly who I appear to be."

"No one is exactly who they appear to be." She placed her palms flat on the table and held his gaze without wavering. "*Everybody* has a secret."

"Do they, now?" He lifted his water glass to his lips, took a sip then set it back on the table. His movements were precise, but his eyes were filled with playful humor.

Savannah didn't find any of this funny. An image of Peter's cold stare flashed in her mind, making her shiver. "In my experience everyone hides something from the world."

"Even you?"

Especially me, she wanted to shout. Instead, she settled back in her chair and spoke calmly. "Even me."

"Then tell me, Savannah. What's your secret?"

There was an unfamiliar ball of...something in her stomach, something astonishing, a feeling that she could trust this man with the truth.

"Savannah?" he urged.

The nerves she'd battled off and on since arriving at the restaurant played havoc with her confidence. She refused to allow them to win. "I was married once before."

There, she'd said it. The truth was out at last.

"Yes. Kate told me."

Well, of course *Kate* told him. Savannah brushed her hands over her skirt, trying desperately to stave off the surge of unexpected emotion that pawed through her. It wasn't her business what relationship this man had with Kate.

Then again, yes, maybe it was her business. She knew firsthand what it felt like to lose a man to another woman. She would never knowingly be the cause of that kind of pain, especially not in the case of a friend.

"Is there something between you and Kate," she asked, "something...romantic?"

"No." He didn't elaborate, didn't stumble over an explanation. His answer had been simple and to the point.

And she believed him.

Did that make her a fool? *Oh, Lord, please, I hope not.*

"Did Kate also tell you that my husband was killed in a car crash six months ago?"

"Yes." Trent twirled his finger along the rim of his water glass. "She did."

Her friend had been quite chatty with the man. "What else did Kate tell you?"

His hand stilled and something like anger crossed his face. "She told me your husband's lover was in the seat next to him when he died."

Instant tears filled Savannah's eyes. She turned her head away, blinking ruthlessly. She would not shed another tear for Johnny Elliott. Not. One. More.

"Well, then, you know my secret." Her lips trembled as she spoke.

"The scandal surrounding your husband's death is not a secret, Savannah." His voice slid over her like a soft, cool, refreshing breeze. "Not yours, anyway."

She felt a familiar fluttering in her stomach again. Longing? Hope? Both? Neither?

"I—" She cut off her own words. Trent was right. The scandal behind Johnny's death was not a secret. Not in this town. "All right, you want to know what I'm hiding from the rest of the world?"

He nodded slowly. "I do."

"My entire life is…" She took a deep pull of air and plunged forward. "My entire life is a lie."

Trent went perfectly still. An overwhelming sense of remorse flooded his mind. Savannah had just confessed to living a lie. He was surprised by the pain her admission brought him.

Dear God, Dear God…

He stopped the prayer before it started and made himself reconsider Savannah's words. She hadn't admitted to anything concrete. Yes, she'd claimed to be living a lie. But wasn't that true of everyone? As Savannah herself had said, every person carried a secret within them.

Taking a slow, deep breath, Trent looked at her without expression and centered his thoughts. The most obvious solution was to ask her what she meant, exactly. She'd been unknowingly submitting to his subtle interrogation ever since they'd entered the restaurant.

Why not continue?

Before he could begin the waiter returned with their food. After a bit of jostling and rearranging of silverware to fit the plates on the table, they were alone once again, the smell of fried catfish floating on the air between them.

The food sat untouched.

Trent continued holding Savannah's stare. She continued looking back, with her hands woven together in her lap, her eyes blinking rapidly and her bottom lip pulled between her teeth.

She did not look like a liar, as she claimed. Or a spy. Or even a Nazi sympathizer. On the contrary, she looked horrified she'd spoken so plainly.

Trent wanted to give her the benefit of the doubt.

But no. He couldn't.

He cleared his mind and applied himself to ferreting out the truth. The full truth. Above all else, he had to remain detached. "What sort of lie are you living, Savannah?"

She lowered her head and sighed. "Johnny's car crash wasn't an accident."

He held perfectly still. Where was she heading with this? "Was there any indication of tampering?"

"What?" Her eyes rounded with genuine shock. "No. *No.*"

Relief washed through Trent like a rush of living water. Certain of where she was heading now, he wanted to offer her comfort. He wanted to tell her not to blame herself, that the car crash wasn't her fault, but he knew in her current state of mind she wouldn't hear him.

He tried anyway. "Of course the crash was an accident."

"It wasn't." She looked frantically around her then leaned forward and lowered her voice so only he would hear her next words. "The crash was my fault."

Trent knew all about guilt over someone else's death, how taking the blame could eat away at the very soul of a person. But in this instance, Savannah was wrong. "You weren't driving that car."

She lowered her hands to her lap and carefully placed one on top of the other. "You don't understand."

How perfectly untrue. "Then explain it to me."

She sighed. "I was out to dinner with friends the night Johnny died. At one point I looked up from the table and there he was, standing in the doorway, with another woman on his arm."

A man dishonoring his marriage vows, the worst possible transgression, in Trent's estimation. He wanted to hit something. Or rather, someone. Unfortunately—or perhaps fortunately—that particular someone was already dead. "What happened next?"

"Johnny didn't notice me at first. He was too..." She looked to her left, looked to her right, then sighed. "Enamored with his date."

He already knew all this; the briefing had been thorough. Yet, the image threaded anger through Trent's calm. No one deserved that sort of betrayal. Wanting to offer comfort, he tried to take Savannah's hand. She shifted out of his reach.

"When Johnny finally looked in my direction I had risen from my chair and was already walking toward him. I had no idea what I was going to do, or say. My steps were fueled by anger. Not shock, not hurt, but unbridled rage. I knew the confrontation would be ugly. I kept walking toward him, anyway."

She paused, fiddled with her napkin in her lap, twisted the

cloth around and around in her hands. "When he finally saw me his face turned white, like he'd seen a ghost."

"I'm sorry, Savannah. I'm really sorry." He meant every word.

"They immediately left the restaurant, but he knew what he'd done. I saw it in his eyes. He *knew* he'd betrayed me. And then…" She drew in a ragged breath. "He wrapped his car around a tree less than an hour later."

"Savannah." Trent spoke very slowly, very carefully. "You aren't to blame for your husband's accident."

"Oh, but I am. He was distraught over seeing me. He was driving too fast and wasn't paying attention." She choked back a sob. "The accident was my fault."

There were all kinds of responses Trent could give. He focused on alleviating what he heard in her voice. Guilt. "You might *feel* like it's your fault, but feelings aren't truth."

He paused and made sure she was looking at him before he continued. "The truth is your husband got behind the wheel of a car and then smashed it into a tree. The whys behind his actions, and the doubts over who's to blame, those are all are based on feelings. Not truth, Savannah, *feelings*."

She gave him a watery smile. He could see she'd heard him and was processing his words. "It's that simple to you?"

"It's that simple, period."

"I…thank you, Trent." Her lashes fluttered and her eyes filled with water, but she didn't give in to her tears. "Just…thank you."

Trent's pulse scrambled in his veins. He shouldn't allow emotion to get a foothold. But it was too late. By showing strength in her moment of vulnerability, by refusing to buckle under her emotions, she'd made him care. In that instant, she'd become a major liability to him and to the mission.

Why she'd affected him so quickly—so deeply—was something he couldn't allow himself to consider. Not for a moment.

To say he was concerned at the turn of events would be a gross understatement. The woman could very well be a traitor.

His brain refused to wrap around the notion.

A movement at the café's entrance pulled at his attention. He swiveled his head in time to catch sight of two athletic-looking men dressed in dark suits standing in the doorway.

Savannah sucked in a harsh breath and proceeded to speak Trent's thoughts aloud. "What is the FBI doing here?"

Chapter Seven

With Savannah's words reverberating in his mind, Trent gathered information at lightning speed. Two men. Dark suits. Probably—*definitely*—FBI. They were standing in the doorway. Surveying the diners one by one.

Trent didn't have time to be surprised. He could only think, plan and evaluate. All while maintaining a relaxed pose.

By the way the two men scanned the restaurant, with single-minded precision, they were undoubtedly looking for someone specific.

But who?

And why here? Why now?

Their presence during a critical OSS operation had the potential for disaster. But what Trent considered the most concerning piece of the puzzle was Savannah's certainty of the men's identities.

"You think they're from the Federal Bureau of Investigation?" he asked, watching her closely, searching for any signs of deception or cunning.

She swung her gaze back to his, her eyes narrowed with indignation. "It's not as though they're trying to hide their identities."

Trent's thoughts precisely.

The FBI shouldn't be here, not now, and certainly not in such an obvious manner. The OSS had taken the lead on this mission. The lines of communication had failed somewhere along the way. It was the kind of blunder that got men killed. Good men like Bobby Gallagher, as well as children like little Heinrich, and countless others.

Trent swallowed back his growing rage and focused on the most disconcerting unknown in the equation. *Savannah*. She seemed overly certain in her conclusion. Too certain.

"What do you mean? I think they look like every other man in this restaurant."

Not precisely true, but Trent needed to decipher the extent of Savannah's observation skills.

"Look at them closely. I mean, *really* look at them." She made no move to do so herself, but waited for him to do as she commanded.

"Notice how their close-cropped, military haircuts are identical under their nondescript hats," she said. "Not only that, they're also wearing ill-fitting black—not blue, not gray, but black—suits in the exact same make and boxy style."

Her description was spot-on, and yet, she hadn't once looked at them since she'd started talking. Trent experienced the swift ache of loss. Loss for what, exactly, he didn't know.

He pushed back the sensation and continued questioning Savannah with nothing more than mild curiosity in his tone. "You're saying they're FBI simply because they dress alike?"

"That's precisely what I'm saying." She lifted a delicate shoulder. "What two men in your acquaintance wear the same suit, in the same style, on the same day?"

Trent hauled in a tight breath. Her question was valid, and one he'd considered with the other pieces of information he'd already gathered.

The FBI *wanted* everyone to know they were here.

Whatever their motive, Trent's job just got harder.

"They could be local cops," he said, primarily to find out what Savannah's response would be to the unlikely possibility. "Maybe detectives of some sort."

"No. They're FBI."

"You seem pretty convinced."

Her fingers began drumming on the table in a rapid tap, tap, tap. "They come to town every week, like clockwork."

She looked the picture of outrage as she watched them move through the restaurant and pick a table on the opposite side of the room as their own.

"Those same men have been here before?" he asked.

"No. Different men, same suit. Like I said, FBI."

He continued probing. "Why would the FBI come to Jacksonville on a regular basis?"

Trent already knew the answer: standard operating procedure during war. However, Savannah's take on the situation mattered. The woman was proving to be a strange mixture of contradictions: her mind was observant—almost calculating—but her eyes were innocent. Heartbreakingly so.

Sighing, she shook her head. "They're here to watch Dr. Klinger and his wife."

She nodded toward a table on her right.

Trent followed the direction of her gaze and took note of the elegantly dressed elderly man and woman.

"As you can see for yourself, that sweet couple is utterly harmless."

Trent agreed. Or rather, he agreed that Dr. Klinger and his wife *looked* harmless. But in his experience, looks were often deceiving.

Regardless of the fact that the doctor had a kind face, a full head of bushy white hair and a ruddy complexion, he could still pose a considerable threat if he was a Nazi sympathizer. The man's wife, although painfully thin and seemingly too frail to wreck any real havoc, could be just as dangerous.

Trent had seen enough in Germany to know what people were capable of in time of war. He shuddered as memories tried to make their way into his consciousness. "Why do you think the government is watching the Klingers?"

"Because they're German, of course."

Of course.

Her fingers started tapping faster, then went perfectly still. She had more to say. He saw the truth of it in her eyes. The hesitation came next, and then the decision to reveal something distressing.

Trent maintained his calm exterior.

"They keep an eye on...my father, as well as several others in town."

So. She knew about the government's interest in her father. What else did she know?

Trent rolled his shoulders, trying to free the knots forming in his muscles. But the tension was there to stay now that the conversation was heading in the proper direction, if somewhat unplanned.

Eyes locked with Savannah's, he chose his words cautiously. He couldn't be obvious in his questioning, but he had to be relentless. "The FBI watches your father on a regular basis? Why?"

"For the same reason they watch Dr. Klinger. Because he's a German-American."

Ah, they'd arrived at a moment of truth. "They watch your father simply because he's German, and no other reason?"

Savannah pushed back from the table with a hard shove and looked at Trent as though he'd missed a valuable point in the conversation.

"Yes, Trent." She spoke slowly, the way a teacher spoke to a student not paying attention. "The FBI watches my father simply because he's German."

Trent leaned forward, trying to read into her very soul. What *were* her loyalties? What role, if any, did she play in all this?

"That surprises you?"

She picked up a dinner roll and proceeded to shred it into tiny pieces. "My father has always been a loyal American."

"You seem very sure of him."

"I'd stake my life on this one thing." She set the roll back on the plate with exaggerated care. "William Klein is completely devoted to his country."

Trent said nothing. He was coming to believe Savannah was innocent. In everything. The plot. Treason. All of it. But he knew better than to confuse his personal hopes with reality. Yes, she'd uttered a few heartfelt words about her father's loyalty. But words were just *words*.

The woman could be a master at deception. Just like Trent. Or maybe even better.

A sick spasm shot through his gut. He broke eye contact and looked over at the FBI agents again. They didn't look back, which was suspicious for a variety of reasons. They should be watching everyone in the restaurant, not just one couple, at one table. They either weren't doing their job properly. Or they had another agenda in mind.

Whatever the reason for their behavior, Trent would have to contact General Donovan and have him pull the FBI back, at least for the next two weeks.

Then again…

Perhaps Trent could use their presence to his advantage. He ran several scenarios through his mind. Discarded one after another, then decided on an approach. The one that would have the added benefit of gaining William Klein's interest, if not his immediate trust.

In the meantime, he needed to continue interrogating Savannah, gently, of course. "I'm sure your father has nothing to worry about. I suspect the government is simply being cautious." The misleading statement flowed off his lips with ease.

"Perhaps you're right."

She seemed calmer. Trent, however, was not. He'd become an expert at lying. Whenever a wave of conscience struck in the past, he would remind himself of the story in the Old Testament where Joshua sent spies into Jericho. Usually that did the trick.

But lying to Savannah didn't feel right. It felt like a betrayal. Especially after all she'd been through with her husband's deception.

Trent felt like a world-class heel.

Feelings weren't real, he reminded himself. And feelings weren't truth.

Maintaining his silence, he picked up his fork and forced himself to concentrate on his food.

Savannah did the same.

She took several bites, then set her utensil back on the table and looked out the window. Her eyebrows slammed together.

"What I don't understand is the government's concern with German-Americans." She spoke the words almost to herself. "The Japanese are the ones who attacked us."

Trent had heard this argument often enough, in countless American homes, as though the war was only being fought against one enemy—the one who'd attacked the U.S. directly.

How incredibly naïve.

The threat of Hitler and his Third Reich was real. The monster regime's desire to conquer the world was real. The remote, secret saboteur school at Quenz Lake in Prussia was *real*.

The reconnaissance pictures Trent had locked inside his briefcase showed a highly developed training program. All indications pointed to the fact that Operation Pastorius—the failed plot against the United States a year ago—was only the first wave. More attempts were imminent. They would be carried out by German soldiers who not only spoke English but had all lived in the United States. Most of the saboteurs were believed to be American citizens.

Was Savannah truly ignorant of the current plot?

Trent's gut said yes, but in reality he was no closer to an answer than when they'd arrived at the restaurant.

He looked at the food left on his plate then set down his fork with cold precision. "Japan isn't our only enemy," he said. "We're fighting a very nasty war in Europe as well."

"I…*know*." She too gave up all pretense of eating and shoved her plate out of the way. "Bobby's death proves that."

Trent recoiled at the reminder of his fallen friend. Flagrant miscommunications had led to a bloodbath in Hamburg. Trent had barely made it out of Germany alive. Bobby had not.

Because of that experience Trent would never be the same man again. His *soul* would never be the same.

"The war with Germany is real, as indisputable as the one in the Pacific." He lowered his voice to a hiss. "Make no mistake, Savannah, Hitler and the German High Command want to conquer this country. They rejoice in *every* American death. And any American citizen aiding the German cause is a traitor."

She stared wide-eyed at him, clearly shocked by his vehemence.

He was shocked himself. Trent Mueller, cold-hearted, unconscionable secret agent, never lost his cool. *Never.*

A chill encircled his heart.

This woman had just made him speak plainly when it was deadly to do so. If she was a party to her father's activities Trent had very possibly overplayed his hand.

He gnashed his teeth together, then just as quickly relaxed his jaw. One blink, a quick smile, and the charming sophisticate was back in place. No worries on his mind other than enjoying a wonderful meal with his lovely date.

Unfortunately, his transformation hadn't been fast enough, and compassion filled Savannah's gaze. "Trent, tell me the truth. How many friends, besides Bobby, have you lost in the European campaign?"

He blinked at the soft lilt of her voice. "Too many," he admitted.

She closed her hand over his and squeezed. "I'm sorry."

With those two words she pushed beneath his sophisticated façade. Again. Her ability to worm past his defenses, past all of his training, was a complication he couldn't afford.

In less than two days he'd revealed more to this woman than he had to anyone before her. What was it about Savannah Elliott that made him want to bare his soul and take dangerous risks?

Why did he suddenly want to believe goodness existed in the world and that God would put His hand on the Allied forces? That victory would be theirs?

Savannah's voice broke through his thoughts. "What you said earlier, about Americans aiding Germany." She pulled her hand back and set it in her lap. "Do you truly believe there are people—American citizens—actually sympathetic to Germany over their own country?"

He answered truthfully. "Yes."

Her gaze locked on his. There was a storm behind her eyes, one that made her look both uncomfortable and slightly angry. "It's not my father the FBI should be watching."

"No?"

"No. They should be watching…" She dragged her finger along the table's edge, then leaned forward. "…his assistant."

The moment the words left her mouth she clamped her lips tightly together. Evidently, she hadn't meant to speak so plainly. Not to him, at any rate. A veritable stranger.

Or maybe she had meant to do exactly that.

If she were a traitor like her father, if she knew why Trent was really here—why he was courting her—it would be a brilliant move on her part to gain his trust by creating a common enemy. A perfect plan to see what he knew.

Then again, she could have genuine concerns about Peter Sorensen that were based on facts Trent could use to forward his own mission's goals.

His best option was to play along. See where this line of questioning led him.

"You think your father's assistant is a…friend of Germany? Isn't he a Norwegian?"

"Yes, he is. Or rather, that's what he claims. But he seems overly enamored with all things German."

"So are a lot of people. That doesn't make them traitors."

"I know that." She leaned back in her chair and blew out a frustrated breath. "I don't know why I'm so suspicious of Peter. There's something about him I don't trust."

"Can you be more specific?"

"Not really. But I think he's using my father. It's just a feeling, nothing concrete."

Her distress seemed far too real to be an act. That didn't mean it wasn't an act. Trent remained silent a moment. And then another. And still another. His gaze never left her face.

Savannah squirmed in her seat.

He continued holding the pause.

She broke at last. "If only I could prove my suspicions."

Now they were getting somewhere. "Any ideas where to start?"

Trent had a few, but this was her game. She needed to take the lead. And he needed to let her, something that didn't come naturally to him but was important in ferreting out her motives.

"Not really, no." Her fingers began tapping on the table again, faster this time. "I figure the best place to start would be to look for a paper trail of some sort."

Brilliant. "Why would you think that?"

"As an accountant I've discovered one fast and hard truth." Her eyes gleamed. "There's always a paper trail."

Trent was really starting to like this woman. Perhaps a little too much. His best course of action would be to test her. To do so could be dangerous, but could also lead to a great reward.

He took the risk. "What if I told you I could get you inside Sorensen's office at night to look around without interruption?"

Her eyes narrowed. "I would have to wonder how a college professor could make such an offer."

He took another, bolder risk and revealed pertinent information about himself. "I was Army Intelligence before I was injured." Easily verified if she—or anyone else—did a little digging. "I have certain, shall we say, skills."

She looked intrigued, rather than shocked. And now he really liked her.

"Skills," she said. "As in the kind that could get me inside a man's, shall we say, private office?"

"Precisely."

"And if I said I was game? Hypothetically speaking, of course."

"Then I'd say you should meet me in the lobby of my hotel tonight and we could *hypothetically* take a midnight stroll through downtown."

"A midnight stroll through downtown." She smiled tentatively at him. "Which hotel did you say was yours?"

"I didn't."

She lifted a single eyebrow.

"I'm staying at the Roosevelt."

"That's one of my favorites."

"Mine as well," he said. "I find the hotel especially lovely as a starting point for a midnight stroll."

A beat passed. And another. Her shoulders finally relaxed. "I'd love to experience such a thing."

"And so you shall." He grinned at her, making sure to put a lot of mischievous boy in the gesture. "This very night."

"I'll wear black."

"Excellent choice."

And with that, the date was set.

Trent would get Savannah inside Sorensen's private office. She was either setting a trap for him or chasing a paper trail as she claimed.

He would know for certain after tonight.

Satisfied with his plan, he looked pointedly at her plate. "Are you finished eating?"

"I…" She looked down, too. "Oh, yes. I guess I am." She set her napkin on the table and smiled. At him. Only him.

His heart twisted in his chest.

Needing air, lots of air, he rose. "Let's go." He tossed down enough money to cover their meals and then stretched out his hand.

She accepted his assistance with her inherent graciousness. The moment their fingers touched her smile widened.

This time, Trent smiled back.

Placing his palm at the small of her back, he escorted her through the restaurant and realigned his priorities.

All eyes watched their progress.

Halfway through the room, Trent put his other plan into motion, the one that relied heavily on people's penchant for gossip. He gave Dr. Klinger a short nod, the gesture nothing more than a slight dip of his head. The doctor gave Trent a very small smile in return, looking as though he was having a hard time placing a name to the face.

The man's expression could also be interpreted as annoyance, which was the precise reaction Trent needed. Only someone watching very closely would have noticed the brief interchange between Trent and the German physician.

Trent needed the attention of two in particular. He shot a quick glance at the far corner of the restaurant. Both men snapped their menus in place, pretending grave interest in to-day's selections.

Satisfaction filled Trent.

The FBI had him in their sights. And he had them in his.

Chapter Eight

Alone in her office once again, Savannah pulled off her gloves then slammed them onto her desk. What had she been thinking, agreeing to commit a criminal act as though it was something she did every day?

Trent must think her a terrible person.

Then again…

Hadn't their "midnight stroll" been his idea? After all, he had *skills*.

Alarm skittered up her spine. Trent. Had. Skills. No, it wasn't alarm rushing through her, but rather a sense of inevitability. Savannah wasn't surprised at all that Trent wasn't what he seemed. He was yet another man in her life harboring secrets. But in his case, the realization didn't make her uneasy. Quite the opposite.

He'd let his mask slip during lunch and she had glimpsed the person beneath the sophisticated veneer. Despite his *skills* and his mysterious answers to some of her questions, she sensed a truly decent man lay beneath all that lazy charm and swagger.

A decent man she could trust, one who had more depth to his character than he'd revealed this afternoon.

Wasn't that why she'd had the courage to broach the subject of Peter in the first place?

She'd been the one to start them down the road of solutions to her dilemma. Trent had merely offered a concrete answer to her problem, one she had all too easily accepted.

On some level—a sane one, perhaps—she knew she should feel more remorse for what she was planning to do tonight. With Trent's help, she was going to break into a man's private office, a man who could be exactly what he seemed.

Not likely.

She must find evidence against Peter that would prove her suspicions were correct.

Would she really follow through tonight?

Yes. Yes, she would. Because this wasn't about breaking and entering, this was about protecting her father from a dangerous association. What was the old saying? "Desperate times call for desperate measures."

Was she really going to go through with this?

Lord, what has become of me?

Sighing heavily, she proceeded to straighten the ledgers on her desk into neat, perfectly balanced rows.

"Savannah, are you in there?" A soft, persistent tapping accompanied the question.

Before she could answer, Kate opened the door and glided into the office with her trademark grace. Wearing a black dress with a sweetheart neckline, a matching hat and pristine white gloves, the woman looked the picture of Southern elegance.

"Darling." Grabbing her by the shoulders, Kate kissed the air near Savannah's cheek and then stepped back. "I've come to finalize our plans for our trip to Atlanta next week."

Savannah stared at her friend. She'd all but forgotten about the shopping trip.

Seemingly unconcerned by Savannah's silence, Kate looked around the office in interest. Her eyes narrowed, but she said nothing about the austere décor. "Is now a good time to discuss the details?"

Savannah hesitated a moment, then remembered her manners and offered her friend a seat.

Kate shook her head at the wooden chair she'd indicated. "I think I'll stand."

A smile tugged at Savannah's lips. "I can't say I blame you." The chair was serviceable but would offer little, if any, comfort. "Now, about our trip—"

"Not a trip," Kate corrected, her finger wagging in the air between them. "A shopping adventure."

"Right. An adventure." Savannah shifted from one foot to another. She couldn't quite pinpoint what, exactly, but something about Kate's visit felt…wrong. Why was her friend here? Why now, at this odd hour in the day? "I don't know, Kate, I—"

Cutting her off a second time, Kate launched into a litany of reasons for the trip. And then drifted into a description of her favorite shops.

Savannah only half-listened. In the past, she would have jumped at the chance to explore the Atlanta stores for the latest fashions. But how could she go shopping now? How could she *want* to go shopping?

Aside from the fact that the country was at war, Savannah had a full-time job that often required her appearance on Saturdays.

None of which were the real reasons for her hesitation. Her lunch conversation with Trent, and the seriousness in which he'd spoken of the conflict in Europe, had gotten to her.

Trent had gotten to her. He'd been fiercely adamant that they were fighting more than one enemy, not just the Japanese. His intensity had started her thinking about traitors living in their midst. Her mind had quickly put Peter in that category.

What if she was wrong?

What if she was *right?*

Her father could be working with a traitor. The possibility made her shiver with dread.

Before today, Savannah hadn't taken the reality of the German threat to heart. Not completely. Even with the death of good men like Bobby Gallagher.

What did that say about her?

Knowing what Kate had lost on the battlefield, Savannah felt a very real sense of remorse. Her friend's only brother had given his life for his country. He'd died a hero's death. While there were Americans, cowards, *traitors,* actually working toward more loss of life.

It was too horrific to consider.

Under the circumstances, why was Kate so adamant to head to Atlanta? Perhaps a "shopping adventure" was her way of coping with the loss of her brother.

"What do you say?" Kate parked a hand on her hip and looked at her expectantly. "Are we going to Atlanta?"

"Yes, I suppose we are." Savannah would be supportive of her friend. She would go for Kate's benefit, if not her own.

"Marvelous." Kate's shoulders relaxed dramatically. "Now, about that other matter we discussed."

"Other matter?"

"Winslow's party Wednesday night." Kate cocked her head at an attractive angle. "You said you received an invitation."

"Oh. Well, yes, I did." Savannah had received several invitations to upcoming parties. She'd had no real intention of attending any of them.

"You can't possibly say no. I hear Winslow's hired a professional caterer and a swing band. It's going to be a smashing good time."

A smashing good time. Savannah doubted that very much, not if Winslow's guest list included the same people from last night's party. Which, of course, it would. Jacksonville society was a closed, tight-knit group. She opened her mouth to decline, then remembered her decision to face the gossips head-on. No more hiding.

She drew upon a favorite verse from Joshua that fit the situation perfectly. *Be strong and courageous...for the Lord your God will be with you wherever you go.*

Savannah might not have planned this new life for herself, but she would be strong and courageous now. Winslow's party would be yet another chance to face the whispers. This time on her own terms.

"Say yes, Savannah. I've invited Bobby's friend as well. He's in town another week." Kate stared directly into Savannah's eyes as she spoke. "You remember Trent, don't you?"

Savannah's heart stumbled against her ribs. What was it she saw in Kate's eyes? Her friend had had the same look last night, an almost crafty, sly glimmer.

"Of course I remember Trent." She suppressed a frown. "In fact, I just had lunch with him today." She didn't add the part about their scheduled midnight stroll. Savannah still wasn't sure she would show.

"Well, isn't that grand? I thought you two had hit it off last night." Kate's happiness sounded genuine.

And yet...

There was that *look* in her eyes again. Was Kate jealous? Was that the reason for the tension in her shoulders?

Trent had said there was nothing romantic going on between them. At least, not on his part.

Was there something more on Kate's end?

"Does it bother you that I went on a date with Trent?"

"Bother me?" Kate's tinkling laugh came out soft and musical. "Of course not. I'm actually quite happy for you. Considering what you've been through these past six months, I think you deserve some masculine attention."

Kate's gaze held no subterfuge, just pure pleasure, and maybe a note of humor.

Trent had had the exact same reaction to Savannah's question. Not so much in words but in looks, all the way down to the amused gleam in his eyes.

Had they rehearsed their response?

What a terrible thought. And one Savannah refused to consider any further.

She was tired of letting one man's betrayal turn her into a skeptic, tired of questioning everyone's motives, even those closest to her. From this moment on, she would take Kate and Trent at their word.

"So you'll join us at Winslow's?"

Why not? "Yes, Kate, I do believe I will."

"Wonderful." Kate took Savannah's hands in hers. "I promise you won't regret this."

No, Savannah thought, she wouldn't regret going to the party. She wouldn't allow herself that indulgence.

Trent had delivered Savannah back to the shipyard at precisely 1320. He'd waited in his car a full ten minutes, with the engine running, until Kate entered the building as planned.

His lunch date with Savannah Elliott had been remarkably successful and had turned in a direction he couldn't have planned any better. Although a potential trap, their scheduled midnight stroll later tonight was ripe with possibilities.

While Savannah searched Sorensen's office, Trent would not only gather his own intelligence, he would ferret out the woman's loyalties. Two birds, one stone.

Did she really believe her father's assistant was the only Nazi sympathizer? That the man who ruled a banking empire so successfully was malleable enough to be outmaneuvered by his own protégé?

Could Savannah be that naïve?

Possibly.

The thought brought a twinge of guilt. Gritting his teeth, he put the car in gear and pulled onto Atlantic Blvd. Anger tried to take hold of him, but Trent wouldn't allow it. No one made him feel guilty. He was a heartless operative. A man without conscience.

He'd better get that straight in his head.

Flattening his lips into a grim line, he checked the rearview mirror. Two separate, unrelated cars pursued him, one following him closer than the other.

Both were playing perfectly into his hands.

With time on his side, Trent drove the speed limit, following the road as it veered west then turned south onto San Marco Blvd.

Keeping half his attention on his prey, the other half on the road, he reviewed the events of his lunch date with Savannah in his mind. He'd been so focused on luring the FBI into his trap he'd left matters tense between them.

Badly done, Trent.

His main goal with Klein's daughter was clear: gain her complete trust so he could gather information from her.

He would do just that tonight. And again at the party. He had no doubt Kate would coax Savannah into attending.

He felt a tug at his lips, for all the wrong reasons. Forcing his mind back to the matter at hand, he entered the picturesque San Marco shopping district.

At this hour, there weren't many parking spaces along the quaint row of shops. He had to make several passes until he found an available space.

Taking note where the other two cars parked, he exited his own car and strolled along the sidewalk at a leisurely pace. The hot, humid air hung heavy around him. The sky was a hard blue, no clouds. And the smell of magnolias wafted along a very stingy breeze.

Trent ignored the heat, breathed in the sweet scent and continued walking. He haphazardly stopped to survey a nearby window display.

The plate-glass window proved an adequate surveillance tool. Like Trent, the FBI agents had exited their car. They were a block and a half behind him on the sidewalk. Their footsteps were easy enough to discern over the melodious sound of the large fountain up ahead and the chatter of the afternoon shoppers. Their heels struck the pavement in military exactness, a dead giveaway they didn't belong.

Trent continued on his way.

One of the agent's feet hit harder than the other's. Trent calculated the man to be ten pounds heavier than his partner. Both were smaller than Trent.

Needing to determine the location of the third player in this unfolding drama, Trent stopped at the next shop. This particular display was centered on a large, wooden dollhouse with impossibly small furniture randomly placed inside.

Trent shifted slightly, just enough that the angle of the sun created a mirroring effect on the window. He easily located Peter Sorensen. The Norwegian still sat in his car two blocks west, apparently choosing to watch matters from a distance.

Trent resumed walking. Although her reasoning was incorrect, Savannah was right to distrust the man. Trent looked forward to helping her find proof that Sorensen was a Nazi sympathizer. Her discovery would be yet another thread of evidence to weave among all the other pieces of information the government had against the Norwegian.

The moment of truth would come when Savannah discovered the facts also pointed to her father.

Putting his focus back on the matter at hand, Trent looked slowly over his shoulder. Both FBI men pivoted to their right and pretended interest in the nearest shop's window. As they'd done at the restaurant, they weren't trying to hide their presence. Trent needed to know why, even though their behavior suited his own plan perfectly.

As an unconventional warrior, he had no illusions about his contribution to the war effort. He would never earn a medal, would never earn praise from his superiors, but his actions would save lives. The sacrifice for the greater good was worth the risks, the forfeit of a few for the safety of the multitude.

There were more dangerous missions, especially in Germany, but this one was highly critical. The U.S. war machine out-produced all other countries combined. If anything hindered that production the war could continue indefinitely.

Trent slowed his pace. The FBI agents closed in. They were less than a block behind him now.

Sorensen remained in his car, making no move to interfere, but he'd leaned forward, his arms cradled on the steering wheel.

The man had seen enough, Trent decided.

He turned down a side street, knowing the walls of the build-ings would hinder Sorensen's view.

Needing to work fast, in case the man decided to get a closer look, Trent focused on the footsteps behind him. The agents were twenty paces back, still walking shoulder to shoulder but not making any move to close the distance just yet.

They were allowing Trent to select the route and ultimate point of confrontation. The question was, why?

He glanced out of the corner of his eye and surveyed the scene as he turned down a back alley.

The FBI agents were now ten paces behind. Sorensen hadn't moved from his car, but he no longer had a clear visual. By the time he decided to join Trent and the FBI agents, *if* he decided to join them, the skirmish would be over.

Ready to end this, Trent cut down a smaller alleyway be-

tween two shops. Several yards in, he spun around to face the
way he'd just come.

One beat passed. Two.

On the third, the agents rounded the corner and stopped dead
in their tracks.

"Hello, boys." Trent glanced at both faces then centered his
gaze between their heads. "Fancy meeting you here."

The two blinked at each other, then regrouped quickly, closing the distance at a rapid pace. However, as they approached,
they kept their hands stretched out by their sides, palms facing
Trent. "We're not here to start a fight."

The calm statement, spoken in that careful tone by the
smaller of the two, was an obvious maneuver to gain Trent's
trust.

Trent trusted no one.

He held his ground without flinching. Perhaps if he hadn't
worked inside the Third Reich, where discovery meant an SS
bullet in his chest, *or worse,* he might be more concerned by
the unfavorable odds in such a small space.

But this wasn't Germany. This was the United States. The
American government was more civilized than the Nazis and
followed gentleman's rules of warfare.

The assumption was that these two were indeed Americans.

Watching for any slight move, Trent spoke calmly, his tone
low and fierce. "What do you want from me, if not a fight?"

They said nothing. But something shifted in their stances, a
gear change. They were patient in their pursuit now, unnaturally
so. Every step became controlled. Deliberate.

These guys weren't FBI.

But were they Americans?

Their builds were leaner than he'd originally surmised,
trained for endurance and stamina, not brute force. Spies, probably.

Balancing on the balls of his feet, Trent narrowed his gaze

over both. He could tell they each carried at least two concealed weapons. Guns hidden in sophisticated shoulder holsters and knives strapped to their legs below the knee. There could be a third weapon on both men, and possibly a fourth on the smaller of the two.

Throughout his inspection, the men kept their hands visible, their bodies unmoving, but their gazes shifted rapidly around the alley. Neither was comfortable with his back to the entrance. Good.

"Who do you work for?" Trent asked, watching only their eyes. Any false move would show there first.

"General Donovan dispatched us to follow you." The smaller of the two spoke again.

"Why?"

The same man continued speaking. "We're supposed to tail you in order to draw suspicion your way."

Trent said nothing.

"The idea is to solidify your cover."

Trent had set out to attract their attention for the same reason. The goal was to convince anyone watching—preferably William Klein or his lackey, Sorensen—that the United States considered Trent a threat to the nation.

"I need proof of your connection to Donovan."

They both nodded, a look of respect filling their eyes at the request, but it was the smaller of the two that spoke yet again. "Thirteen, one."

The address was a convincing start, but not enough for Trent to trust them. "Go on."

Sighing, the man did as commanded. "Then I stood on the sand of the sea. And I saw—"

Trent held up his hand and fixed his gaze on the man that had yet to speak. "Let's hear the rest from you."

"And I saw," he repeated clearly, precisely, with a good dose of impatience, "a beast rising up out of the sea."

At last, Trent was convinced. These were Donovan's men. They'd accurately recited the mission's secret code, Revelation 13:1.

"Well, now." Trent smiled grimly at one, then the other. "Since you're here to solidify my cover, let's make this look good."

Chapter Nine

❧❧

Herr Klein's private office was nineteen floors above the bank he owned, and occupied the entire top floor of the downtown Copeland Building. With its wood-paneled walls, oriental rugs and expensive furnishings, the oversize room was the ideal bank president's sanctuary. And the one place in America where Hans-Peter felt the most uneasy.

He was trained to make war against the enemy, not play games. Regardless, he always performed his duties at the highest level of excellence.

Case in point: Herr Klein had given him two days to uncover Trent Mueller's identity. Less than sixteen hours later, Hans-Peter entered his boss's office, final report in hand.

Sitting behind a large mahogany desk, his forearms resting on the edge, Herr Klein looked pointedly at the thick file. "You've had success."

"I have." Hans-Peter moved deeper into the room, set the report on Herr Klein's desk and then stepped back. "Mueller appears to be exactly who he says he is."

And yet, Hans-Peter still had his doubts. No one was exactly who they appeared to be, no matter how neatly the facts fell into place.

Holding his gaze a moment longer, Herr Klein pulled the file closer to his side of the desk, but didn't flip open the top cover. "Expand, please."

As if he were still reporting to the German High Command, Hans-Peter puffed out his chest and clasped his hands behind his back.

"As you already know, Trent Wilhelm Mueller is the second son in a rich, prominent New England family." Hans-Peter stuck to the facts he'd learned from his source in the U.S. Pentagon. For now. "His father has two brothers and an uncle in Hamburg, but he doesn't keep in regular contact with them. The family money comes from the mother's side."

Other than a ridge of concentration digging between Herr Klein's eyes, there was no indication of how he was receiving the news so far.

Hans-Peter continued, "The oldest son, James, joined the RAF two days after Britain declared war on the Fatherland. Six months later, he died a…hero." He nearly choked on the word.

"A hero, you say." Herr Klein leaned back in his chair. A late-day shadow curtained most of his features. "From what perspective?"

"Before his plane was shot down, James Mueller took out a brand-new munitions factory outside the German city of Frankfurt." Hans-Peter's chest grew tight with hatred. In his estimation, James Mueller got off too quickly. He should have suffered a more painful, prolonged death.

Leaning forward, Herr Klein flipped open the file and skimmed the first page of the report.

"Mueller has an impressive educational background." He ran his finger to the bottom of the page. "He's fluent in four languages, including German."

Hans-Peter said nothing. His report had far more interesting information concerning Mueller's education than the man's affinity for languages.

"Ah, now this is interesting," Herr Klein commented, almost to himself. "Mueller earned his degree in record time."

"He has a photographic memory," Hans-Peter confirmed. "Consequently, throughout his years at Princeton he put most of his energies into making a name for himself as the stereotypical, wild second son."

"I see." From his scowl alone, it was evident Herr Klein's shrewd mind filled in the blanks quickly. "What is the man's vice? Women?" He was clearly thinking of his daughter's interest now. "Or perhaps alcohol?"

"Neither," Hans-Peter admitted, if a bit grudgingly.

"Then what is the man's weakness?"

The answer was on page four of the report. "Fast cars. Boats. Anything built for speed. He's made a name for himself taking unnecessary risks."

Herr Klein lapsed into silence, his fingers splayed flat on either side of the report. "So he's reckless."

"As well as careless, with his life and others'." Not the type of man Herr Klein would want involved with his daughter. Savannah had better tread carefully. "He supposedly had a change of heart after his brother's death."

"I see he was in the military less than a year."

"He was discharged after an incident behind German lines. For medical reasons."

"Medical reasons?"

"A thin piece of shrapnel is still embedded in his right eye. It's left him with inferior vision."

"He hides the disability well."

"Agreed." The man he'd met last night, and followed this afternoon, had shown no physical defects.

"Even with the vision issues." Frowning, Herr Klein looked back at the file. "His language skills are impressive, usable. Why wasn't he recruited by any of the intelligence branches of the military?"

"He was. By all of them."

Herr Klein's eyes turned hard as steel. "Which one did he join?"

"None. Mueller went back to teach at Princeton and has lived a life above reproach since then."

"Indeed." Herr Klein smiled, just a little, the gesture giving him a sinister look. He turned to the next page, read silently, then caught his breath and looked up quickly. "Is this true?"

Hans-Peter flicked his gaze down to the file, determined precisely what page Herr Klein had stopped on, then answered the question at once. "Yes. Mueller is one of the world's foremost experts on Guido von List and his prophecies."

Specifically the one that proclaimed a super race, led by the German Messiah, would soon take its place in the sun.

"Mueller and I have a common interest." Herr Klein's eyes lit up with the zeal of a true believer as he continued reading.

"So it would seem." Hans-Peter didn't bother hiding his skepticism. Mueller's expertise in the very discipline that would tweak Herr Klein's was a little too…*convenient.*

"Ah…yes, this explains why he's in the area now."

Again, Hans-Peter said nothing. Mueller was scheduled to speak at a symposium on religious prophecy at the University of Florida. He'd arrived a week early in order to visit Bobby Gallagher's family. All of which was right before the largest Nazi sabotage plot to date. How…very…

Convenient.

"I've read enough." Herr Klein snapped the file shut. "Set up a private meeting with Mueller."

"At once." Hans-Peter looked forward to it. There were a variety of ways to pull the truth out of a man, some subtle, others not so subtle. All very effective.

He turned to go, then reconsidered. "There's something else you should know."

A slight lift of one eyebrow was the only indication his words had been received.

"I took it upon myself to follow Mueller after his lunch date with your daughter."

The eyebrow lifted a fraction higher.

"I wasn't the only one following him. Two men in dark suits tailed him into the San Marco shopping district as well."

"Did he know he was being watched?"

Hans-Peter reviewed the afternoon's events in his mind, the way Mueller casually climbed out of his car, how he strolled slowly along the sidewalk and haphazardly stopped to check out the window displays. His behavior hadn't been that of a man addicted to speed, reformed or not, it had been...

Convenient.

"Yes, I believe he was aware. He led the two agents in a game of cat and mouse for approximately ten minutes. He then lured them down an alleyway behind a row of shops. Mueller came out, alone, five minutes later."

"And the agents?"

"They returned to their car not long after he drove away. They looked decidedly worse for the encounter."

Herr Klein's lips spread into a cold, ruthless smile as he rose from his chair. "Your conclusions on the man?"

Hans-Peter allowed every bit of his distrust to show on his face. They were too late in the game and had far too much at stake to make an error in judgment now.

"Without speaking with Mueller, directly, it's hard to say for certain. All indications point to the possibility that his sympathies align with our own."

"But you don't believe he's one of us."

"No." Hans-Peter flattened his lips into a hard line. "I do, however, believe he's a dangerous man. To us. To the mission. *And* to your daughter."

"Set up the meeting at once."

"Yes, Herr Klein." Hans-Peter felt his patriotism stirring. He resisted the urge to toss out his arm in salute, but couldn't stop himself from saying. *"Sieg Heil."*

Five full minutes before midnight, Savannah arrived at the Roosevelt Hotel. She stood just outside the lobby, shifting from foot to foot. As if to mock her uneasiness, the night sky was completely clear, not a cloud in the sky.

Should she enter, leave? Stay, go? Even now, Savannah wasn't sure what to do.

For all intents and purposes, she was already on a criminal path, one that could get her arrested.

She'd never been to jail.

Had Trent?

Surely not. Or Kate wouldn't have introduced them in the first place.

Savannah peered inside the building and spotted the man in question. He was exactly where he said he would be, waiting for her in a wingback chair a few feet to the right of the main atrium.

He hadn't seen her yet, which was perfectly fine with her. She needed another moment to gather her courage.

Do not be terrified...for the Lord your God will be with you wherever you go.

The Bible verse was one of her favorites, but Savannah was pretty sure the Scripture didn't apply to tonight's outing. Against all she believed as a Christian, she was setting out to commit a crime. Willingly.

But if Peter was a traitor—and she believed that he was—how could she not follow through with her plan? Wasn't it her civic duty as an American citizen to do whatever it took to stop him?

But stop him from what?

She didn't know for sure. Wasn't that the point of this...midnight stroll?

Procrastinating a moment longer, she continued eyeing her coconspirator. He was dressed head to toe in black. Just like Savannah. But where she'd chosen to wear a casual, nondescript dress, he'd donned a pair of elegant pants and long-sleeved shirt that appeared tailor-made for him. He looked nothing like a criminal.

In fact, with his long legs stretched out in front of him, and his hands resting lightly on either side of his chair, he seemed entirely harmless. And not at all concerned he was about to conduct a little breaking and entering.

Why wasn't he more nervous?

Perhaps he had his own agenda for tonight's midnight stroll, one that involved searching Peter's office for purposes she couldn't begin to fathom.

No, that was ridiculous. Trent was a college professor now. He'd simply seen a woman in distress this afternoon and had offered to help her by utilizing skills he'd learned in the Army.

Feeling better about her decision, Savannah offered up a prayer for forgiveness and pushed into the hotel lobby.

Eyes on Trent, only him, she took slow, careful steps. One foot in front of the other, no hurry. They had all night to accomplish their task.

The moment Trent saw her he stood and began moving in her direction. But unlike Savannah's hesitant journey across the lobby, his footsteps struck the hardwood floor with purpose.

All Savannah could think was: *It's happening again.*

She was utterly powerless to stop her visceral reaction to the man. Her head grew light. Her pulse picked up speed. Her mouth went dry.

What was this strange hold Trent had over her? And why couldn't she make her lungs work properly whenever she was near him?

The questions bounced around in her head a few seconds longer before he stopped in front of her and took her hand.

"You came," he said, pressing his lips to her knuckles. "I wasn't sure you would."

Enjoying his touch far too much for their short acquaintance, Savannah pulled her hand free and then clutched her palms tightly together in front of her. "I wasn't sure I'd show, either."

"Ah, honesty." Humor lit in his eyes. "I must say, I find that particular trait in a woman irresistible."

The compliment echoed around in Savannah's head, sending her thoughts spinning into chaos. The man really did have… *skills*.

And now Savannah's legs threatened to give way completely. She locked her knees.

He smiled.

"The sky is especially clear tonight. Shall we enjoy some fresh air and go for a…" He gave her a slow wink, the charming rogue fully in place. "Midnight stroll?"

He was so calm. So infuriatingly calm. And that made Savannah all more the more anxious.

On a conscious level, she knew she should run back to the safety of her bed and forget all about this insane plan of hers. Desperation was fueling her actions, making her rationalize a very real crime in her mind. She just wanted everything back to normal. But she feared that wouldn't happen as long as Peter was in her father's life.

"Yes, Trent." She shoved the remaining shreds of her conscience aside. "I believe a midnight stroll is quite in order."

"Wait here."

He returned to the chair he'd recently vacated. Looking neither left nor right, he reached underneath the seat and pulled out a black canvas bag large enough to hold a variety of tools for, oh, say, breaking and entering into a bank assistant's private office.

Savannah's pulse hammered through her veins.

She tried to feel remorse for what she was about to do, tried to drum up some sense of self-reproach. She came up empty. Her heart was void of all emotion, save one. Resolve. She *must* protect her father from Peter's continued influence. There would be time for self-recriminations later.

Knowing she was rationalizing her bad behavior yet again, and still unable to feel a sliver of guilt, Savannah spun around and exited the hotel ahead of Trent.

Once out on the sidewalk, she turned toward her father's office building.

Trent was already beside her, facing in the proper direction.

"You know where we're going?" she asked, more than a little surprised.

"Of course I know." He slung his arm over her shoulders and pulled her close. "When I agree to help someone, I come fully prepared."

She blinked up at him, rendered speechless.

He expanded, "Aside from packing a few necessary tools," he rattled the bag in his hand, "I've done my research as well."

She blinked again.

"I asked Kate where your father worked."

Well, that made perfect sense. Except…it also brought up another concern. "Does Kate know why you asked about my father?"

"No." His eyes grew serious, dead serious. "This business tonight is between the two of us, Savannah. Just the two of us."

Although she sensed his words had a deeper meaning, she took him at his word. He hadn't told Kate anything about this outing. And the fact that he hadn't done so made Savannah feel a little less alone, as though she had a genuine ally in this dangerous matter.

In silent agreement, they started walking down the sidewalk, their steps perfectly in sync with one another. It took Savannah a moment to realize Trent still had his arm wrapped around her shoulders.

A little shocked at how good it felt to be this close to the man, and how his spicy scent soothed her completely, she tried to pull away.

He tightened his hold.

Why wouldn't he release her?

She tried again.

He kept his hand firmly in place.

Apprehension roared through her. "You…you can let go now."

"Not yet." His voice washed over her, a smooth, warm blanket of calm. "We aren't alone. Look behind you, about ten yards to your right."

She glanced over her shoulder and gasped. A police car was parked across the street, with two tired-looking officers staring straight at her.

Was she about to be arrested? Already?

"Relax, Savannah," Trent said. "We haven't done anything wrong yet."

Yet. She tried not to hyperventilate.

"We're simply a man and a woman taking a midnight stroll."

A man and a woman taking a midnight stroll. It sounded so innocent, when it was anything but.

A spurt of panic made every muscle in her body tense.

"Deep breaths, Savannah. Take slow, deep breaths."

She obediently drew in a long pull of air. Blew it out slowly. Then repeated the process three more times.

"And try to look happy to be with me."

Trent was so at ease next to her, so solid, she obeyed without question. Pasting an agreeable smile on her face, she leaned into him.

After a moment, her feet wavered under her. He slowed their pace to a crawl. "Are you having second thoughts?"

Yes. "No."

"We can turn around," he offered. "Just say the word and this…stroll is over."

"No. I want to do this. I *have* to do this."

"Why?" His hand tightened on her shoulder. "Why is tonight so important to you?"

She recognized the suspicion in his voice, felt the tension growing stronger in his body. Confused by the odd shift in his behavior, she closed her eyes a second and then opened them again. "I told you. I don't trust my father's assistant. I believe Peter is…he's…a threat."

She didn't expand any further, didn't explain how her father's blind faith in Peter had grown to unnatural proportions of late. Primarily because she wasn't sure how to put her concerns into words without sounding trite, or maybe even ridiculous.

Seemingly satisfied with her answer, Trent increased their pace. "Put your arm around me, too."

His voice was pleasant once again, his gait smooth and relaxed. He had a remarkable way of sliding into character. One of his…skills?

She hesitated.

"Come on, Savannah. We have to make this look authentic."

Right. Perfectly logical.

She did as he suggested.

But the moment she roped her arm around his waist a sense of contentment filled her. And that made her more uneasy than before.

Still linked, they completed the first block of their journey in tense silence. The streetlights illuminated their path, creating a golden, almost romantic glow around them. Any other time, under any other circumstances, Savannah might have enjoyed herself. She was in the company of a handsome man who appeared to adore her.

An illusion, she reminded herself, so they could *look authentic.*

"There's the Copeland Building," she said. "Up ahead on your left."

"I see it."

She started to cross the street.

Trent tugged her back. "Wait."

"Why?"

"The doors will be locked at this hour. I need a moment to determine our best way in, one that won't draw attention to our presence." He craned his head toward the back of the building.

She couldn't help but smile. "Oh, Trent, you're not the only one who came prepared."

He kept his gaze forward, looking up the building then down. "No?" His voice sounded preoccupied.

"No. I have something that will allow us to walk straight through those front doors over there."

His eyebrows slammed together. "And what, precisely, do you have with you?" At last, he looked at her, his eyes filled with amusement. "A hammer to smash a panel of glass?"

"Nothing that drastic." Still smiling, she dug into the pocket of her skirt and retrieved the small item she'd swiped from her father's desk earlier this evening. "I have the key."

Chapter Ten

Trent stared at the piece of metal dangling from Savannah's fingertips. A wave of distrust crashed through him. How simple and easy, that she would have a key to a twenty-story high-rise in the heart of downtown Jacksonville.

There was an obvious explanation, of course. Her father owned the building.

Simple and easy.

Trent's face grew hot. A bead of sweat trickled down his back. Every time he started to believe in Savannah's innocence, she pulled a stunt like this.

"How did you acquire that?" he asked in a cold, bland voice.

"I took it from my father's desk at home." She waved the key close to his nose. "Without permission."

She looked so pleased with herself, so *innocently* pleased, Trent couldn't help but smile back at her.

The urge to pull her into his arms—and kiss her soundly on the lips—came fast and hard. The sensation had nothing to do with the mission, and everything to do with his own disturbing feelings toward the beautiful, resourceful woman. To make tonight personal, on any level, was to ask for disaster.

Yet, Savannah looked so innocent, so beautiful, so *appealing,* as she stared at him with glee. For a moment, Trent wanted to forget her father was a traitor and that they were about to break into the office of the man's most trusted assistant, a dangerous man in his own right.

Emotion had been trained out of him for moments such as this. He let his training kick in and gave Savannah the boyish grin he'd introduced at lunch. "I like the way you operate, Mrs. Elliott."

Her smile widened. But then her hands began to quiver. "I can't seem to stop shaking." She thrust the key at him. "You... you better take this."

She'd either had a sudden case of nerves, or she was setting him up to be the one caught in the act of breaking and entering.

Don't trust her, Trent. Not yet.

He took the key and walked across the street. Surveying his surroundings one last time, he fit the key in the lock. A turn of his wrist and the heavy metal door swung open on its hinges.

With no time to dawdle, he pulled Savannah inside the building with him. The door closed behind them with a loud, resounding click.

An eerie, almost hollow silence filled the interior of the building. Unable to see more than five feet in front of him, Trent retrieved his flashlight but didn't flick on the switch yet. Not until they were farther away from the street.

Clearly familiar with her surroundings, Savannah took the lead in spite of the darkness. Her heels clicked on the marble. The sound reverberated through the silence like a jackhammer, alerting her presence to bugs, mice and any other creature deigning to listen.

An amateur mistake on her part? Or a calculated ploy to determine his level of training?

Either way, Trent wrapped his fingers around her arm and pressed up against her from behind.

"Take off your shoes," he whispered in her ear.

He stood close enough to get a whiff of her hair, a sweet, fresh, floral scent that reminded him of springtime.

He swallowed. Hard.

"Oh. Right. My shoes." A shiver pulsed through her and landed straight inside him. "I wasn't thinking."

She sounded truly regretful.

Wanting to trust in her but knowing better, Trent kept his grip on her arm while she slipped off her shoes and handed them over to him.

He stuffed both in his bag.

"The elevators are straight ahead," she said.

"We'll take the stairs."

"But Peter's office is on the twelfth floor."

"We'll take the stairs," he repeated, wondering again at her lack of concern for stealth. "The elevator is too conspicuous."

She stiffened under his grip. "You seem to know a lot about sneaking into a locked building at night."

Yes, he did. He not only knew how to break *in* to a building at night but also how to break *out* of one as well. His particular gift included jail cells and impenetrable prisons. Information he wouldn't share with Savannah unless the need arose.

He prayed the need would never arise.

"Let's go," he said.

This time he took the lead, moving at a clipped pace. Savannah glided along beside him. Her feet whispered across the floor without a sound. The woman was proving a quick study.

Trent refused to be impressed.

Savannah held the flashlight steady while Trent went to work on the lock outside Peter's office. They'd climbed the twelve floors without speaking to one another.

Now, just outside Peter's office, Trent's hands worked quickly, with expert precision. He'd obviously done this before.

The thought gave Savannah a tiny thrill. The man's heightened awareness, physical abilities and deliberate movements made Trent more appealing to her, not less. She should have been ashamed of her reaction to the man. She'd only known him two days. And most of that time he'd worn the mask of a worldly sophisticate.

Although she'd caught glimpses of his true character, Savannah doubted she'd met the real Trent Mueller yet. She needed to take a step back from him, literally and figuratively. Instead, she leaned in closer.

Was she attracted to dangerous men? Was that the fatal flaw that would doom her to a life of misery and potential separation from the Lord?

No, if that were the case she would have been attracted to Peter Sorensen. The very thought made her shudder.

A soft click filled the air.

Trent stood and retrieved the flashlight from her hand. The moment he shoved the door open he turned off the flashlight, plunging them into darkness.

Savannah trembled.

"After you," he said softly next to her, his voice overly polite, as if they were walking onto the dance floor for the next waltz.

Still shaking and needing a moment to calm down, Savannah paused at the threshold. She ordered herself to stop thinking so much. She'd come this far. No turning back now. What she was doing was for her father. For her country. And maybe even for herself.

Because Savannah needed to prove that her instincts were intact, that her mistake with Johnny had been a one-time error in judgment, not the beginning of a pattern. Maybe then she could mourn him properly and put the past behind her.

Trent placed his hand on her shoulder. His presence alone had an oddly soothing effect.

"We'll do this together," he said against her ear.

"I…yes." She blew out a tiny breath. "Excellent suggestion."

He lowered his hand to the small of her back and guided her forward.

He shut the door behind them.

The interior of the office was dark, too dark to make out any objects. Peter must have drawn the curtains before he'd left for the evening.

Savannah took several steps forward, then stopped and waited for her eyes to adjust. Just as shapes began to form, Trent turned on the flashlight again. She blinked at the sudden, blinding light.

"Take it," he said, pressing the metal cylinder into her hand. "I have another one in my bag."

Steadying the instrument in her hand, she directed the small beam of light in a wide arc. Peter's office was large and military neat.

Where would he hide important papers from prying eyes?

"I'll start at his desk," she said.

"I'll keep watch."

"Perfect." She started forward.

"Savannah?"

She froze. "Yes?"

"You need to work quickly. There might be a night guard making rounds."

"Oh." The flashlight bobbled in her hand. "I hadn't thought of that." She should have.

Trent made a sound deep in his throat. "Get moving, Savannah."

"Right."

With his warning playing in her head, she sat at Peter's desk and tried to decide where to start her search. She still didn't know what she was looking for.

She could hear, rather than see, Trent moving through the room. He slid open a filing cabinet, rummaged around a bit and then slid the drawer shut again.

Working quickly, she investigated Peter's desk. Wishing she'd brought her glasses with her, she moved to the final drawer, tugged on the handle once, twice. It wouldn't budge.

"Trent, I need your help. This one's locked."

He was by her side in a flash. He'd moved without making a sound, proving his *skills* were rather extensive.

Just what had he done for the Army as an Intelligence officer? She'd assumed he'd been a researcher. Someone who'd gathered information and then wrote it up into a coherent report for others to act upon.

Now she wondered.

"Which one?" he asked.

She pointed to the drawer at the bottom right-hand side of the desk.

"Shine the light on the lock." He crouched down until he was at eye level with the drawer.

After a moment, he retrieved the tools he'd used earlier from his back pocket. He fit one of the two pieces of metal in the lock and then guided it around with the other.

His movements were quick, smooth, precise. There would be no marks on the lock when he was through.

Seconds later the drawer slid open.

Who *was* this man?

"You're very good at this," she said in a quivering voice.

He didn't respond.

Leaning over him, she peered inside the drawer. Her heart sank. Nothing appeared out of the ordinary. There was only a stack of files lined up on top of one another in an ordered pile.

Had this trip been for nothing? Was Peter just her father's trusted assistant after all?

Trent opened the top file.

Wishing again that she'd brought her glasses, Savannah squinted at the glossy paper. "What is that?"

"A photograph." The word came out hard and flat. Trent was not happy.

Savannah was confused. "A photograph of what?"

"Blueprints."

"Blueprints?"

"Of a…" He paused. "Building."

Savannah tried to get a better look. Why would a bank president's assistant need a picture of blueprints to a building? Her mind simply wouldn't make the connection.

Despite the fact that she'd told herself Peter might be a threat to the country, Savannah had expected to find only evidence of him stealing from her father. Was he into something far worse?

Trent opened the next file.

Even without her glasses Savannah recognized the folded papers inside. Shipping charts.

Her mind whirled.

Blueprints. Shipping charts. What was Peter up to?

Lips pressed together, impatience riding her hard, she reached past Trent and flipped open the next file herself. This one was a typed report of some sort, with words she couldn't quite make out in the dim light without her glasses. Leaning in for a closer look she realized the paper was a dossier.

The person's name at the top started with a P or an F or a T or a—

Trent snapped the file shut and killed the light.

"Why did you do that? What—"

He placed two fingers over her mouth. "Someone's coming."

What? She hadn't heard anything.

"Don't say a word. Understand?"

Eyes wide, she nodded.

Trent pulled her to her feet. One hand on her arm, he made quick work of returning the files exactly where they were in the drawer, locked it and then tugged her deeper into the office.

Fear clogged in her throat. Where was Trent leading her?

As soon as the thought ran through her head, he opened a door. She hadn't realized there was another way out of Peter's office.

There wasn't.

Trent had shoved her in a closet.

She stumbled over a stack of boxes, threw her hands out to steady herself and instantly collided with a wall.

She swiveled around and slammed into another wall. This one made of hard muscle. "Trent, what are you doing?"

"Shh."

Feeling the strain rolling off of him in waves, she shuddered. Too scared to think clearly, Savannah leaned all her weight into him.

He wrapped his arms around her waist and held her close.

Shutting her eyes, Savannah prayed to the Lord for help, for release from the panic tying her stomach into knots. A futile attempt, she knew. The Lord wasn't in the business of helping criminals escape detection.

Flattening her hands on Trent's chest, she took in a silent breath. His heartbeat raced against her palms, proving he wasn't as calm as he was letting on.

The thought gave her no comfort.

The sound of boot heels striking the floor reverberated inside her head. Savannah stifled a gasp. She knew that purposeful gait. It belonged to Peter.

Why was he here so late?

A sliver of golden light shot through the seams of the closet door, heralding his arrival. Next came the creak of a chair, the sound of a lock turning and then...

The slide of a drawer pulling slowly open.

Thankful she wasn't alone, Savannah held her breath and listened to Peter's movements.

Please, Lord, please don't let him decide to open this closet.

Trent remained an unmovable statue against her. She could feel his heartbeat, but not much more. Was he even breathing?

For what felt like hours, but could have only been a minute or two, the sound of Peter poking around in the drawer continued. Then there was a loud thump and the slide of metal against metal. A click.

Another round of footsteps filled the air before the light snapped off.

And then…

Nothing.

Two agonizing minutes passed. And still…*nothing.*

Savannah didn't dare move.

Trent didn't, either.

They stayed locked in each other's arms, unmoving. Each second was endless, each minute an eternity.

At last, Trent removed his hands from around her waist.

Savannah released a slow whisper of air through her lips. "That was close."

"Too close."

There was something in his voice, something hard and ruthless. "Trent, what's wrong?"

"How often does Sorensen come to his office this late at night?" The question was full of anger, anger directed solely at her, as though she'd become his enemy instead of his coconspirator.

"I…I don't know."

"Don't you?"

Did he really think she'd *known* Peter would show up tonight? Why would he think that? Before she could ask him, he opened the closet door and took a step back. Away from her.

Without his solid support, Savannah tumbled forward, losing her balance in the process. She righted herself in time to see Trent heading for the exit.

"Wait," she called after him, making sure to keep her voice barely above a whisper. "Where are you going?"

He yanked open the door, looked left, right, then stepped into the hallway. "We're done here." He looked back over his shoulder. "It's time to go now."

No. She rushed after him, then stopped halfway to the door. "I don't have my proof." She glanced back at Peter's desk. "Not in hand, at any rate."

"Nevertheless, we're through." With slow, measured movements, Trent turned back to face her. "It was a mistake to come here tonight."

This was the second time she sensed his words had a doubling meaning.

"But I might never get a chance like this again." She hated the desperation she heard in her own voice.

Trent's expression turned hard, and he remained in the hallway. "You saw the photographs, the charts. What more do you need?"

"I *need* concrete evidence and time to read through it so I can determine what it all means." She moved closer to him, touched his arm. "Please, Trent."

He moved out of reach. "No. Savannah, you can't take anything out of this office. It's too dangerous. Sorensen would know."

That was why Trent was so angry? Because he was afraid for her?

"What if Peter is a threat to this country?" She thought about what they'd found in the drawer. "We *have* to stop him."

"Not tonight."

"Why not?"

His expression softening, Trent reached out and touched her face with the tip of his finger. "It's not safe."

But they were so close. She'd had her hands on the evidence.

Why was Trent refusing to help her, when the proof was mere feet away from them?

Was he truly that concerned for her safety? Or was there some other reason?

"Trent. Please. Help me do this."

"No."

"But—"

"No." Frowning, he reached out and pulled her against him. She could feel the tension in him, the same pent-up emotion that had been in his eyes a moment earlier.

He lowered his head. His face moved closer to her. Closer. For an instant, she thought he might kiss her, but then he pressed his forehead against hers.

"When the time is right," he said softly, "I'll make sure you have your proof against Sorensen."

He sounded so sure of himself, and yet, so very grim.

"I'm warning you, Savannah. You won't like what you find."

Perhaps not. But if Peter was as dangerous as she believed, and he was a threat to the country, he could do considerable harm to her father. If only by association.

"I'm willing to take the risk," she said in a firm voice.

"Are you?"

"Yes."

"All right." He set her away from him. "Give me a few days."

That wasn't the answer Savannah wanted to hear. She wanted the proof now, before her father spent another moment under Peter's influence. But the way Trent stared at her—with raw honesty in his eyes—she believed he would do exactly as he promised. He would get her the evidence she needed to prove Peter was not who he seemed.

After only a two-day acquaintance, she was putting her faith in a man who could turn out to be worse than Peter. Savannah only hoped she wasn't making a mistake.

Chapter Eleven

Savannah Elliott had officially become a problem. That was the thought that ran through Trent's mind as he waited for her to appear at Winslow Chapman's party. Their aborted attempt to break into Sorensen's office the night before had revealed much about the woman. And yet, nothing substantial at all.

Although he had a strong hunch, Trent still didn't know where her loyalties lay, not completely. Not definitively.

The fact that they'd been interrupted while searching Sorensen's desk—by the man himself—could have been a coincidence. Missions never went as planned. However, Sorensen's arrival could have also been a perfectly timed trap to prove that Trent was more than a college professor.

If Savannah was any other woman, if her father was simply a well-respected bank president, Trent would lean toward the first scenario. She'd seemed truly frightened when Sorensen had shown up unexpectedly, and all the more determined to leave his office with proof in hand.

But if Trent had opened that drawer a second time, she'd have seen the report on him, the one that had been fed to Sorensen by their man in the Pentagon. Trent could not have allowed her to read the briefing. She must continue to think he was merely visiting a fallen friend's family.

Trent was spared further speculation by a small commotion at the front door. Savannah had arrived.

Trent didn't miss the way his heart dipped in his chest at the sight of her. He'd had an entire day to prepare for this moment, and yet, it took several moments of deep breathing for his erratic pulse to settle into a smooth rhythm once again.

In the short time he'd known Savannah Elliott, Trent had formed a strong opinion in his mind, one that he admitted came from personal feelings rather than objective facts.

Last night had proven that she had an inner strength he found highly appealing.

Nevertheless, he had to remain objective. And uncover her true loyalties as soon as possible. Preferably tonight.

With various ideas running through his mind, Trent allowed a small smile to spread across his lips. He wasn't the only one watching her entrance. She drew interest, but not the same kind she'd garnered in the restaurant the day before. Tonight, the gazes thrown her way were filled with admiration. The male gazes, at any rate.

She wasn't dressed all in black like the last time he'd seen her, but she was just as spectacular. She wore a green dress cinched tight at the waist, the flared skirt hitting just below her knees. With her blond hair illuminated under the soft indoor lighting, the woman shone like a bright star in a midnight sky.

Why not enjoy the view a moment longer?

Trent leaned a shoulder against the wall, crossed his arms over his chest and settled in to watch her make her way through the room.

He liked how she moved. Her steps were fluid and graceful. Gone was the ice princess from the country club. In her place was a warm, smiling woman who greeted people with genuine affection in her manner.

Was it a sophisticated act on her part? Another weapon in her arsenal?

He couldn't say, which didn't sit well. Trent was uncommonly gifted at reading people; it was one of the reasons the OSS had recruited him. But Savannah Elliott, with her many complicated layers, was proving a challenge.

Trent caught her eye and something passed between them, something he barely understood on a conscious level. Something permanent and life-altering.

He swallowed, then got hold of himself and smiled back. She stumbled and his smile broadened. He liked catching her off guard, liked knowing he'd been the one to make her feet miss a step.

Impatient to be with her, he pushed from the wall.

Kate stopped him with a hand on his arm. "Trent, no." There was a hard warning in her voice. "Stick to the plan. Savannah must feel in charge tonight. She *must* come to you."

Knowing Kate was right, he relaxed back against the wall, forcing himself to appear casual. Nonchalant. A man with little on his mind save the next moment of pleasure.

Inside, he seethed. At himself. At Savannah. At them both. For a deadly second, he'd forgotten why he was pursuing the woman. He'd forgotten the mission.

He'd *forgotten* his hard-and-fast rules. Nothing personal. Nothing permanent. Just work the plan.

Helping Savannah break into Sorensen's office had been a calculated risk. And, quite possibly, a mistake. What had started as a means to uncover the woman's loyalties had ended with Trent discovering nothing he didn't already know. He'd expected to find blueprints, charts, even the dossier on him. He had *not* expected to create a strong personal bond with Savannah Elliott.

"We can't afford any more complications," Kate added. "Not after last night."

Trent leveled a cool glare her way. "We've already had this conversation." After he'd informed Kate of the aborted break-in attempt, he'd suffered through her lecture on the danger of taking unnecessary risks. Again, nothing he didn't already know.

"Yes, we have," she said. "And yet, I find I have to remind you, *again,* that Savannah isn't like other women. She's different. Special."

"Is that a warning? Or a recommendation?"

"Don't be contentious, it's beneath us both. Remember, Trent, your head needs to be clear for later tonight."

"I'll say the same to you."

Kate smiled. Her eyes did not. "I'm not the one with the... situation. Look, you're just a man. You—"

"I'm *just a man?*"

"Oh, you know what I mean." She patted him condescendingly on the forearm. "I'm merely trying to make a point."

"And that is?"

"When men like you," she poked him in the chest, "fall for women like Savannah, well, they fall hard. Be careful, my friend. You're close to crossing a line. Savannah's the kind of woman who turns men stupid. If she's working with her father—"

Trent raised a hand to stop the rest of her words. "I know the stakes, Kate." He gave her a look meant to quell further discussion.

"Then we understand one another."

"As always."

Lifting her chin, she started to speak again, but stopped herself. "There's my cue. Savannah's coming over." She nodded toward her friend, then departed without another word.

Trent barely noticed. His gaze was fixed on Savannah. For a dangerous second, the world slowed down. Air left his lungs in a painful *whoosh.*

She's the kind of woman who turns men stupid.

He didn't doubt that for a minute.

Caught in a moment of indecision, Savannah slowed her steps. A young couple passing by misunderstood and stopped to speak with her. She tried her best to give them her complete attention. Unfortunately, her gaze kept straying across the room.

A mad thrill skipped along her spine.

Trent was alone now, Kate having left his side seconds before. He waited patiently for Savannah to finish her conversation, but she could hear his silent call.

With one shoulder leaning against the wall in a casual pose, his intense eyes made all sorts of promises she didn't quite understand. Despite the warning bells going off in her head, Savannah wanted to be with him. Now. Last night had not gone as she might have hoped, but she wasn't sorry she'd made the attempt. She wasn't sorry she'd chosen Trent to help her, either.

Every time she was in his company their bond grew stronger. She knew he respected her. After all, he hadn't once dismissed her concerns over Peter. Yes, they'd left empty-handed last night, at Trent's urging. But he'd agreed to get her the evidence she needed. She'd give him the days he'd requested, but she would still try to formulate a solution on her own.

The couple finally said their farewells, and Savannah resumed walking across the room.

Lord, am I trusting the right man? Do I take a risk or beat a hasty retreat before I get in too deep?

Silence greeted her questions, the same disturbing silence she'd experienced for six long months.

Well, then. She would have to do this on her own.

Eyes fixed on Trent, she ignored the rapid beating of her heart and continued forward.

He was dressed in another perfectly tailored suit, this one a dark navy blue, set off by an expensive silk tie. The only relief from his somber attire was a crisp white shirt and the slash of his lazy smile.

Looking at him now, no one would suspect he was capable of sneaking into buildings at night, picking several different kinds of locks, as well as utilizing other unexpected…*skills.*

On one level Savannah knew she shouldn't be this intrigued by a man, *any* man, not so soon after her husband's death. On another, she wanted to be bold and find out why Trent fascinated her so.

Her head told her to proceed with caution. Her heart told her to take a chance.

She listened to her heart and closed the distance between them. "Hello, Trent."

"Savannah." He pushed away from the wall, took her hand in his and raised it to his lips. The gesture was both sweet and familiar. "I'm pleased to see you again."

"And I, you."

Regardless of her nerves, she'd spoken the truth. She'd been thinking about this man ever since he'd escorted her home last night, or rather early this morning. They'd ended things rather abruptly, but that had been due to the unusual events prior to their parting.

All day, Savannah had been anticipating seeing Trent again. It would be pointless to lie to herself, even in the privacy of her own thoughts.

"You look as stunning as ever." He lowered his gaze to her feet and then back up again. "The modern cut of that dress suits you."

Her cheeks warmed under the compliment and a pleasant shiver flowed through her. She'd like to think she'd dressed for herself. But she realized that the appreciation she saw in Trent's eyes had been her ultimate goal.

Savannah could no longer think of this man as a stranger. Last night they'd crossed an invisible threshold. The danger had brought them closer and bonded them in a way fifty lunch dates never could.

So why was she suddenly nervous in his presence?

For what seemed like endless seconds, they continued staring at one another, neither speaking, neither making a move to put a polite distance between them.

The moment should have been awkward. It felt...

Exhilarating.

What was it about this man that made Savannah want to toss caution to the wind? Why did her stomach flip inside itself whenever she stood close to him?

She'd never been this fascinated by a man. She knew so little about him, except that he had...*skills* not normally found in a college professor. She also knew he dressed well and smelled wonderful, an enthralling mix of spice, cedar and pure male.

Tonight, Savannah decided, would be about getting to know this man better. On a personal level.

She would start with the mundane. "Did you enjoy the rest of your day?"

She asked the question in a conversational tone. However, she truly wanted to know how he'd filled his time since their escapade.

"My time has been...productive." He didn't expand. And Savannah didn't ask him to, mainly because she wasn't sure what she saw in his gaze.

Satisfaction? Something a little less gentlemanly?

"Have you been working on my...problem, then?" It was a leading question, she knew, but time was slipping away. She *must* find a way to convince her father Peter was dangerous.

Trent obviously saw through her casual tone, because he chuckled softly. "Ah, Savannah, you are a delight."

Despite her impatience, the compliment spread warmth all the way to her toes.

In a casual move, he leaned back against the wall and let his eyelids drop to half-mast. The charming sophisticate was firmly back in place. Last night might never have occurred.

Savannah sighed. "You have nothing for me."

"Not yet."

"Then how *did* you spend your day?" She was genuinely curious.

"If you must know," he said, "I spent most of my time putting the finishing touches on a lecture I'm scheduled to present at a nearby university next week."

A lecture. Well, of course. A perfectly suitable endeavor for a college professor. After last night, she'd nearly forgotten what he did for a living. "What topic will you be speaking on?"

She truly wanted to know.

"Nothing you'd find interesting."

"Try me," she said, her interest piqued. "I might surprise you."

He chuckled again, the sound rumbling from deep within his chest. "Of that, I have no doubt."

Beneath the charm and smiles—what she was starting to think of as his mask—Savannah sensed he was holding something back from her. No. Not some*thing,* but rather a part of himself. A secret part he shared with no one.

She desperately wanted to dig, to press for information, to *make* him open up to her. An odd reaction, to be sure. She'd never been one to push.

Then why was she compelled to do so now?

Why was it so important to discover Trent's secrets, his thoughts, his…everything? Was it only because of the closeness they'd shared last night, or was it something more? Something that went beyond a mild flirtation?

"You truly want to know?" he asked.

"I do."

Still propped against the wall, nothing moving but his eyes, he said, "My lecture will be on prophecy."

Savannah blinked, then remembered he was a professor of philosophy and theology. "Oh, yes. You mean Biblical prophecy. Like in Daniel, Isaiah and the Book of Revelation."

"No."

"No?"

"I'll be speaking on German prophecy." He held the pause a fraction too long. "Have you heard any of the predictions?"

"Well…yes. Yes, I have." In fact, her father was overly fascinated with the subject. Peter kept him well supplied with books, essays and articles. It was propaganda, as far as Savannah was concerned, and one of the main sources of her concern over their association.

"Have you heard of Guido von List?" Trent asked.

Her eyes widened. Peter had recently given her father one of von List's books to read. They'd passed it back and forth for weeks, spent hours locked up in her father's study discussing the material. When Savannah had finally had a chance to peruse the contents of the book, she'd confronted her father over the disturbing subject matter.

The conversation had not gone well.

As if he could read her thoughts, Trent's shoulders visibly stiffened. "You know of von List, don't you?"

"I…" She gave a nervous laugh, not sure how to proceed. This wasn't the direction she'd expected their conversation to go. "I hadn't realized the prophecies of von List would be considered a serious academic subject."

"On the contrary, they're *very* serious." He bent his head until his lips nearly touched her ear. "Don't you think it's invaluable to know how the enemy thinks?"

She shivered. This time the sensation was not a pleasant one. An image of Peter's face shot through her mind. Perhaps she should bring Trent into her confidence. "That's what my father said when I discovered him reading von List's book, *The Secret of the Runes*."

Trent's eyes narrowed. "You've spoken of von List with your father?"

The argument still fresh in her mind, she breathed out a hiss. "Yes. Once."

When she'd pressed, her father had claimed he didn't believe any of the nonsense in the book. He was only researching the rise of the Nazi party, as a historian would study the Roman Empire's rise and fall.

Savannah shook her head. "The idea of a master race, one derived from the Ancient Germanic people, is absurd." She spoke her thoughts aloud. "No, it's appalling. It's…" She let her words trail off when she realized Trent's eyes had widened. Had she spoken too freely?

He was silently searching her face, but for what?

What was he hoping to find?

"Surely you agree with me," she said, wondering why his gaze had gone a bit hard.

A moment of silence stretched endlessly between them. "Yes, Savannah, I…agree."

Something in him had changed. He was more tentative. Yes, that was the word. "Trent?"

"Come, Savannah. Let's not talk of von List or a master race any longer." He touched her cheek gently, his smile lazy and a little lopsided.

The charming rogue was back in full force. She should be leery, but there was suddenly an authentic feel to his behavior. "Trent, I—"

"Tell me another one of your secrets." He made the command in a low, caressing whisper. "Then I'll tell you one of mine."

She blinked at the shift in his mood. He was clearly trying to lighten the moment. He'd become approachable again, almost playful.

Well, if he wanted to *play*…

Placing her hand on his arm, she batted her eyelashes at him. "I hate coffee."

"You hate…pardon me?"

At the genuine confusion on his face she felt a tug at her

heart. "You asked for one of my secrets. Well, there it is. I hate coffee."

"Ah, yes." His lips quirked. "A failing, indeed."

"Now it's your turn." She moved her hand farther up his arm. "Tell me one of your secrets."

He opened his mouth to speak, but looked around him and shook his head. "Not here."

"But—"

"Outside." He took her hand from his arm and then braided his fingers through hers. "I'll tell you once we're completely alone."

With their hands locked palm to palm, he tugged her out the double doors that led onto the lawn. Feeling a little light-headed, she followed along without protest.

They walked toward the river in silence. The grass, left slightly wet from an afternoon shower, tickled her ankles. The lapping water against the bulkhead covered the sound of their footsteps. The night air weighed heavy with humidity. And tension.

The bright, full moon in the cloudless sky illuminated their path. With each step they took the sound of the party grew distant.

When muffled laughter was all she heard, Savannah pulled to a stop and withdrew her hand from Trent's.

"All right, we're alone now. Tell me one of your secrets, Trent."

He stared into her eyes, no more masks. No more flirting, no more playful smiles. This was the man who'd helped her break into Peter's office. A man she sensed she could trust.

"My brother was killed in the war three years ago." His words came out in a fast tumble of clipped syllables.

"But we weren't in the war three years ago," she said out of reflex.

"No. We weren't. He joined the RAF, the Royal Air Force,

back in 1939, right after Hitler invaded Poland. He died a handful of months later."

"Oh, Trent." She touched his arm lightly. "I'm sorry."

Moonlight played across his face, cutting hard angles into his already chiseled features. "Me, too." He turned away to face the water directly. "But that's not my secret."

His face, still easily discernible in the moonlight, was bathed in emotion. Savannah had thought she wanted to know him better, but not if the exercise caused him pain.

She squeezed his arm gently. "You don't have to tell me, Trent. Not tonight."

"I *want* to tell you."

Trying to process what she heard in his voice, she nodded. "All right."

"My secret isn't that my brother died a hero." He continued staring out over the river, his breathing a bit erratic. "My secret is that I fear I'll never live up to his example."

Chapter Twelve

The moment the words left his mouth, Trent turned to face Savannah directly. He could see her reaction glittering in her eyes. He'd not only captured her attention. He'd gained her sympathy.

He told himself that had been his main objective in revealing his secret. She wouldn't trust him if he didn't give a piece of himself. But he could have told her a lie. He'd done it often enough in the past. Instead, he'd shared the truth, a very deep, personal concern he'd never admitted to another human being.

"Oh, Trent." She moved closer, close enough for him smell her clean, fresh scent. "I can't imagine how hard it must be to carry a burden like that."

He blinked down at her, realizing she'd done it again. She'd slipped past his defenses, to the very core of who he was as a man. Not by trying to talk him out of his feelings, but by acknowledging them.

He was in serious trouble with this woman.

She's the kind of woman who turns men stupid. Kate had been dead wrong on that point, at least in his case. Savannah hadn't made him stupid. She'd made him…*feel.* A far more dangerous prospect.

He'd met other women in his role as a spy. Silly women. Selfish women. Courageous women who risked their lives for the German Resistance. Yet, none of them had been able to slip below the sophisticated shell he wrapped around himself.

Before he could think too hard about what he was doing, or rather *why* he was doing it, his arms snaked around her waist. "Come here."

When she didn't resist, he pulled her closer.

The plan was to win her affection at all costs. In order to take their relationship to the next level, he was *supposed* to kiss her tonight. In normal times, he'd be moving too fast. But the world was at war, and they'd created a strong bond in Sorensen's office.

Stronger, perhaps, than Trent wanted to admit.

He rested his forehead against hers, struggling to stay in control of the moment. A primitive desire to protect this woman—even from himself—rose within him.

But just like last night, when Savannah had been wrapped in his arms and they'd been seconds from discovery, Trent had experienced an adrenaline rush. The same one he used to feel when he raced cars.

He wanted to take unnecessary risks with this woman. To be careless. To claim Savannah for himself.

Lord, help me to remember my duty.

Their breathing joined in a patchy cadence.

Trent's mind emptied of all thought, except one. Savannah felt good in his arms.

The need to kiss her nearly brought him to his knees. But he wanted the moment to last a bit longer.

Just…one…more…moment. Where time didn't matter. The world didn't matter.

Nothing mattered but the two of them.

In the end, it was Savannah who moved first. She pulled her head back and looked directly into his eyes. "Trent, I didn't mean to push. I never meant to upset you. I—"

He pressed his lips to hers. He didn't want to hear the rest of what she had to say, didn't want to think about his brother.

He kept the kiss slow, casual. A woman like Savannah needed tender handling.

She stiffened slightly in his arms and started to pull away. But then her fingers curled into his shoulders.

The moment things started to get interesting, Trent knew he'd officially crossed a line. Not because he was kissing Savannah—that had been part of the plan—but because he was *enjoying* the moment far too much.

He lifted his head and took a step back. And then another.

Savannah stared up at him. Eyes round, breathing erratic.

Her fingers slowly lifted toward her lips, but stopped midway. Her hand fell back to her side and she sighed. Then her face scrunched into a frown.

Not wanting to see regret in her eyes, Trent pulled her back in his arms and she immediately relaxed into him.

For an endless moment, they simply stayed where they were, wrapped together as they'd been in the closet.

Savannah broke the silence first. "Trent, do you ever wish you were still in the Army?" she asked, her cheek pressed against his chest. "You know, fighting in the war like other soldiers?"

How was he supposed to answer that question? He *was* fighting in the war, although the irony of doing so while in the arms of a beautiful woman wasn't lost on him. A beautiful woman, he reminded himself, whose loyalties were not yet fully clear.

The argument was becoming harder to make.

He lowered his head, enjoying the moment for one, single heartbeat.

The woman is a mission, he reminded himself. *This isn't about you, what you want or what you can't have.*

The kiss might have been part of the plan, but reacting as though it had been real was not.

"Savannah—"

"No. Don't say anything." She touched his lips with the same finger she'd pressed against her own mouth. "Please. It's not important."

She had the soft look of a woman falling in love. Satisfaction filled him, then quickly turned to concern.

Trent was supposed to be following orders. He was *supposed* to court Savannah. But he had to remember, no matter how much he wanted matters to be different, he wasn't courting just any woman.

He was very possibly courting the enemy.

Savannah watched in confused silence as Trent took a rather large step away from her and then raked his fingers through his hair. The familiar mask slid quickly into place, turning his features into a beautiful, blank sculpture void of all emotion.

Oh, but she wasn't fooled. She'd seen the split second of yearning in his gaze. The craving. The unmistakable longing.

Or was she kidding herself? Was she reading in him emotions she was struggling with herself?

She hated that she didn't know the man well enough to determine what was really going on inside his head, hated that her own thoughts were a giant tangle of confusion in her mind.

Even with his mask firmly in place, Savannah saw the battle waging behind Trent's eyes, as though he didn't know whether to proceed or pull back.

She understood his quandary. Although Johnny hadn't been faithful to her, shouldn't Savannah have felt at least a little sorry she'd kissed another man?

If only she could blame the whole thing on Trent. But no. She'd been a willing participant.

Giving both of them a moment to sort through their thoughts, Savannah moved to the edge of the lawn and leaned her hands on the waist-high retaining wall running along the river's edge.

The smooth marble felt warm under her hands, the day's heat having yet to dissipate fully from the structure. The downtown skyline twinkled in the distance, while light from the waxing moon danced along the river blown into choppy ripples by the wind.

As Savannah waited for Trent to join her, she felt a little uncomfortable. But also excited. No matter what came out of his mouth next, lie or truth, Savannah knew one thing for certain. That kiss had been real. For both of them.

Another moment passed before Trent moved to a spot next to her along the wall. He didn't try to break the silence, which was just as well. Savannah wasn't sure that she wanted to hear what he had to say. Not yet.

There had been a moment in his arms when her world had finally made sense. Perhaps for the first time in her life.

With her mind in a state of confusion, she needed the Lord's discernment. But she couldn't hear His voice like she once had, back when her life had been simple and uncomplicated. Now, there was too much noise in her head to decipher *right* thinking from *wishful* thinking.

Savannah had fallen for the wrong man once before. She didn't want to head down that same fruitless path again. In her professional life she was smart, analytical, measured. She always worked through a problem one step at a time. In her personal life she was proving impetuous.

Stifling a sigh, she angled her head to look at Trent directly.

He was so handsome she found it difficult not to gape as he stared out over the water, blinking slowly, the breeze playing in his hair.

With his eyebrows drawn together in concentration, he looked entirely too serious for a man who'd just kissed a woman under the moonlight.

"You're thinking too hard," she said in an effort to lighten the mood.

That earned her a chuckle. "Shouldn't that be my line?"

"Why? Oh, right. Because it's usually the woman who over-thinks these sorts of things."

"Something like that."

He turned to face her at last, his eyes smiling down at her with genuine humor lurking in their depths.

Her heart filled with an emotion she hadn't felt in a very long time. Joy.

Reflexively, Savannah took a step toward him. He shifted slightly, then opened his arms in silent invitation. She went into them without question.

They stayed locked tightly together, their heartbeats joining in perfect rhythm.

Everything in Savannah relaxed.

But then a soundless whisper of warning gripped her. She was falling too hard, too fast. No good could come of this attraction she felt for Trent.

She'd met this man only days before. She should pull away, put some distance between them.

She stayed right where she was.

Tightening his arms around her, he lowered a kiss to the top of her head.

Her heart sighed.

"I want to see you again," he whispered against her hair.

"You…" Her tongue stumbled over the word, adding several unnecessary syllables. "…want to see me again?"

Afraid of the intense emotions flowing through her, she *really* wanted to pull away now. She found herself clinging to him instead. If only her confusion would disappear.

Oh, Lord, why does this have to be so hard, so impossible, so doomed for failure?

Shouldn't romance be easy?

Not if it's worth keeping. The reply came from deep within her heart.

"Dinner, Savannah." He shifted and then gently touched her cheek before dropping his hand. "Friday evening. Just the two of us." He dropped his hand from her face. "Make me a happy man and say yes."

Yes. Oh, yes.

She nearly shouted the words out loud. Dinner. Friday evening. Just the two of them. No other worries on their minds but getting to know one another better. It would be a perfect opportunity to move past the awkwardness that showed up at unexpected moments like these.

Parting her lips to give her response, Savannah suddenly remembered her mother's invitation. A ball of disappointment formed in her throat. She'd didn't want to share Trent, not with her family. Not with anyone.

But perhaps it would be wise to have her parents get to know him better. Their opinion, especially her father's, could be very enlightening.

"Actually," she said, her disappointment evident in her voice, "you're invited to dine at my house that night."

"Dinner at your house?" He looked dubious. "With you *and* your parents?"

After her father's behavior at the country club Savannah couldn't fault Trent's skepticism. "Well." She attempted a smile. "The offer was originally my mother's idea."

"And your father? What are his thoughts on the matter?"

"When he heard about the invitation he insisted I extend it to you at once." She didn't add the part about his accompanying scowl or his continued warnings that Savannah tread carefully with Trent, a man she barely knew.

A wordless moment passed between them. Trent's manner was relaxed, but his eyes had grown more intense. Not quite predatory, but close.

"Your father insisted?" he asked, taking one of her hands and stroking the knuckles at the base of her fingers.

"Yes, he did. He finds you..." Her eyes closed as he continued to caress her palm. "...intriguing."

"Is that so?"

Unable to think with Trent rubbing her hand in those slow, mesmerizing circles, she popped open her eyes. "Yes."

"And you, Savannah." He released his hold on her. "What do you want?"

You, her heart shouted. Her mouth said, "I want you to accept the invitation."

"Then how could I possibly refuse?" The satisfaction in his voice brought a strange reaction in Savannah's stomach. One that wasn't altogether terrible. Actually, she felt...fluttery.

If Trent could make her feel like this after one kiss, what could he do if he put a little more effort in his pursuit?

"Should I bring anything with me when we dine?" he asked.

She wanted to tell him to bring the evidence against Peter he'd promised to find for her, but she didn't want to ruin the moment. She had to trust he'd deliver his promise before Friday night. If not, she'd think of a way to get the proof herself.

In the meantime, she'd keep things simple between them.

"No." She shook her head slowly, hoping to appear nonchalant and in control. "Just yourself."

"Can you think of nothing that will put me in your father's good graces?" He gave her a wry grin. "He didn't particularly warm up to me when last we met."

Swallowing a sigh, Savannah didn't bother arguing the point. "He's very protective."

"As any man would be with such a lovely daughter."

A string of knots tightened in her stomach. Savannah wanted her father to like Trent. She wanted to be right about him, to know her judgment of his character was correct.

"There is one thing you can do to win my father's interest," she said with a sigh. "If not his immediate approval."

"I'm listening."

"Talk to him about German prophecy."

Chapter Thirteen

Four hours and twenty-six minutes after kissing the beautiful Savannah Elliott under the pale Jacksonville moon, Trent entered the Roosevelt Hotel. The woman had played right into his hands. She was, indeed, falling for him.

Perhaps their midnight stroll the night before hadn't been a mistake, after all. Savannah clearly felt a bond with Trent.

And he with her.

She'd invited him to dinner at her house Friday evening. It would be the perfect opportunity to study William Klein in his natural habitat, without interruption.

Satisfaction filled him. The mission was proceeding as planned. Nevertheless, Trent's mind wanted to go back to that moment when he'd held Savannah in his arms and kissed her. Not for the sake of the mission, although that was part of it, but for his own pleasure as well.

Savannah tempted him to believe she was innocent of her father's treachery.

He would not. Not yet. They'd merely shared a kiss. A kiss, he reminded himself, that had been part of the overall plan. There was still much to do tonight.

Shoving aside the rest of his thoughts, Trent focused on his surroundings.

Unlike the other tall hotel buildings in town, the Roosevelt was built in the middle of the block rather than the corner. This gave the hotel an unassuming outer façade.

The interior was another matter entirely. The lobby had scrolling, multicolored floral wallpaper that worked well with the brocade furniture. Focusing beyond the décor, Trent looked to the east, south, west and last to the north.

Nothing out of the ordinary caught his attention.

He continued toward the elevators, keeping his gaze focused straight ahead, aware the clerk was staring at him from behind the registration desk. Calm and loose-limbed, Trent moved at a quick pace without appearing as though he was in a rush.

At the last moment, he shifted direction. Only slightly. But it was enough to steer him away from the elevators and toward the stairwell. He took the stairs two at a time up to the ninth floor and then made his way quickly down the hall to his room. Like the hotel lobby, the décor inside the elegant suite was upscale and tasteful.

Before removing his coat and tie Trent checked to see if anyone had made an impromptu visit during his absence. He shut the door with a soft click and began the systematic search. Circling the perimeter in a clockwise direction, he checked the nearly invisible strands of hair he'd strung across random drawers and doorjambs. All were intact.

His back muscles looser, he moved into the adjoining bath, and then went out onto the balcony. So far he'd found no signs of unwanted entry. Or tampering.

He finished his search in the large bedroom.

Satisfied all was at it should be, he lowered to the floor and retrieved one of two suitcases from under his bed. Beneath a hidden panel in the side lining was the false identification badge he'd spent all afternoon creating. He'd used the one he'd taken from the shipyard as an example.

Still unsure if he would use the forged identification, he studied his handiwork. The badge would get him inside Pembroke tonight, as long as other factors played out to Trent's satisfaction.

No one suspected a man who didn't try to hide.

Trent studied the ID a moment longer. He'd done an exceptional job, very professional, but his instincts warned against the simple route tonight. Trent had learned long ago to trust his instincts. Unfortunately, he wasn't sure what they were telling him now.

He would discuss the matter with Kate. The whole point of having a partner in a mission like this was for shared information and insight.

Stuffing the badge in his pocket, Trent sealed the hidden panel. He then pulled out several file folders, a writing pad, pencils and an academic journal.

Every detail, no matter how miniscule, must be addressed. Earlier tonight, he'd told Savannah he'd spent the past few days writing a lecture on the one topic he knew would get a reaction out of her. Though she hadn't given him the one he'd expected. In fact, her hatred of the Nazi agenda to create a Master Race had seemed genuine.

Trent paused. His pulse grew thick in his veins. Every sign pointed to Savannah's innocence. An inner voice told him to trust her. His training told him to reserve judgment.

He went with the latter and arranged the items he'd pulled out of his suitcase on a desk near the window overlooking the city's skyline. He made sure to put the "lecture" on top of the pile. If Savannah was working with her father, if she relayed information from her conversation with Trent and someone came looking for proof, the evidence would be in plain sight.

Exiting the room, Trent chose the stairwell that led directly into a back alley behind the hotel. As he made his way down the nine landings, he allowed his mind to review the events from earlier in the evening.

The plan to win Savannah's affection was working brilliantly. But if she ever found out the real reason he'd set out to pursue her—

He cut off his thoughts with a soft growl.

A bolt of guilt shot through him, anyway, a slow ripple of remorse that brought unbearable pain.

Lord, what sort of fiend have I become?

Sacrifice one for the many, he reminded himself. In times of war, the end always justified the means. And yet, his guilt refused to dissipate.

When this mission was over, Trent had to make sure Savannah was the one who broke things off between them. No matter what, she could never know he'd set out to use her to get close to her father.

All this was assuming, of course, she was innocent.

And if she wasn't?

The question whispered through his thoughts, making his breathing hitch in his chest. If Savannah was a traitor to this country, would that make Trent's actions acceptable? Perhaps even noble?

Sacrifice one for the many. The end justifies the means. There were always casualties in war. And…

And…

Trent was rationalizing.

Exiting the building with a frown pulling at his lips, he shut off his emotions, hardened his heart and found Kate waiting for him in her car at the exact place they'd planned.

Nodding a silent greeting, he climbed into the passenger seat.

Kate pulled away from the curb. "Where to first?"

"Pembroke." The blueprints in Sorensen's office had been of the shipyard. Trent wanted to see if they were current, or if there were other secrets to be found in Savannah's office.

"Right." She swung the car onto the next street. Two blocks

later, she took another turn and then another, until they were headed in the proper direction at last.

At this hour, there was an empty stillness on the streets. Jacksonville, a river city by the sea, was a growing metropolis by day, more than a little eerie at night. Split in two by the St. Johns River, the city was connected by three closely positioned bridges that kept traffic flowing between the neighborhoods on either side.

Kate chose the most central of the bridges to cross over the river.

"How are we going in? Like we talked about earlier?" She angled her head to look out over the steering wheel. "Or is it too bright out tonight?"

Trent studied the black sky that had been whipped clean by the wind. The moon, though not completely full and looking almost lopsided, shone boldly, illuminating even the nooks.

That meant climbing over the fence was out.

"There's a new plan. I'm going in alone."

Kate gripped the steering wheel so hard her knuckles turned white. "Why?"

Since she was smaller and more agile than him, the original plan had been for Trent to boost Kate over the fifteen-foot fence. Then she would open the back gate for him and they would catalog the shipyard's weaknesses together. Now, with the moon out in full force, the idea was too risky.

One thing he'd learned in Sorensen's office last night was that they weren't dealing with amateurs.

"I want you waiting in the car," Trent said. "Engine running."

She nodded, but didn't look happy. "And you? How will you get in the shipyard now?"

"I'm going to walk straight through the front gate."

"Not a good idea." Her face pulled into a glower. "There might not be a lot of security at Pembroke, but the night guard won't just let you walk straight through the front gate."

"I have credentials."

Kate drew the car to a quick stop. "Let me see."

He dug in his back pocket then handed over the ID.

She pulled out a tiny flashlight from under her seat and proceeded to examine the card. She turned it over, studied the other side, then handed it back to Trent. "Nicely done."

He lifted a shoulder. "I was trained by the best."

"No argument there."

Trent smiled at her droll tone, hearing the irony beneath it. General Donovan had not only recruited ex-soldiers, language specialists and beautiful women to work for the OSS. He'd also brought in world-class thieves, safecrackers and the best counterfeiters in the world. As a result, just as Trent had told Savannah, he had several unconventional skills in his bags of tricks.

"Normally, I'd agree that walking in the front gate is a good idea, but not at Pembroke." Kate sighed. "Not anymore."

"Why not?"

"I did some additional checking this afternoon. The current night guard used to work during the day, as a welder, but his wife took ill two weeks ago. He had to switch shifts so he could care for her during the day."

A noble reason to change hours, Trent silently conceded. Unfortunately that presented a problem for tonight. "After working days he probably knows all the employees."

"More importantly, he'll know you're not one of them, despite your official identification badge."

His mind working quickly, Trent glanced at the sky once again. All clandestine battles involved improvising. This part of the mission, it appeared, would be no exception. "It's a lovely night for a swim."

"It is, indeed." Kate put the car in gear and pressed on the gas pedal. "But that means no camera to document your findings."

"I'll make do." He tapped his temple. It wasn't the first time he'd have to use his photographic memory. Once he explored the entire shipyard he would re-create the layout on paper.

Ten minutes later, Trent stood on the river bank just south of Pembroke. Stripped down to his pants and undershirt, he took a deep breath and dove into the brackish water.

The cool water was a shock to his system and he gasped on impact. Within minutes of hard swimming the water's temperature was bearable, if not completely pleasant.

Having made similar trips, Trent broke the water's surface in the southernmost bay of the shipyard in record time. Hands flat on the retaining wall, he kicked out once then pulled himself into a flatfooted crouch on the concrete floor.

Water dripping in his eyes, he stayed low and listened to the sounds around him. Iron hulls scraped against the bulkheads. Ropes and chains groaned in the wind. In the distance came big band music, muffled but distinct. The guard probably had a phonograph in the gatehouse. A lucky break.

Trent rose to his feet.

Shook the water out of his eyes.

Drew in a bracing breath.

And set out to discover Pembroke's secrets.

By the time Trent had all the information he needed stored safely in his head, a band of low-flying clouds had rolled in from the west, dimming the moonlight to an unnatural haze.

The lack of light wasn't a problem at this point. Trent already had the layout of the shipyard memorized, including the points of weakness. All of which were contained in the dry docks and dockside sheds.

Peering up at the giant crane above his head, an uncomfortable feeling pricked at his senses. And made him think he'd missed something important here tonight.

He lowered his head and glanced around him, taking in the shipyard slowly, methodically. The dry docks held a cold, uninviting air, as did the rest of the shipyard. Perhaps it was the subdued lighting of the moon, or maybe the out-of-place swing music wafting in the air that set Trent on edge.

The wind kicked up, slapping him in the face. He needed to return to his hotel room and re-create Pembroke on paper.

Before slipping back into the river, Trent decided to check Savannah's office one last time. He'd missed something significant. He felt the truth of it deep in his gut.

Moving slowly, with the stealth he'd honed from sneaking around German shipyards, he entered her office. The door, as he'd noted the first time he'd pushed it open, hadn't been locked. A clear indication Savannah wasn't trying to hide anything momentous.

Yet the uneasy feeling persisted. Trent stopped on the threshold, once again noting the fact that the woman kept a tidy work area completely free of clutter.

This time, as he moved to her desk, his instincts started humming. Savannah was hiding something here, after all, something vital. Something that would either incriminate her or, perhaps, exonerate her.

Eyes narrowed to slits, Trent circled around to the other side of the desk and sat in Savannah's chair. The ancient springs creaked in protest.

He glanced at the window overlooking the river, the one facing Anderson Shipyard, and let out a slow hiss of relief. From this angle, he couldn't see out the window at all. If Savannah was gathering information for her father it wasn't from sitting behind her desk.

Not that something so minor would make a difference. All she would have to do was rise and she would be able to see out the window.

Lowering his gaze, he ran his palm flat across the desktop then opened the row of drawers on his left. Like the first time he'd searched their contents, he discovered ledgers, loose papers, invoices—in short, everything necessary for a bookkeeper to do her job successfully.

Turning his attention to the drawers on his right, Trent once again found nothing out of the ordinary.

On high alert, his instincts batting at him with hard blows, he opened the center drawer and dug around. When he shoved his hand to the back, his fingertips came in contact with something cold and smooth. A quick flick of his wrist and he pulled the item free of the drawer.

What he held in his hand made Trent smile.

Savannah Elliott, the perfect blond aristocrat, had imperfect eyesight.

He looked through the lenses and immediately realized they were designed for deciphering fine print. His heartbeat stalled in his chest then revved up to full speed.

Could this be the proof he'd been searching for? Proof that Savannah wasn't helping her father, at least not in the way Trent had originally suspected. The Nazis would never trust the gathering of vital information to a woman who needed this powerful a prescription. Whether she needed the eyeglasses to see down the river or not, there were too many potential errors she could make.

The discovery didn't make Savannah innocent, not by half. But Trent knew he'd opened a door to the possibility.

As soon as the sun rose, he would seek her out and give her a little test. Hopefully—*finally*—he would have his answer as to where her true loyalties fell.

Chapter Fourteen

The morning after Winslow's party, Savannah waited for her father to leave the house before she emerged from her own room. Although she wanted to dwell on that lovely kiss she'd shared with Trent last night, something far more disturbing competed for her attention: German prophecy.

Savannah found it odd that Trent was an expert in one of her father's favorite subjects. Nevertheless, parts of their conversation had started her thinking in a new direction, one that had her insides vibrating with anticipation.

Perhaps the evidence she'd been seeking all along had been right under her nose, buried in the books and papers Peter had recently given her father.

The possibility was probably nothing more than wishful thinking on her part, but worth investigating further. And now that her father had finally left for the day and her mother was off to an early hair appointment, Savannah seized the moment. This was her chance to conduct a little uninterrupted snooping.

Unfortunately, she had to leave for work soon herself. With time of the essence, she rushed out of her room and down the back stairwell without making a sound. No need to alert the household staff to what she was doing.

Praying for quick, undisturbed success, she slipped into her father's office without catching anyone's notice.

Wanting solitude for several reasons, none of them wholesome, Savannah shut the door behind her. She was becoming quite proficient at sneaking into places where she didn't belong. What had happened to the obedient, Christian woman she'd once been?

Probably not the best time to ask such a question.

Outside, a light rain misted in the sky, turning it a dull gray. It was a perfect accompaniment to Savannah's current mood. Cold despite the June heat, she rubbed her palms together for warmth and moved deeper into the room.

The smell of leather and her father's cigars wafted on the air. A quick glance around the study revealed nothing out of the ordinary. William Klein did not tolerate clutter in his house. His office was no exception.

The very moment the thought materialized Savannah's gaze landed on a pile of papers lying askew and off-center on her father's desk.

Odd.

Two steps closer and she realized the stack was held in place by a well-worn, tattered book. From this distance Savannah was unable to read the title.

Squinting past the dim lighting, she took a step closer and then gasped at the bold words splayed across the front cover.

"*The Secret of the Runes,* by Guido von List," she whispered. The very book she and Trent had discussed last evening.

An inescapable feeling of dread shot through her as she drew her fingertip along the binding. She'd thought the book would be gone by now, back in Peter's possession. Why was the offensive thing still in her father's office? And why was it lying out for anyone to see?

Didn't her father realize the disturbing subject matter alone could draw unnecessary suspicion his way?

Frowning, Savannah picked up the book and flipped from one random page to another.

Handwritten notations were scribbled throughout. The words were in an unfamiliar language. Norwegian, perhaps? German? Whichever, the handwriting did not belong to her father.

Savannah turned to another page.

The word *Aryan* jumped out at her. She didn't need to understand the rest of the notations to know what that word meant. Despite their argument on the subject, her father couldn't possibly believe in a Master Race. The very idea was inhuman, unchristian and entirely too awful to contemplate.

The sound of the door swinging open barely registered in her mind before a hard, angry voice spoke. "What are you doing in here without permission?"

The harsh tone made her jump. "I… *Oh.*"

Caught. She'd been caught, by the one man she was beginning to fear most in this world. *Peter.*

Hands shaking, heart beating wildly against her ribs, Savannah spun around and connected her gaze with his.

The book dropped from her fingers and hit the top of her foot. She swallowed then lifted her chin, determined to show no weakness in front of this man. This bully, as she was coming to think of him.

Without taking his eyes off hers, Peter bent to the floor and retrieved the book.

He snapped the cover shut and straightened to his full height. "Does your father know you're in his private office this morning?"

Bristling at the accusatory tone, Savannah desperately tried to think up an excuse for her presence.

But in the next instant, her anger reared. This was her home. Not Peter's. *He* was the intruder, *not* her. "I don't have to explain myself to you."

His lips twisted into an unpleasant sneer. "Actually, in this situation, you do."

How bold he was. How arrogant. Savannah's breath caught in her throat, but then she remembered who she was. Her father was this man's employer.

"I'll ask the questions, not you." She kept her breathing even, her voice as emotionless as his had been. "How did you get inside our home, Peter?"

"With my key. The one your father gave me."

Without waiting for her response, he pushed past her and then stopped midstep. His eyebrows pulled together. "Your perfume." He breathed in slowly, his nose inches from her hair. "I have... smelled it before. Recently."

Eyes locked with his, she fought against the urge to shudder. He reminded her of a snake. His nearness disconcerted her and made her voice shake. "We danced together at my party only a few nights ago. Surely that was when you smelled it last."

"No." He grabbed her arm, his grip brutally tight. "*More* recently than that."

"I—"

"In my office. The other night."

Had he been able to smell her perfume when she'd been trapped in his closet?

No. *No.* She hadn't worn any fragrance that night. But perhaps it had lingered on her dress. Or perhaps...

He was trying to trick her.

"I have never been in your office," she said, pleased to hear the calm pitch of her voice.

He released her so suddenly she nearly stumbled against the desk. "My mistake."

He walked to her father's desk without another word. Face void of all expression, he gathered the stack of papers von List's book had recently held in place.

"What are you doing?" she demanded before she could censure herself.

He glanced at her, his expression bland, innocuous and yet, so very frightening at the same time.

"Your father forgot these when he left this morning." The papers crackled as he stuffed the stack under his arm. "He sent me to retrieve them. As well as this." He indicated the book in his other hand.

"Oh, of course." She sounded like an idiot, but couldn't make herself think of a smart response. What he said made perfect sense. As her father's most trusted assistant, Peter would be the one sent to retrieve forgotten papers.

Yet, all that talk about her perfume had left her head whirling with alarm. What would Peter do if he discovered she'd been in his office two nights ago?

He would do nothing. Because he would never know.

"After you, Savannah." He moved by her side, standing far too close as he looked pointedly at the door.

Clearly, Peter wanted her to leave the room ahead of him.

She would not give him the satisfaction.

"I'm sure you're very busy this morning, so please go on ahead." She gave him the most pleasant smile she could muster. "I'll only be a moment behind you."

He didn't budge.

Refusing to cower, she lifted her chin a fraction higher. "Give my father my best when you next see him."

At last, Peter gave her a terse, insolent nod. "As you wish."

To her surprise, he left the room without further argument.

Heart in her throat, Savannah stared after his retreating back. If she'd ever doubted her suspicions, she knew the truth at last. Peter Sorensen was a very dangerous man.

And Savannah was more determined than ever to get him out of her father's life.

No matter the cost.

* * *

Still reeling from her troubling encounter with Peter, Savannah sat in the shipyard parking lot with her car's engine still running. She needed to go inside the building and focus on her work. But her mind wouldn't settle.

What sort of hold did Peter have on her father? And why was she starting to fear it was something she didn't want to know? Trent's warning came back to her. *You won't like what you find.*

Did he know something she didn't?

Sitting here alone, fretting over the problem all by herself, wouldn't bring her any concrete solutions. She wanted to tell Trent about her encounter with Peter this morning but thought better of it. What could he do anyway? Peter hadn't actually done anything wrong or given her anything to use against him.

She was back to square one, with nothing definitive to prove any of her suspicions. Perhaps Trent had had better luck. She would contact him this afternoon, if he didn't contact her sooner.

Feeling marginally better, Savannah exited her car and stopped dead in her tracks. Her mouth fell open. The man in question was sitting on a bench outside the main building of the shipyard, lounging casually, one ankle crossed over the other, as though he didn't have a care in the world.

Wearing no jacket, no tie, just a pair of well-made tan pants and a plain, white button-down shirt, Trent should have looked woefully underdressed.

He looked spectacular.

When he saw her approach, his face broke into a charming smile. "Good morning, beautiful."

Heart lodged in her throat, she snapped her mouth shut. "Trent. Do you have something for me?"

"Not yet." His smile didn't waver. "But soon."

She sensed he was putting her off. *You won't like what you find.* Perhaps not, but it was up to her to decide that on her own.

She couldn't continue this awful state of not knowing what Peter was up to much longer.

"If you're not here to share any information with me, what are you doing here so early?" Despite her tardiness, it was not yet nine o'clock in the morning. "And how did you get past the front gate?"

Seeming in no hurry to answer her question he rose slowly, reached for her hand and then cradled it in his palm.

She forgot to breathe. Just. Simply. Forgot.

"The guard remembered me from the other day." He released her hand and smiled. "He said I could wait for you as long as I stayed within eyeshot and outside the main building."

Well, that certainly made sense. And yet…it didn't. "But *why* are you here now? I don't understand."

He continued grinning at her from behind the all-too-familiar mask of his. "I found I couldn't wait until Friday evening to see you again. Surely you missed me, too."

With all that masculine attention directly solely at her, words backed up in her throat.

Why did the man have to be so…so…charismatic? And so…very…handsome? He wore an aura of power with the natural ease of a man comfortable in his own skin. The sort of confidence that was highly appealing.

There were a dozen men in Savannah's acquaintance that could have caught her eye, men who would have been both easy and convenient to allow into her life.

Lord, must I always take the difficult route?

His smile turning playful, Trent leaned in close. "Want to play hooky with me today?"

"No." Her answer was immediate, if spoken with a large dose of regret. "I can't."

Although…

She was tempted. She wanted to forget her recent encounter

with Peter, wanted to watch Trent's insufferable mask slip away, just as it had last night when they'd kissed.

Oh, that kiss.

"Are you absolutely certain you can't break away?" he asked. "I was thinking of heading out to the beach."

Well. That explained his casual attire.

She parted her lips to say something, anything, but nothing came out. Absolutely nothing.

Trent didn't seem concerned by her silence. On the contrary, he appeared amused. "The concierge at the hotel told me Ponte Vedra Beach is only a thirty-minute drive and is worth exploring."

"It is lovely," she agreed.

"You've been there?"

"We have a house right along the coast, near the country club."

"Ah." His eyes filled with interest. "Sounds like you have special feelings for the place."

"Oh, I do." She shifted her purse strap more solidly on her shoulder and sighed. "The house is situated in the dunes. It's a perfect setting that provides a great deal of solitude. It was my sanctuary when I first arrived home after…well, when I came home."

She closed her eyes a moment, remembering the raw pain she'd suffered during those first weeks after Johnny's death. The vast ocean stretched as far as the eye could see, beckoning her daily. She'd walked along the shore. She'd tumbled in the waves. She'd healed.

As a result, she was no longer the person she'd been before knowing Johnny. She'd changed. But not enough, she realized now. Not nearly enough. Perhaps that was why she couldn't hear the Lord anymore. Why it was so hard to pray. Why she was starting to doubt her own father, just a little, when it was his assistant who needed watching.

"Take me there, Savannah. Take me to your beach house." Tenderness gleamed in his eyes as he spoke. He looked large and invulnerable. An immovable rock, yet imminently safe. "Show me where you found the peace I see on your face now."

Trust him, a small voice in her head said. *Let this man be the one.*

Madness. Such thinking was sheer madness and completely beside the point.

Yet, the temptation he presented was too much to resist. She was tired of all the worry about her father and Peter. She wanted a day just for herself, selfish as that might seem.

"All right, Trent." It was an easy capitulation on her part. She wanted to show him the place where she felt both safe and the most like herself, where worries didn't exist. "But I can't leave right away. I have a few pressing matters that I must address this morning."

"I understand." His eyes turned a blue so rich and deep they held hints of purple. "How about I return in a few hours? Will that be enough time for you to clear your desk?"

Anticipation turned her voice low and husky. "Plenty."

"Splendid. I'll be back in two hours to pick you up." In the next beat, he pulled her in his arms and pressed his lips to hers in a quick, bone-melting kiss.

Then he was gone.

Approximately fifteen minutes after leaving Savannah in the shipyard's parking lot, Trent entered the Roosevelt hotel once again. Unlike the previous evening, the lobby was filled with people of all ages and sizes milling about. Some looked frazzled. A few walked with measured purpose, while still others meandered at a pace reserved for holiday.

Trent had witnessed the same scene in countless hotels throughout his life. Yet, this morning, a cold, unsettling shiver ran up his spine.

Someone was watching him.

A rush of adrenaline had him shifting his stance. Alert now, eyes tracking left to right, right to left, he was in mission mode, prepared to react at any moment.

The air around him pulsated with danger.

Another quick, all-encompassing sweep of the lobby and Trent found the source of his sense of foreboding.

Peter Sorensen.

The Norwegian stood just off the main lobby. Cast in a mix of shadow and light, his sculpted features looked unnatural, misshapen.

The controlled stillness of his stance and hawklike survey of the room confirmed what Trent already suspected. Sorensen was no bank assistant. He was a trained soldier, on a mission, and looking for someone in particular.

Trent had no doubt who that *someone* was.

Avoiding a family of four and a man dressed in an expensive business suit, Trent shifted two precise steps to his left, balanced on the balls of his feet and faced Sorensen head-on.

One beat passed. Two. By the third their gazes locked.

Sorensen's mouth curved into a sinister smile.

Trent's pulse thickened in his veins. It was if he was looking directly in the face of evil.

A shudder passed through him, the sensation one he hadn't felt since the last time he'd been in Germany. When Bobby had died at the hands of the SS.

The uncomfortable feeling settled deep in his soul, like an arctic wind blowing through him.

Too many regrets.

Too many secrets.

The only true refuge in times of darkness is God. The sudden thought came strong and bold. An undeniable truth Trent found himself wanting to cling to, now more than ever.

All the lies. All the subterfuge. They were taking their toll, making him doubt whether good would overcome evil in this ugly war.

All things work together for good to them that love God.

The Truth whispering through him brought immediate comfort. Warmth spread where the cold had settled in earlier.

And then...

Sorensen began his approach.

Trent held his ground.

A few more steps and Sorensen closed the distance between them.

Face blank, holding to his silence, Trent waited for the other man to speak first. It would be interesting to see how Sorensen handled this interview, especially since they'd never actually met face-to-face before this moment.

"You are Trent Mueller?"

"Who's asking?"

"My name is Peter Sorensen. I am William Klein's...assistant."

Trent nodded, filing away another valuable piece of information about his adversary. Sorensen's American accent was perfect, *too perfect,* with the kind of flat Midwestern inflection only language specialists acquired through years of practice.

"Mr. Klein requests a meeting with you."

"Now?"

"Now."

Anger surged at the arrogant assumption he'd simply come along as commanded. It would be easy to match Sorensen's patronizing tone, easier still to allow his annoyance to show.

However, Trent's role as the reckless son of a wealthy American family required a jaded, flippant response. "And if I'm unavailable at the moment?"

"You will make yourself available."

Ah, yes, there it was. The hint of Austria hovering beneath

the words, undeniable proof that Sorensen was not the man he pretended to be.

Had the slip been a mistake borne out of frustration? Frustration over Trent's refusal to comply without question? Or perhaps it had been a calculated ploy to draw out his expertise with languages?

"Since you put it that way." He allowed a provoking smile to play at the edges of his mouth. "I'm all enthusiasm."

"You will follow me."

"But of course."

Without speaking further, Sorensen turned on his heel and walked out of the hotel. He did not look back to determine if Trent followed. Nazi arrogance taken to the extreme. If Trent had had any lingering doubts about the man's allegiance, they were gone now.

Once outside, Sorensen maintained his cold silence. He led the way down the busy sidewalk, head held high in military exactness.

Trent drew alongside the man. Still in his role of entitled, wealthy American he pitched his voice to a sarcastic level. "I take it we're walking to our destination?"

"As you can see." Sorensen's abnormally straight posture conveyed a man barely holding on to his patience.

Well, then, time to determine just how far Sorensen would allow Trent to push him. "Tell me, my good man." Trent put a dose of sarcasm in his voice. "Where, exactly, is this impromptu meeting of ours to take place?"

"You are to meet Mr. Klein in his office on the top floor of the Copeland Building."

Ah, yes. "I'm honored."

Sorensen's mouth flattened into a hard line. The gesture made him look like a man pushed to his limit yet able to maintain his outward control.

Impressive, and valuable information for the future.

They completed the rest of the three-block jaunt with few words and short, succinct phrases.

Trent, however, used the tension floating in the air to toy with his adversary. He pushed for a mistake, a slip, a revelation.

Sorensen returned the favor with zeal.

Neither balked.

Neither gave an inch of ground.

The game of espionage was fully underway, played by two well-trained operatives refusing to show any sign of weakness.

By the time they entered the Copeland Building and rode the elevator to the top floor, Trent had discovered three things about Peter Sorensen, none of which came as a surprise.

The man was arrogant. He was highly intelligent. And he was quite possibly the most formidable foe Trent had ever encountered.

Chapter Fifteen

William Klein's secretary turned out to be an average-looking woman of indeterminate age. Her hair was cut shorter than was fashionable and the plain, red-brown color reminded Trent of rust. She had an earnest face and tired eyes, the personification of a hard worker putting in long hours.

Her desk was filled with eleven stacks of papers and the latest version of the Smith Corona Sterling typewriter. There were no photographs of family. No personal items. Not even a nameplate. It was the most functionally sterile work area Trent had seen outside the Pentagon.

"Trent Mueller to see Mr. Klein," Sorensen informed the woman in his perfectly bland American accent.

She stabbed a glance in Trent's direction. "He is anticipating your arrival."

Sorensen answered for him. "Very good."

Without waiting for further instruction, the Norwegian stepped to the door behind the secretary's desk and tapped lightly.

There came a muffled reply before Sorensen opened the door with a flick of his wrist. Moving aside, he allowed Trent to lead the way. But rather than joining him inside the office, he pulled the door shut with a hard snap.

So. This was to be a private conversation. Man to man.

Trent couldn't have planned it better himself.

Smiling ruefully, he moved deeper into the room. The smell of rich tobacco assaulted his senses, reminding him of his grandfather's study. In that moment, it occurred to Trent that he'd been closer to Heinrich Mueller than he had his own father. His brother had been the favorite in their home growing up. But in his grandfather's eyes Trent had been the real golden boy.

An odd memory. And immaterial at the moment.

Or perhaps not.

Trent's close relationship with his German grandfather was one of the reasons he'd been assigned this task of infiltrating Klein's inner world.

Donning the role of German-American, emphasis on the *German,* Trent continued forward. He stopped a foot in front William Klein's desk, and centered himself directly between two identical wingback chairs.

Klein did not invite Trent to sit. Nor did he look up from his desk. A subtle attempt to establish control.

Trent was not impressed.

Instead, he took the opportunity to carry out a more thorough inventory of the room. As he swept his glance along the perimeter, he noted the sound of a clock ticking directly behind him.

The office was bigger than he'd expected, the walls painted a muted blue accented by rich mahogany trim. Several Oriental rugs in bold, swirling colors sat atop wood floors that were polished to a shiny finish. The furniture was made of aged leather that had been worn to a fine patina.

The paintings on the walls were all landscapes.

The art was not good. Wretched, in fact. Knowing Klein, the artists were probably German.

Eventually Klein set his pen aside. He spent another seven seconds rearranging the papers on his desk.

At last, and with more formality than Trent deemed necessary, he spoke. "Savannah tells me you have accepted my wife's dinner invitation for tomorrow evening."

"I have indeed." Trent smiled, putting a mixture of respect and gratitude in the gesture. "With great pleasure on my part."

Klein made a noncommittal sound. He was obviously reserving judgment, in the way a caring father would. The man clearly loved his daughter. Trent found himself admiring that sort of devotion. Even sympathized with it. Savannah was, after all, a remarkable woman.

Nevertheless, the thought that he might actually have something in common with this *traitor* made Trent's shoulders knot up.

He forced himself to relax.

"My daughter seems to have taken a liking to you." The reserve was still firmly in place, along with a good amount of concern.

Assessing his options at lightning speed, Trent knew he could handle the situation in several ways. Placate. Aggravate.

Or mollify.

He chose none of the obvious routes and went for direct honesty. Not for the father's sake, but for the daughter's.

"I can assure you, the feeling is mutual."

A sound of dismay slipping past his lips, Klein rose from his chair. "You are treading on dangerous ground, Mueller. Other men, with finer backgrounds than yours, have dared to say the same and have fallen short."

"With all due respect, sir, I'm not like other men."

"No, Mueller." Klein laughed, a cold-blooded gurgle of contempt. "You are not."

"Sir, I have no intention of—"

Klein held up his hand to stop the rest of his words. "Take a seat." His tone brooked no argument.

Deciding to mollify now, Trent obediently eased into the chair on his left.

Klein came around his desk, hands clasped behind his back. He stopped mere inches from Trent and hovered over him with a menacing scowl on his face.

Trent recognized the ploy. The superior warning off the inferior. Or rather, the protective father threatening the upstart playboy who dared to sniff around his daughter.

Tread carefully, Trent told himself in the same words Klein had used. *This is no game to the man.*

Contrary to the tense situation, Klein leaned back against his desk, his arms hanging loose by his side in a deceptively casual manner. "My daughter has not always had the best judgment in men. As such, it is my duty to ensure she doesn't make another mistake."

Trent felt the other man's frustration. And his resolve. "I understand your concern."

"Do you?"

"Yes, sir, I do." *Tread carefully.* "Savannah told me about the night her husband died."

A look of surprise crossed the other man's face. "How much did she tell you?"

"Everything, including the part about the other woman on his arm when he first arrived at the restaurant."

A range of emotions crossed Klein's face: bafflement, unease, outrage and then…nothing.

The man had his emotions back under control.

"Savannah tells me you are a professor at Princeton University."

The change of subject didn't surprise Trent. Under normal circumstances, Klein's tactic might have been effective.

However, these weren't normal circumstances. And Trent wasn't actually courting the man's daughter.

He was here to catch him in the act of treason.

"That is correct. I teach a combination of philosophy and theology courses to Princeton undergraduates."

All of which Klein already knew. General Donovan's man in the Pentagon had been instructed precisely what to reveal to Sorensen when he'd called for information on Trent three days ago. Sorensen had been unaware his "contact" inside the American government was actually an OSS agent.

It had been a perfect bait and switch, with Sorensen completely unaware he'd been duped.

"Philosophy and theology?" Klein rubbed his chin in consideration. "Do you have a specific area of expertise?"

Again, Klein already knew the answer.

Again, Trent played along as though he didn't.

"For the past year I have focused my studies on prophecy." He propped an ankle on his knee and composed his features into a bland look. "German prophecy, to be precise."

"An unusual specialty, especially in these precarious times."

Trent nodded, but said nothing more.

Ball in your court, Herr Klein. Let's see how far you're willing to go with this.

The man appeared to consider his next words carefully. "Although I'm no expert on the subject—" his arrogant tone said otherwise "—I do consider myself somewhat of an enthusiast on the subject of German prophecy."

"How utterly fascinating," Trent said with zero inflection. "We share a common interest." He waited a beat. "Beyond your daughter, of course."

Despite the slight flinch at the mention of Savannah, cunning filled Klein's eyes. "Don't you think it odd that we share such a unique common interest?"

And there it was. One card laid metaphorically on the table, faceup, played with a bold stroke of the hand. And Trent had thought Sorensen a formidable foe? The man was no match for William Klein.

"Perhaps it's not odd at all. Perhaps it's…" He smiled a very small smile. "Fortuitous."

"Indeed."

It was Trent's turn to reveal a portion of his hand now. "Considering the nature of our common interest, I'd go so far as to say we share other...sympathies as well."

"That remains to be determined." A muscle shifted Klein's jaw. "However, my schedule is full this morning." He pushed away from his desk. "We will discuss the matter in greater detail tomorrow evening, before we dine with the women."

The game of cat and mouse had come to an end.

For now.

Satisfied he'd set the stage for the next step in his plan, Trent rose. "I look forward to our upcoming discussion."

He turned and headed for the door.

"Mueller."

Trent turned around slowly. Very, *very* slowly. "Yes?"

"There is one final point I wish to clarify before we continue our...association."

Eyebrows lifted, Trent waited for Klein to continue.

"I am sure you know that Savannah returned home only a handful of weeks ago."

"Yes. I am aware of that."

"Then I should also inform you that she shares none of my... *sympathies,* as you put it."

Caught off guard for the first time during their interview, Trent found himself blinking in surprise at the other man.

Did he realize the magnitude of what he'd just revealed? In the process of declaring his daughter innocent he'd all but incriminated himself.

Except...

Klein hadn't actually said anything concrete. Nothing that could be used in court, at any rate. In fact, the man could be intentionally misleading Trent in an effort draw to him away from the daughter he adored.

Even knowing William Klein was a liar *and* a traitor to the

United States, Trent wanted to believe he was telling the truth in the case of his daughter's loyalty. He wanted to believe Savannah was innocent.

He did not have that luxury.

"I'll take what you said under advisement."

He turned to leave once again.

Klein wasn't through with him yet.

"Given the reality of my daughter's...innocence, I expect you to proceed accordingly in the future."

Translation: walk away now or suffer the consequences.

Trent resisted the urge to ball his hands into tight fists. "Understood."

This time, when he turned to go, Klein did not stop him. Trent left the office with a heavy heart.

He desperately wanted to believe Savannah was loyal to the United States. But without concrete evidence he had to *proceed* in the same manner as before.

He would continue courting Savannah, because for all intents and purposes she was still a threat to national security.

Trent almost believed it, too. Almost.

Although Trent had been charming and full of compliments when he'd arrived at the shipyard, Savannah couldn't shake the notion that he wasn't completely in the moment with her now. He seemed...distracted. And he kept checking the car's rearview mirror.

What was he looking for?

She glanced over her shoulder, too, but found nothing out of the ordinary, just a line of cars heading in the same direction as they were.

She turned back around and sighed. Even knowing he needed to pay attention to his driving—the road had a treacherous curve up ahead—Savannah still wanted to touch Trent's arm, to make him look at her and give her that oh-so-familiar smile.

She wanted to see his blue, blue eyes run along her face then fill with masculine appreciation.

She wanted him to be the man who'd only this morning said he couldn't wait until tomorrow evening to see her again.

What could have possibly happened since she'd seen him last?

Drawing her bottom lip between her teeth, Savannah folded her hands in her lap and watched the scenery crawl past. He was driving awfully slow, something she hadn't expected from a man like him. She'd assumed him to be addicted to speed.

What else didn't she know about him?

She knew he filled the entire space with his scent. His controlled breathing. His large presence.

Needing air, Savannah wound down her window and breathed in the scent of sea and marsh. The smell alone told her they were close to the bridge that would take them over the Intracoastal Waterway and on to their destination.

Her suspicions were confirmed a moment later when the bridge came into sight.

Savannah slid her gaze back to Trent, once again sensing something had changed since this morning. There was a strange new feeling between them, one that left her torn between alarm and anticipation.

As Trent continued concentrating on the road, the sensation intensified.

Had he found out something about Peter? Something she could use?

Surely he would have told her by now.

Her heart thumped hard against her ribs.

When they cleared the bridge she found she could bear the silence no longer. "You'll want to take a right turn at the end of this road."

Not the best conversation starter, she knew, but at least he angled his head toward hers and smiled.

"All right." He returned his attention to the road.

Suddenly, Savannah wasn't sure she wanted to share her private sanctuary with him. She'd found peace in the house on the beach. Would Trent understand? Would he care? His expression had been so impassive just now. She couldn't imagine what had put him in such a strange mood.

Or why he kept looking surreptitiously over his shoulder when he wasn't checking the rearview mirror.

What did he hope to find?

And why did she sense it had to do with something altogether unpleasant?

Lord, please let me be right about this man. Let him be trustworthy.

For a prayer, it wasn't fancy. And it certainly wasn't pious. But it came from the heart.

Wasn't that enough?

In the past, whenever she'd felt distant from God she'd gone through the motions, anyway, eventually finding her way back.

Would she be able to do so again? Or had she allowed circumstances to lead her down a path of no return? Had breaking into Peter's office been a momentary lapse borne of desperation, or a sign of worse things to come?

Perhaps God had already taken His hand off her.

Refusing to accept such a calamity, Savannah decided to trust the Lord to reveal Himself in time. "We're only a few miles away now."

"Good." Trent reached out and squeezed her hand. The reassuring gesture calmed her nerves.

Whatever was happening between them, and she knew *something* was happening, Savannah would wait until they were on her turf to explore it further.

After two more turns, and several miles of driving parallel to the coast, she pointed out the window. "There. That's our house up ahead. The third one on the left."

Trent looked over his shoulder one last time then pulled into the drive and cut the engine. He didn't make a move to exit the car. "I need to tell you something, Savannah."

"You have found evidence against Peter."

"No. It's something more personal."

Every muscle in her body tensed. He sounded so serious, so *determined.* What could he possibly have to reveal?

Nothing good could come from that kind of tone.

She closed her eyes a moment, swallowed, then gave him her undivided attention. "All right, Trent. But not here. On the beach."

The faintest trace of unease crossed his face. But he exited the car without question and came around to her side to open her door.

She accepted his assistance and joined him on the drive. For a moment they stood staring at one another, their individual breathing shallow and hectic.

Smiling, he brushed a hand down her arm and her skin felt suddenly alive. Why? His touch had been casual.

"Savannah." He managed to make her name an apology. "I—"

She cut him off before he could speak further. "Not here. Follow me." She spun around and headed toward the ocean.

He took her hand as they made their way around the house, holding firm as they crossed over the lawn, then down the wooden stairwell that led onto the beach below.

They were not the only ones enjoying the beautiful day. Several families had set up chairs, blankets and umbrellas. Everyone was consumed with their own fun, and no one paid them any attention.

The tide was out, leaving a large expanse of sand and shells and random pieces of driftwood.

Savannah was too interested in the man holding her hand to pay much attention to the crunch of shells beneath her feet. Or the waves crashing to shore in an unending cadence. Or even the seagull diving for his daily meal.

They walked in silence for several moments before Trent pulled her to a stop and pivoted to face her directly.

He glanced to the woods on his left then gave her the lazy smile she'd seen often enough. The sun made his eyes glitter a pale, iridescent blue. There were so many emotions staring out of him she couldn't begin to decipher any of them.

The wind shifted his golden hair around his outrageously handsome face. A dangerous man, she thought, and wondered: Where was the panic?

Another moment passed then he gave one firm shake of his head and his gaze cleared.

He'd come to some sort of a decision.

And she knew—just knew—she wasn't going to like what he had to say.

"When I first laid eyes on you at the country club, I only saw what others said about you."

He touched her cheek and her concern increased. She didn't want to know, but found herself unable to resist asking, "What... what did you see that first night we met?"

"A beautiful ice princess who could freeze a man with a single look."

She gasped, shocked. Except, not so very shocked. She'd known the gossip about her had been unkind.

"But then I asked you to dance and every preconceived notion I had fell away."

His words should have insulted her, but her mind went in a completely different direction. They'd met only four days ago. Four. Short. Days. And he was on the verge of making some sort of a declaration.

She knew wartime accelerated relationships, but this was America. The war wasn't here. And it certainly wasn't a part of either of their lives. However, there was an unmistakable urgency in Trent that she couldn't ignore. He made her feel things, deep and confusing things, in a way she'd never felt before.

She forced back a wave of panic. It was too soon for her feelings to be stirred so completely. Johnny had been gone only six months. Despite the way he'd died, where was her loyalty to the man she'd vowed to love a lifetime?

"I was wrong about you, Savannah." Trent took her hand in his and rolled it over until her palm faced upward. "Completely wrong." He placed a gentle kiss in the center of her hand. "Not the beautiful part, but the—"

"Ice princess part."

He gave her a wry smile and rolled his shoulders. She expected the familiar mask to slip into place. But his eyes filled with tenderness, the kind that stole her breath away.

"Forgive me. You're not what I expected. I—"

"No, Trent. Don't apologize." She cupped his face with her hand. "I'm well aware of the gossip about me. You couldn't have known the truth."

"I never want to hurt you."

Savannah braced herself. Whenever a man said *I never want to hurt you* it was a sure sign he was about to do exactly that.

But he didn't speak again. He simply pulled her into his arms and rested his chin on the top of her head.

"I can't make promises to you," he said in a strange, tight voice. "I...*can't*."

Of their own volition, her fingers curled into his shirt and she pressed her cheek flat against his chest. His heartbeat was strong and fast.

"I'm not asking you to," she whispered, wondering why he sounded like a man heading off to a war zone.

"You should, Savannah. You should demand—"

He stopped abruptly and pulled back. Not wanting to see whatever was in his eyes, she kept her head lowered.

"Savannah." He placed his finger under her chin and applied

light pressure until she was looking him straight in the eye. His gaze was sharp, measuring, weighing. "You should demand complete honesty from me."

"Would you give it to me if I asked?"

"No."

All pretense was gone between them now. There was only clear, raw honesty. And yet, she felt out of step, confused, as though she'd missed a key portion of the conversation.

Trent had just told her he would always lie to her. But she sensed he was trying to tell her something important about himself, something real. Something she should already know but had missed along the way.

"I don't understand. What are you trying to tell me?"

He dragged a frustrated hand through his hair. She could tell this conversation was not going as he planned.

A ball of panic knotted in the vicinity of her heart.

"I need you to know that this is the most truthful I will ever be with you."

Softly, tenderly, he covered her mouth with his.

She prayed her knees would hold out under the gentle, warm onslaught.

This kiss was different than the others, more tender and full of unspeakable, beautiful emotion. Was Trent showing her how he felt without saying words?

She'd never been a woman who needed fancy declarations. She only needed this. This silent declaration of…of…

Tears of joy welled in her eyes.

Several seconds passed before he finally drew away.

They stared at one another, both breathing hard now. And then he smiled. *This,* she thought as she stared into his eyes, was the real Trent Mueller.

Savannah smiled in return.

He blinked once, twice, then shook his head. "Now that we

understand one another, why don't you show me around your house and the surrounding dunes?"

"Oh. I…" She stared at him, unable to gather her thoughts into coherent sentences. They understood one another?

How, exactly?

Understanding was not the word she'd use for what she felt at the moment. *Confusion. Puzzlement. Concern.* Those fit the moment far better.

Trent was, after all, a stranger to her. And yet…

That kiss had been filled with far more emotion than a simple gesture between strangers.

Perhaps he would explain himself after the tour.

Feeling more hopeful than she had a few minutes ago, she took his hand and pulled him in the direction of the house. "Come. Let me show you my personal refuge."

Chapter Sixteen

Stick with the plan, Mueller. Savannah is supposed to fall for you.

Trent had no doubt she was doing precisely that. But with the realization of his success came very real guilt.

She wanted proof against Sorensen, proof Trent could easily hand over to her at any moment. But if he did that, Savannah would discover the truth about her father as well.

Trent must continue to put her off. And if she pressed him for the information, he would lie to her. Without hesitation. Without question.

What did that say about him?

Certainly nothing gallant.

Not that it mattered. There was no room for heroism in espionage.

As they walked parallel to the water, Savannah turned her head and smiled at him, her feelings for him evident in her warm gaze.

His heart took a quick, extra thump. He felt a dangerous tenderness for this woman, a bone-deep desire to protect her from harm.

The force of his feelings was so strong they infuriated him. There was something about Savannah that drew him to her, a force that defied reason. It was not her beauty alone. But her light as well. He'd been immersed in darkness so long he found himself craving what she offered. Peace. Hope. A future free of guilt and lies and pain.

In four short days Savannah had reminded Trent he had a heart. One that yearned for things he could never have. He would never forget her.

But he had to remember they weren't alone.

Every moment of this outing had been planned down to the minute.

Per his instructions, the other two OSS agents still posing as FBI had tailed them to the beach.

So had Sorensen.

Even now, the Norwegian was perched behind a tree in the dunes near the Kleins' house, watching their every move. The OSS agents were in a similar position, better hidden, but there, in a spot several hundred feet to the south.

Trent kept all three men in sight, while his mind worked through the very real problem walking beside him.

Kate had warned him he would fall hard for Savannah if he wasn't careful.

He'd scoffed at the idea. Emotion had been trained out of him, that's what he'd told himself. Over and over again.

He'd been dead wrong. Savannah had gotten to him the moment he'd laid eyes on her.

When he'd held her in his arms just now, he'd kissed her as a man kissed a woman he adored. In the process, he'd crossed so far over the line he'd landed at a point of no return.

Trent knew enough of Scripture to know the dangers of allowing himself to fall for a beautiful woman. Even King David, a man after God's own heart, had been led astray by his obsession with a woman. Before this mission, Trent had always thought David weak. If he'd only tried harder to resist temptation he'd have avoided the resulting disasters.

Trent had been arrogantly naïve in his assumptions.

The temptation of a beautiful woman, one who had the power to get below a man's defenses, was the deadliest weapon known to man.

Many men—men far better than he—had been led to their ruin by a beautiful face. They'd also been saved.

The thought gave him a sliver of hope.

Perhaps Savannah would be his redemption.

Or my ruin.

Unaware he was only half-listening to her, Savannah chattered on about the glory of watching a nor'easter blowing in off the water.

Trent smiled and nodded and made various sounds of agreement.

He looked up to the dunes, finding Sorensen easily enough through the thick underbrush. The man wasn't as stealthy as he presumed.

But he was deadly all the same.

Sorensen could never know Savannah had broken into his office. Assuming she wasn't working with Sorensen and drawing Trent into their web. It would be the perfect double-cross.

Had that kiss been a mistake? No, not the kiss—that had been part of the plan. Trent's *personal* participation was another matter entirely.

He could not let his guard down again. Never again.

Eyes open, he filtered out the chaos in his mind, ignored everything personal and focused on his surroundings. The saboteurs were supposed to land on the beach close to where he and Savannah were now.

Out of the corner of his eye, Trent noted the endless expanse of water. The view was uninterrupted for miles, not only straight out over the horizon, but also to the north and south.

Nothing of strategic importance lay to the south. However, Mayport Naval Base was only a handful of miles to the north.

The Nazis had chosen a prime spot to begin their treachery. There was nothing beyond privately owned residential houses and two hotels lining the coastline between this point and the base.

"Look, Trent, up there. That's our house." Savannah pointed to a spot directly to their right.

He turned and took in the view.

The house, a large, two-story structure made of wood, was nestled between rolling sand dunes peppered with sea grass, thick underbrush and spindly oak trees. The first and second floors were dominated with black-shuttered windows, giving every room a perfect view of the ocean. The attractive, sloping roof was made of perfectly square wooden shingles.

"It's very inviting," he said, even as his eyes moved to the surrounding forest. Sorensen was no longer in sight, but Trent knew he was still watching them.

The OSS agents had moved deeper into the woods as well.

A small, wooden structure several feet to the right of the house caught Trent's eye. "What's that over there?"

Savannah followed his gaze. "Oh." She planted a fist on her hips and shrugged. "I'm not sure. Some sort of gardening shed."

"A gardening shed?"

Staring at it a moment longer, she lifted her shoulders again. "Yes, I think so." She sounded sincerely unsure. "I've seen our gardener tinkering around in there."

"You have a gardener on staff down here?" The report hadn't mentioned a gardener for the beach property.

"No, of course not. Well, I mean, my father does employ a gardener, yes, but Winston only comes out here once a week."

Accepting her explanation with a brief nod, Trent studied the wooden shed. The structure was small by most standards, about four feet by six. However, it was large enough to hide a considerable amount of explosives, detonators, ammunition and other supplies necessary to blow up several shipyards.

Would Savannah realize this?

Deciding to test her, Trent gave her an expectant look. "Want to go check it out?"

Her eyebrows slammed together in obvious confusion. "You want to explore a gardener's shed?"

"Any reason why we shouldn't?"

"No, but…" She angled her head and studied the shed another moment. "What could you possibly expect to find in there?"

"That's the fun of it." He tapped her lightly on the nose.

"Fun?"

"Yes, fun. Not knowing what we'll find is the point. The joy of discovery and all that."

"The joy of discovery, indeed." She let out a short, happy laugh. "I don't know why I keep forgetting who you are."

An odd sensation dug deep inside his heart, grabbed hold and squeezed. He couldn't pinpoint what he heard in her tone. Amused understanding? Admiration, perhaps?

The reflex to hold her came fast. He shoved it aside and pretended confusion. "I'm not sure I catch your meaning," he said.

"I keep forgetting you're a college professor. It makes perfect sense that you would be interested in exploring a shed most people would overlook."

Trent searched her face for any indications of deceit. There weren't any. There never were. Savannah Elliott was an open book. No pretext. No subterfuge. An innocent woman enjoying the company of a man she found attractive.

Then again, if she was attempting to lead him astray, he probably wouldn't be able to tell if she was lying right now. She could be a master in the art of deception.

He didn't believe she was. Nor did he believe she was working with Sorensen or was part of her father's treason. Not because William Klein had all but said so in his office this morning, but because of Savannah herself. She was turning out to be sweet, sincere and straightforward.

No one was that good of an actor.

And Trent was starting to trust her.

He looked away. Counted to five.

Trusting this woman was the worst thing he could do at this point.

Always err on the side of suspicion. The axiom had kept him alive in situations far more precarious than this.

The last thing he needed was to lose his impartiality.

With that in mind, he placed his palm on Savannah's shoulder and dropped a light kiss on her lips. The move was a calculated show of affection, nothing real, just a part of the plan.

That was what he told himself, anyway.

"Let's find out what's hiding in that shed, shall we?"

"Sure." She smiled up at him. "Why not?"

Hand on the rickety doorknob, Savannah stared and shook her head and finally managed, "I don't understand."

The shed was empty.

Completely empty. There wasn't a single hedge shear, or hoe, or anything remotely resembling a gardening tool. Stranger still, there wasn't even a dust mite or cobweb.

"You seem surprised."

At the sound of Trent's voice coming from directly behind her, she jumped slightly forward. Her hand lost its grip on the doorknob. She hadn't heard him approach. But he was standing so close, practically on top of her as he peered over her shoulder into the darkened, empty shed.

"I am surprised." She blinked into the stingy light. "Like I said, I just saw the gardener tinkering around in here last week."

"Perhaps he was clearing it out for some other purpose."

Trent's voice sounded colder than usual.

Feeling disoriented, Savannah held perfectly still, her back facing Trent. She couldn't figure out why she felt something had gone terribly wrong.

"This is all so—" she sucked in a tight breath "—strange."

"Did your father mention anything that would explain this?"

"My father? No. No, he didn't." Why would he?

"And you find that odd."

There was that tone again. The one Trent had used the other day in her office when he'd questioned her about Anderson Shipyard, and again in Peter's closet when he'd shown up unexpectedly. "I honestly don't know what to think. There must be an explanation. And yet…"

"Yet?"

"Something about this feels…wrong." All of it, including Trent's participation.

She was suddenly afraid to look directly at him, afraid to let him see what was behind her eyes. Distrust. Suspicion.

This empty shed was somehow important to him. What she couldn't understand was why.

Why did Trent care about a tiny toolshed that wasn't a toolshed after all?

Trent touched her shoulder. "Savannah."

She swung around and tilted her face up to his.

Having joined her in the shed, his features were hidden in shadow. She told herself it didn't matter. She didn't need to see his face clearly. This was Trent. The man who'd kissed her so tenderly on the beach moments before.

Yet now, he came across as calm and coolly in control of the situation.

Savannah felt anything but.

In fact, her breathing had quickened, as had her heartbeat. The sound roared in her ears, and she prayed her knees would hold up.

"I'm sure there's a perfectly logical explanation, Savannah." Trent ran a gentle finger down her cheek. "Spring cleaning, perhaps?"

A shiver swept through her. "It's June."

His smile was a hard, white slash in the midst of the shadows. "Close enough."

"Why are you pushing so hard to see the shed up close?"

"Simple curiosity, nothing more." A beam of light caught floating dust particles behind him, creating a hazy backdrop for his broad shoulders.

"No, Trent, it's more."

She knew she was right when he dropped his hand and blew out a long, audible breath instead of answering.

Before she knew what was happening he turned and started striding toward the house. Warning bells rang in her head, urging her to follow.

"Trent. Wait." She caught up to him and grabbed his arm. "I know when a man is holding something back. What are you hiding from me?"

To his credit, he didn't argue the point. "Are we having our first fight?" He punctuated the question with his most cocky grin, the one she was coming to recognize as his mask.

A burst of annoyance spread through her. "Don't patronize me."

"All right, Savannah. I won't." His words came out grave, serious. There was no pretense in his eyes, no smiling mask covering his features.

She realized this was the second moment of honesty between them. The other had been after their kiss on the beach.

Unfortunately, she didn't feel triumphant in the knowledge. She felt cold.

So. Very. Cold.

Her reaction worried her, but not enough to let the matter drop. "Tell me the truth, Trent. Why did you want to see inside the shed?"

If Trent answered her truthfully she would trust him from this point forward. If he did not, they would be finished.

As though sensing she was putting him to the test, he ran a hand down his face and swallowed hard.

When their eyes met again, she knew he was going to be completely honest with her. "I thought you were hiding something in there, something you didn't want me to see. I wanted to know what it was."

Hiding something from him? In the shed? What an odd thing to say. "What did you think I was hiding?"

"Weapons?" His eyes went dark and turbulent, in a way she'd never seen before. "Explosives?"

She sniffed at the absurdity of his answer. "No, seriously, Trent. What did you think was in there?"

His gaze cut to the beach, the faraway look in his eyes as vast as the ocean. "I didn't know what to expect."

She heard only truth in his speech. And yet...

Was there a hidden meaning his words?

Surely not.

This was Trent. *Trent.* The man who'd let her see past his mask.

"Now, then." His face relaxed into the pleasant smile she'd grown to expect after a tense moment between them. "Why don't we put this unsavory business behind us and you can show me the rest of the house?"

Relieved the tension had lifted, even if she didn't understand where it had come from, she was only too happy to comply. "We'll start on the first floor."

Chapter Seventeen

Hans-Peter waited until Mueller's car pulled out of the drive before he circled around to the back of the house.

He let himself in with the key Herr Klein had given him months ago. With the door shut behind him, the sound of the ocean was only a dull roar in his ears. Or perhaps the noise came from the pounding of his heart.

Dark satisfaction filled him.

Mueller had taken the bait.

Impatient for his eyes to adjust to the lack of light in the room, Hans-Peter stabbed a glance through the darkness. He could make nothing out yet. He blinked rapidly. At last, random shapes became clearer and more distinct.

He moved deeper into the darkened house and stopped in the middle of the large, open area used as a living room.

The wood floors creaked beneath his feet.

Drawing in a deep breath, he smelled leather, dust and salt air. Bars of sunlight flickered across his feet.

With a quick snatch, he picked up the telephone receiver and dialed Herr Klein's private number. Urgency made his movements quick and precise.

Herr Klein picked up on the first ring.

Without preamble, Hans-Peter explained the situation. "Mueller discovered the empty shed."

He made sure to use enigmatic wording, in case anyone was listening to their conversation.

"As you said he would."

"Yes." A wave of contempt crested. *Mein Gott,* he thought. It was abundantly clear Mueller was working for the American government and had come to stop the sabotage plot.

He would not succeed, no matter how many plans he made. He was arrogant to think he could try. Hans-Peter's heart beat hard with a promise of retribution.

"Mueller's snooping will come to nothing," he vowed.

"Have you checked out the other set of coordinates for a similar breach?"

"It is secure." And quite evident Mueller had no idea an alternate hiding place for the explosives existed.

The night of the landing, the Americans would be waiting outside the empty shed on this piece of beach property.

They would be waiting at the wrong place.

"You've done well, Peter."

Yes, he had. "What next, Herr Klein?"

"Return to town. We have much left to plan."

"Very good."

Hans-Peter replaced the telephone receiver in its cradle and expelled a slow, hard breath.

Despite Mueller's interference, they were on schedule.

In a matter of days, the American government would discover the full might of the Nazi war machine.

The strikes would be simple yet stunning, coming in one wave after another.

And when his mission was over, Hans-Peter would return to the Fatherland a hero.

Once Trent crossed back over the Intracoastal Waterway, a comfortable silence fell over Savannah. Compelled by her serenity, he took her hand and lifted it to his lips.

She smiled but didn't attempt to break the silence.

Just as well. Trent needed to think. He let go of her hand and focused on the road once more.

His mind ran through the past two hours he'd spent at the beach with Savannah.

One thought kept emerging.

The shed was a decoy.

Not that he'd thought so at first. He'd believed it to be the perfect hiding place for the saboteurs' supplies. Until he'd considered various possibilities for Sorensen's presence here today. Only one scenario made sense. Trent was supposed to find the tiny structure empty and swept clean.

Well played.

But ineffective. Trent wasn't so easily fooled.

Now he had two days to uncover the real drop zone.

He knew William Klein was the mastermind behind the plot and the obvious key to finding the correct coordinates.

How fortunate Trent would be having dinner at the man's private residence tomorrow evening.

All because he was courting the woman beside him.

He glanced over at Savannah and smiled. She smiled back, and his heart twisted with guilt.

More and more, Trent was becoming convinced she had nothing to do with her father's treason.

She'd been actually surprised to find the shed empty. She'd also been smart enough to realize there was something not quite right about the discovery. The tiny structure should not have been swept clean. Not so thoroughly.

Mulling over how to proceed, Trent steered into the shipyard and cut the engine. He slid a glance in Savannah's direction once again.

His heart filled with remorse. She would suffer when she discovered the truth about her father. She would be undeniably hurt. Betrayed.

Devastated.

Unavoidable fallout, Trent tried to tell himself. This was all in the name of the greater good.

Unfortunately, he couldn't find peace in the thought anymore. He and Savannah had created a bond over the course of their short acquaintance. If he was honest with himself, he would admit that their closeness had begun even before they'd shared those tense moments in Sorensen's office.

From the start, the woman had gotten to him. Her soulful eyes. That smile that grabbed at his heart and twisted.

For the past year Trent had been so busy policing the world he'd forgotten how to care, had actually thought himself incapable of the emotion. He'd even accepted the cost of what he did for the war effort. His own personal fallout.

When Savannah discovered the truth about his motives she would hate him. The realization made his head swim with confusing thoughts.

Before knowing her, he'd lied, cheated and seduced, all in the name of war. Somewhere along the way he'd lost his moral compass. He couldn't imagine a Lord merciful enough to forgive him all he'd done.

He cursed himself for wanting things to be different.

He had a job to do, one that would save countless lives.

Not if you allow your scruples to get in the way. He had one objective now: Discover exactly where the Nazis were scheduled to land on the beach in two days' time.

To accomplish his goal, he had to continue courting Savannah.

"What time is dinner tomorrow evening?" he asked, refusing to allow his conscience to take hold.

Savannah blinked at his abrupt tone. "Oh, yes, dinner." She flattened her palms on her lap. "Eight. Dinner is always served at eight."

Realizing he was going to botch this if he didn't get a handle on his emotions, he took one of her hands and slowly caressed her palm. "Should I arrive early?"

"That would be nice." She stared at their joined hands. "Say, seven?"

"Seven it is." He didn't let go of her just yet. "I'll see you then."

"I'm looking forward to it." She sounded sincere, but he saw the quandary behind her eyes when she lifted her head. He knew she was going to broach the subject of the shed once again.

He was prepared.

"Trent? Can I ask you a question?"

He pretended not to know what was coming. "Certainly."

"You...that is, this afternoon..." She swallowed several times. "You didn't seem...surprised when we found the shed empty."

Smart woman. "I wasn't."

He didn't allow any hesitation in his answer, didn't allow anything to show in his eyes. It was imperative to keep Savannah from suspecting he had a hidden agenda.

"Why is that?"

He reluctantly dropped her hand. "I'd like to give you a good reason, but I can't." *That,* at least, was the truth. Or rather, a portion of the truth.

"I...you can't give me a good reason? Why not?"

"Call it instinct, a gut reaction, something in between." He shrugged. "But, no, I wasn't surprised when I looked inside the shed and there was nothing there."

His answer was a well-orchestrated lie, just enough truth mixed with just enough evasion to sound sincere. In the eyes of God, his actions were still a sin.

"Well, then." Savannah shook her head and laughed softly. "You are quite insightful."

"So I've been told. Occupational hazard."

"You mean, as a college professor."

"Sure."

At last, she seemed satisfied with his answer, enough to let the matter drop.

A good spy knew when to pull back before he overplayed his hand. Less was often more. "Regrettably, I have a full day ahead of me tomorrow. So I won't see you until seven tomorrow night."

She nodded, looking slightly bereft, but managed to pull herself together enough to lean over and press her lips to his cheek. "Until tomorrow evening."

At least she hadn't broken their date.

Before he could respond, she scrambled out the car and headed toward her office in a brisk pace. Trent had lost his chance to escort her inside. He willed her to look back in his direction.

She never once turned around.

Chapter Eighteen

The next evening, a few minutes before seven, Savannah put the finishing touches on her makeup, then stepped back from the mirror to study her handiwork. She tried to tell herself that tonight was only dinner with a friend. *A friend.* But the fact that she'd spent two hours dressing for the occasion said otherwise.

After discarding several options, she'd gone simple with her hairstyle, a loosely coiled chignon, and had chosen to wear an ice-blue fit-and-flare dress. The popular style made her waist appear tiny, while the soft color made her eyes sparkle two shades lighter than usual. Her skin actually glowed.

She looked—and felt—better than she had in months, due in part to her recent acquaintance with Trent.

It's only dinner, she told herself, a little wistfully this time. She really shouldn't have felt this excited, this full of anticipation, for a simple evening in the company of a man. After all, Johnny had been gone only six short months.

Struggling with a surge of guilt, Savannah allowed her mind to travel back in time. What would she have done had her husband survived that night? Would she have worked hard to salvage her marriage? Would she have forgiven Johnny his infidelity?

She'd have liked to think so.

After all, wasn't forgiveness at the very core of the Christian faith? Unfortunately, she would never know if she could have moved past Johnny's betrayal. That was the trouble with death. It was so final. She didn't have to worry about forgiveness anymore. Or did she?

A lump formed in her throat as something disconcerting tugged at her, something that felt an awful lot like remorse. Or perhaps conviction? Uncomfortable with the sensation, Savannah prayed she wasn't making the same mistake twice.

Was Trent different from Johnny? He'd certainly slipped beneath her well-honed defenses faster than any man. Trent Mueller was an amazing man. Handsome, smart, insightful. Both enigmatic and charming.

But was he honest?

That she couldn't say for sure. His answers concerning the empty toolshed had been evasive. Not outright lies, no, but not the truth, either. What Savannah couldn't understand was why he would feel the need to prevaricate in the first place.

What sort of threat could a woman like her pose to a man like him? She was a bookkeeper, he a college professor.

Neither of them was dangerous.

Although…

There had been a moment in the shed yesterday, one similar to their time together in Peter's office, when Trent had been cast in shadows and Savannah had feared he would eventually hurt her. Physically? No. *No.* But Johnny had taught her that a man could hurt a woman in ways that didn't involve bodily harm.

Now she was just being paranoid and putting entirely too much stock in an insignificant matter.

Yet, no matter how many times she told herself to let the matter drop, she couldn't shake the notion that the empty toolshed was important. Especially to Trent.

Despite the feeling he was holding something back from her, some vital piece of information that would explain his fascination with the tiny building, the decision to trust him would be so easy. Too easy.

Trust only in the Lord.

Always the wisest move. But how could she put her trust in a God who'd been so distant these past six months?

Perhaps you *need to take the first step.*

The thought whispered through her mind as a still, small voice.

"Savannah, darling, are you almost ready?" Her mother popped her head in the room and smiled. "Well. Don't you look especially lovely this evening?"

The compliment filled Savannah with warmth. "What a nice thing to say, Mother."

"I never tell a lie." Alma Klein glided into the room and pulled Savannah into a fierce hug.

She relaxed into the warm embrace and breathed in the smell of her mother's perfume, a familiar blend of wild flowers, lavender and white spice. The scent reminded Savannah of happier days, when her biggest worry had been which shoes to wear with what dress.

After another quick squeeze, her mother pulled away but kept her hands clasped on top of Savannah's shoulders. "I know I've said this before, but it's good to have you home."

Her heart filled with emotion, Savannah smiled at her mother. For a woman nearing fifty, she still looked young and beautiful in her blue silk dress and upswept hair. The perfect wife to a successful banker and businessman.

Had her mother ever wished for something more out of life? Something beyond the role of wife and mother? Probably not. Savannah couldn't think of a more contented woman. Or a more happily married one.

"Oh, Mother." She pressed a happy kiss to her cheek. "It's good to be home. So very good."

Tapping into the cheerful girl she'd once been, she broke

away and twirled in a slow circle. This room had been her sanctuary as a child. The décor didn't fit her anymore. The frills and pink lace were better suited for a young girl on the cusp of becoming a woman, her head full of dreams and possibilities.

Savannah would never be that innocent or carefree again. It was time for her to discover new dreams just for herself. Once she ensured her father was no longer under Peter's influence, she could focus on her own future. Perhaps *then* she would grow close to the Lord once more.

Caught in her thoughts, she jumped at the sound of her mother's voice.

"As much as I'd love to stay here and chat all evening, I've come to tell you that your friend has arrived. He's with your father in his study, talking about—" she laughed "—well, whatever it is men talk about in private."

Hoping to capture her mother's easy attitude, Savannah smoothed a hand down her hair. Unfortunately, the gesture failed to settle the nerves clenching in her stomach.

She didn't like the idea of Trent and her father holed up together in a small room talking about…about…

Whatever it was men talked about in private.

A cold sense of foreboding shivered along the base of her spine.

What was her father discussing with Trent?

What was Trent discussing with her father?

Too many dreadful possibilities came to mind. What if Trent brought up the subject of Peter? What if her father grew angry at Trent's meddling and forced out the truth about their midnight stroll?

What if, what if, what if.

"Maybe we should go rescue him," she said in an unsteady her voice.

"Which one, dear? Your father or Trent?"

Savannah swallowed back a sigh. "Both?"

* * *

William Klein's study was decorated in the same bold, masculine style as his office in the Copeland Building, all the way down to the bad art on the walls.

Interesting. And worth looking around with a careful eye.

However, when the older man directed him to sit in a leather chair facing his desk, Trent feigned only mild interest in his surroundings. His instincts told him he was in the right place at the right time. The coordinates to the alternate landing site were somewhere in this room.

From Klein's arrogant manner alone, it was clear he had no idea Trent had figured out there *was* a new drop zone.

That overconfidence gave Trent the advantage.

He *would* find the coordinates.

But would he find them in time?

An increasing sense of responsibility weighed on him. All the intelligence coming out of Washington indicated that the next forty-eight hours were crucial.

Proving consistent, Klein dispensed of the pleasantries and got straight to the point. "Tell me, Mueller, from one enthusiast to another, do you favor a particular German prophet or prophecy? Or are you a generalist?"

The question was a ploy to uncover Trent's sympathies—or lack thereof. This was not get-acquainted time, nothing so benign. This was an interrogation.

Trent had no doubt William Klein would be thorough in his questioning.

So be it.

"I'm no generalist," he said in a solicitous tone. "At the present, my interest is in Guido von List and his extensive writings on the social occult."

"Ah, yes, von List." Klein rubbed his hands together. "I have found a renewed interest in his book, *Das Geheimnis der Runen*. His conclusions are very...enlightening."

Of course he did. The more obsessed Nazis held a morbid fascination with von List and his study of the runes, especially the most famous of the ancient symbols, the swastika.

"Have you read von List's book in the English translation?" Trent asked, sensing the question would spark a passionate answer. "Or in the original German?"

"The original German, naturally."

Naturally. Trent maintained his outward calm. But his heart raced at an alarming speed. Klein's admission to reading von List's book in the original German spoke volumes. Not an admission to treason, per se. But not innocent, either. "That's certainly impressive."

"It is nothing." Klein drummed his fingers on his desk in a military-precise beat. "A mere hobby."

They both knew reading von List's book—in the original German—was no hobby. Trent dropped his gaze to Klein's desk. The man rested his hand on top of the book in question. The beating fingers slowed. Then stopped.

Trent whipped his gaze back to Klein's.

Klein smirked at him.

This was all a game to the other man. Klein slid the book across the desk. Slowly. Deliberately.

Trent reached out and flipped open the front cover. He did not, however, look at the contents.

Yet.

"I'm curious." Klein spoke in a slightly goading tone. "What are your thoughts on the assertion that a Master Race is not only possible, but…desirable?"

The question was meant to bait him. All part of Klein's plan. Trent was a step ahead. Before his true feelings showed on his face, he tapped into the college professor he was purported to be.

"I believe…" He made a loose gesture with his shoulders.

"That there are sound arguments for and against the notion of a Master Race."

"The notion?" Klein slammed his fist on the desk, the impulsive gesture revealing far more than his words.

Trent had hit a nerve.

He smiled.

Klein gathered air in his lungs, and then continued in a calmer voice. "Do you deny the scientific proof that there is not only a superior race of human beings, but consequently inferior ones as well?"

Trent forced back a wave of disgust. Operating under the assertion that *they* were the superior race, the Nazis had begun to rid the world of the so-called inferior people groups. Their goal was the actual extermination of entire races.

Trent could hold his tongue no longer. "I would say *the notion* of a superior race is impossible to reconcile with a Christian worldview."

"Is that your personal belief?"

Trent's fingers curled into fists. He willed himself to relax, but a Bible verse came instantly to mind, the one his German grandfather had taught him as a boy.

Do nothing out of selfish ambition or vain conceit, but in humility regard others as better than yourselves. Better, not inferior. But better!

"I am merely a college professor." He spoke in his best teacher voice. "I make observations, not judgments."

As Trent spoke he realized the cost of his cover story. He had to pretend he didn't have an opinion on a matter that had birthed unspeakable atrocities in Europe.

When this was over, he prayed God would allow him back into the Light because he feared he couldn't find his way back on his own. He'd strayed too far.

Please, Lord...

He didn't know what else to pray.

Smiling smugly, eyes full of menace, Klein pressed his fingertips and thumbs together until he created a diamond shape with his hands. "You are very careful with your words, *Professor* Mueller."

"It goes with the territory."

"Indeed." Klein drew in a measured breath and redirected the conversation once again. "I understand you spent the afternoon with my daughter."

The sudden change of topic was a calculated ploy to throw Trent off his guard.

He smiled again.

"I did. Savannah was excellent company, as always. We drove to the coast and explored your property in Ponte Vedra."

"And was this trip your idea or hers?"

"Mine."

Rising from his chair with deliberate slowness, Klein moved to a small wooden cabinet on his left, pulled out a half-full crystal bottle and poured a shot of clear amber liquid into two glasses.

He returned to his desk and handed one of the glasses to Trent.

A non-too-subtle test.

Trent took the glass without hesitation.

Klein settled back in his chair. "And what did you think of my second home, *Professor?*"

"I found the entire set-up to be…" He twirled the fiery liquid around in his glass, watched it catch the light. "Extremely functional."

"True enough."

Setting his untouched drink on the table beside him, Trent picked up von List's book and flipped through the pages at random. He absently reviewed the handwritten notations. Most were scribbled in German. A few in English.

All revealed an obsession with the notion of a Master Race.

William Klein's sympathies were clear.

"Savannah tells me you have a fondness for your beach property," Trent said, lifting his attention from the book. "For what I think is a vastly different reason than your wife and daughter."

"You are correct. I enjoy, shall we say, the convenience of the location."

Trent hid a smile at the heavy-handed answer. Klein was intentionally misleading him to think that the saboteurs' landing site was indeed near his beach property.

"My daughter, on the other hand, enjoys the peace and solitude she's found there since returning home."

Book still in hand, Trent turned to another page, glanced through more notations. "You mean, since her husband's betrayal."

Klein frowned at his boldness. "Yes."

"In my experience," Trent continued with his own heavy-handed taunting, "I've found that deception hurts those closest to us. I'm sure you agree."

Angry shock leaped into the other man's face.

Good. He had not missed Trent's point.

However, he pretended that he had. "My daughter might be getting on with her life, but she is still vulnerable. For a man without scruples, she would be easy prey."

Easy prey. Those had been the exact words Trent had read in the OSS briefing a week ago. The description hadn't set well with him then. It still didn't.

Holding back a snarl, he shoved at his hair. Dark emotions threatened to steal his composure. After a moment of fruitless struggle, he decided to let his anger come, let it show on his face.

"You think Savannah can't determine when a man is being sincere or not? You think that little of your daughter."

"I think that much of her." Klein leaned forward. "I will not stand back and watch another man betray her."

"This? From you?" Trent growled the words. A protective

instinct surged inside him. "How do you live with your hypocrisy?"

"You go too far, Mueller."

"As do you."

Angry silence fell between them.

Trent had just laid all his cards on the table, practically admitting he knew about Klein's treason. The time for games was over now.

Klein set his glass on his desk, his eyes narrowed in contempt. "Though it is none of your concern, Savannah and her mother are quite safe in my care. They will be even better off once this war is over and the proper side has won."

So, the OSS briefing had been correct. Klein was funding the Nazi war machine, the assumption being he would be greatly rewarded once the Third Reich ruled the world.

Needing a moment to calm his revulsion, Trent flipped through several more pages of von List's book. A series of handwritten notations caught his eye. The scribbled words were put together in two groupings of six letters each. Trent wasn't familiar with the language, wasn't sure it was a language. Sensing he'd found something important, he committed the notations to memory and then shut the book with a snap.

"You realize that among certain circles—" Trent slid the book back across the table "talk of Guido von List could be considered an act of treason."

Klein's lips peeled away into a sneer. "Whether a man is guilty of treason depends on which side loses the war."

"Spoken like a man certain his side will win."

"As you say." Klein rose.

Trent did the same.

Neither made a move toward the door.

"Now that we know where one another stands," Klein said, "let me speak plainly."

"I would expect nothing less."

"After tonight, I expect you to redefine the nature of your relationship with my daughter."

"Meaning?"

"You will no longer pursue her for any reason, personal or otherwise. I want your word, Mueller."

"My word?" Trent released a harsh laugh. "You would trust my word?"

"In this particular matter, yes, I would."

"Listen, Klein, I—"

A light tapping on the door cut him off before he could finish the thought.

"Father, Trent? We are ready for you now."

"Ah. Summoned, at last." Klein emptied the contents of his drink in one long gulp. "Before we depart, I will have your answer to my demand."

Trent considered telling the man what he could do with his *demand.* He settled for something far more polite. "I will continue my relationship with your daughter as my conscience sees fit."

Very slowly, very carefully, Klein set his glass back on the desk. "And that is all the answer I am to receive?"

"It is."

"Then I will proceed as *I* see fit."

Trent nodded. "Understood."

"Now, then." He directed Trent toward the door. "Let us join the women."

Chapter Nineteen

To Savannah's way of thinking, dinner was an excruciating affair. Tension had been high from the moment the first course had arrived at the table. Now, several courses later, she wanted to grit her teeth in frustration.

It was clear Trent and her father disliked one another intensely. She should have seen this coming, of course. Both men were too dominant and strong willed to give an ounce of power to the other.

She shot a pleading look at her father.

He ignored her completely.

There was nothing more trying than pretending all was well when all was not well.

Whatever had happened in her father's study had left both men on edge.

Savannah knew the feeling.

She felt strangely dizzy and unable to pinpoint the specific problem between the two men. Probably because there wasn't one specific problem. The atmosphere simply felt off-kilter, lopsided.

By the time the dessert dishes were cleared away the two men had exhausted the topic of sailing and were now on to the more serious pursuit of golf.

Her mother appeared not to notice the tension permeating their conversation. In fact, Alma Klein seemed perfectly happy sitting back and watching the two men spar with one another.

Spar. Yes, that was the correct assessment of the situation.

Trent and Savannah's father were tossing warnings and threats at one another in the guise of golf scores. Trent was being far more subtle in his technique. Her father was holding nothing back.

Stifling an annoyed sigh, Savannah set her napkin on the table with great care.

Enough of this. *Enough.*

"Trent!"

All eyes swung in her direction. No wonder. She'd practically barked his name.

Smoothing out her expression, she pitched her voice to a more pleasing octave. "Would you care to walk with me down by the river? We have a spectacular view of downtown."

"What a grand idea." She could see the humor lurking in his gaze, as though he knew she was trying to rescue him and found her efforts…endearing.

She felt both patronized and adored. The ache of unshed tears fluttered in the back of her throat. She pushed the shocking reaction aside.

Smiling at her, Trent rose from the table but then turned to face her mother instead of taking Savannah's offered hand.

"Mrs. Klein." He sketched a short bow, the formal gesture softened by his relaxed charm. "Thank you for the dinner invitation." He bent over her hand and dropped a light kiss to her knuckles. "The food and company were spectacular."

"Oh, my." Alma let out a girlish giggle, the same one she'd given him that first night at the country club. "The pleasure was mine, I mean *ours.* You will come again soon."

"I'd be delighted." Trent nodded in her father's direction.

Her father nodded in return. Neither man actually spoke to the other.

The underlying strain between them was evident in their similarly bunched shoulders. There was something ugly going on between them. Something that Savannah couldn't fathom completely.

She hated feeling one step behind.

Hastening out of the room before she said something contrary, she led Trent through the kitchen to the outdoor marble deck overlooking the river.

Looking around him with interest, Trent followed her down the stairs and onto the lawn.

Strategically placed outdoor lighting illuminated their path. The wind had kicked up, she noted, punching hot, stifling air in their faces. The trees swayed and groaned in angry protest.

Still silent, they climbed the slope of the lawn in tandem. Trent stepped ahead of her and moved an errant branch out of her path. He really was quite the gentleman.

Savannah could smell the storm coming in, could hear it pounding against the side of the house.

The trees continued rattling overhead.

Trent looked up into the night sky, now blackened by a bank of thick, charcoal-colored clouds. "Storm's brewing."

"Yes." She noted the large, choppy whitecaps rolling atop the river. "It'll probably leave damage in its wake."

"I'm afraid you're right."

Their stares met.

His breathing slowed. Hers quickened.

And then a gust of wind whipped between them, throwing Savannah slightly off balance. She flayed around a bit.

He reached out to steady her. "Don't worry, I've got you."

But as quickly as he'd grabbed her, he let her go. Unprepared for the loss of his support, she stumbled again.

This time, he caught her around the waist. "I'm not going to let anything hurt you," he whispered in her ear.

He'd spoken so softly she wasn't sure she'd heard him correctly. "Promise?"

He let her go without answering, then looked up at the darkened sky above. "We better not linger."

If only she understood what had happened to put this new tension between them. The sensation was different tonight. It had a feeling of…of…finality.

Wrapping her arms around her waist, she shook her head at the depressing thought.

She was overthinking again.

Trent had been the perfect dinner guest this evening. Respectful, polite, he'd handled her father's hostility with composure.

It was that composure that set her on edge.

Savannah suddenly wanted to shove Trent, just a little, enough to break through all that Ivy League refinement and uncover the real man underneath.

His careful façade of easy smiles and impeccable manners had lost its appeal. She wanted the dangerous man, complete with *skills,* the one Trent kept hidden below the false outer shell.

Trent propped a foot on the lip of the bulkhead, then shifted slightly to face her.

Her heart fluttered. He was so good-looking. The white of his shirt was a striking contrast to his tawny skin.

And then he smiled. "Thank you, Savannah, for inviting me to dine with your family." He spoke with a natural ease, even as the wind swirled around them with a furious growl. Why was he so calm? "I won't soon forget this evening."

"That I believe." She laughed despite herself. "My father wasn't exactly restrained."

He chuckled. "No harm done. See." He opened his arms wide. "Not a single battle wound to take with me."

Take with him? That sense of finality wrapped around the moment. Was Trent telling her goodbye? Would she never see him again after tonight?

She searched his face for the answer.

A thousand words passed between them, none of them easily discerned.

Maybe he *was* leaving her.

No, Lord, please, not yet.

Not only would she miss him, he'd agreed to help her with the problem of Peter, had already done so, at great risk to himself. Surely Trent wouldn't have helped her break into a man's private office merely to walk away without following through to the bitter end.

No. Trent did not seem like a man who left matters dangling.

Savannah had to trust she was misreading the situation. Nevertheless, she grappled for a new topic, anything to keep him with her a little while longer. She needed the time to convince him there was more between them than a casual attraction.

And, yes, oh, yes, there was more. Much more.

The thought should have scared her.

After Johnny's death, Savannah had feared she'd never find love a second time in her life. She'd feared she was incapable of feeling the emotion ever again.

But she'd been recovering for months, rebuilding her inner strength. And her life.

Then she'd met Trent.

And he'd shown her the truth. She could love again.

Could a woman really fall for a man so quickly?

Maybe, yes. Maybe there was a divine hand involved. Maybe she and Trent had found each other for a reason bigger than themselves, a reason only the Lord knew. And not simply to help her prove Peter was a genuine threat.

"Savannah, it pains me to say this, but I must leave. I have an early morning." He placed a light kiss on her lips. "Good-bye, my darling."

No. He couldn't leave. If she let him go now she feared she would never see him again.

"Trent. Wait. Don't go." She gripped the lapels on his suit and pulled him to her.

He didn't resist. A victory. A very small one.

"Will I see you again?"

He smiled that lazy smile of his, dropping both eyelids to half-mast. "Absolutely. We have unfinished business."

"You mean the situation with…Peter?"

"Among other things."

He wrapped his arms around her then and kissed her with exquisite tenderness. He cared about her. She felt the truth of it in his kiss.

Only a cruel man could pretend such intense emotion. Trent was not a cruel man. She knew it as sure as she knew her own name.

Tears of joy sprang to her eyes. She squeezed them tightly shut, kept them closed when he released her.

She reluctantly opened her eyes and caught him staring at her. He looked smitten—*with guilt*.

"Trent?"

"Tomorrow, Savannah." He lifted his hands to her face and rested them lightly on her cheeks. "We will meet again. Tomor-row."

What an odd tone in his voice. Nevertheless, she believed him. They would, indeed, see one another tomorrow.

Despite her confidence, she decided it wise not to question precisely when, exactly, that would be.

Early the next morning Savannah hurried to the kitchen in hope of catching her father before he left for his office down-town, where he would put in several hours of work, even on a

Saturday. She'd stayed up most of the night, alternating between worries about her father, concerns over Peter and unanswered questions regarding Trent.

She'd been especially preoccupied with thoughts about Trent.

Originally, she'd been attracted to the mystery of him and all the things she didn't know about him yet. From the first moment, Savannah had detected the hidden depths of character beneath the charming façade.

Now she wanted him in her life, whatever that looked like.

But too much stood in their way.

It was time for complete honesty. On all sides. No more secrets. No more subterfuge.

She would start by facing the one man she could always count on to tell her the truth.

"Father," she called out before he could open the back door, "I'd like to speak with you before you leave for the day."

Hand on the doorknob, he froze. "Can't it wait, Savannah? I have a meeting with Peter this morning and I'm running late."

Her father never ran late.

The fact that he claimed to be doing so now made her wonder. Was he hiding something from her?

Ridiculous.

"Please, Father." She used her softest voice, the one that always got to him. "This will only take a moment."

Releasing a sigh, he dropped his hand, turned around but didn't set down his briefcase. "If this is yet another attempt on your part to warn me about Peter, now is not the time."

"But—"

"He told me about your altercation in my study the other day."

Her mouth dropped open.

"You were out of line, Savannah." Her father's tone matched his gaze, very cool, very assessing. And far too much like the way Peter looked at her.

"Peter should not have been in your private study."

"He was operating under my orders."

What an odd choice of words. In that moment, Savannah realized her father would never take her word over Peter's.

It was a humbling realization.

And left her all the more determined to find concrete evidence to back up her argument.

She sighed, and let the matter drop for now. Instead, she redirected the conversation to an equally troubling topic. "What did you say to Trent last night when the two of you were in your study?"

Her father rubbed a weary hand down his face and she realized he looked older this morning. He never looked old.

Something was wrong.

"What did Mueller say we discussed?"

"He didn't mention anything about your conversation." She pulled her bottom lip between her teeth. "But I get the sense that he's pulled back from me."

And wasn't that the problem?

Trent might have said they would see one another today, he might still follow through with his promise to help her find the evidence she needed against Peter, but Savannah feared he was no longer committed to pursuing a romance with her. Not like he'd been prior to last night.

How could his affections for her change so quickly? Her father must have said something to him.

"Pulled back, has he?" The flash of satisfaction in his eyes was impossible to miss. "Perhaps that's for the best."

Savannah's heart sank. "You warned him off, didn't you?"

"Now, Savannah, don't upset yourself. I merely—"

"You threatened him."

"Not in so many words, no."

"Oh, Father, how could you?"

"If Mueller has pulled back, it wasn't because of me." He

looked away, but not before she saw the relief in his eyes. "He is his own man."

There was unmistakable respect in her father's words, reluctantly given but there all the same.

Then why was he so against Savannah dating Trent? "You're not telling me everything."

Eyes on her, he set his briefcase on the ground and placed his hands on her shoulders. "Trent Mueller is not the man you think he is. He will hurt you."

"Is he…" She prayed for the courage to ask the question haunting her. "Is he…like Johnny?"

"No." He dropped his hands and sighed. "I can assure you, Mueller is *nothing* like your dead husband."

So why the warning?

"But, Savannah, there are many forms of betrayal. Some far worse than what you suffered at the hands of your husband."

How could anything be worse than what Johnny had done to her? What sort of betrayal was her father trying to warn her against?

Her confusion must have shown on her face, because he touched her cheek with the backs of his fingers. "Never doubt, my child, that you are worthy of being loved by a good man."

"Trent *is* a good man."

A sad look entered her father's gaze. One filled with genuine regret and something else, something not altogether nice.

"You must walk away from him." His eyes bore into hers. "Promise me you'll stop seeing him at once."

She'd never heard or seen such intensity in her father. It was as if he was afraid for her. "But you said he was nothing like Johnny."

"He will still hurt you."

Of course he could hurt her, because love was inherently dangerous. It wasn't supposed to be easy or simple, at least not at the beginning. That had been the mistake Savannah had made with Johnny, and he with her.

Everything about their relationship had fallen neatly into place. There had been no great effort on either of their parts. They'd met, dated, spent time learning each other's likes and dislikes. Marriage had been the reasonable next step.

Savannah had been comfortable with their arrangement. But had she been in love with her husband? Had she fallen madly, deeply, in love with him?

No. No, she hadn't.

The truth shamed her.

She'd loved Johnny. She just hadn't been in love with him.

Perhaps that was why he'd looked elsewhere for happiness. His behavior had been wrong, so terribly wrong, but understanding his motives made it easier for Savannah to forgive him.

With forgiveness came a surge of hope. Hope for the future. Hope that this time Savannah had found something larger than herself, something real. Something worth fighting for.

A relationship with a man like Trent would not be easy, or simple. And, yes, as her father said, he could hurt her.

Was he worth the risk?

She blew out a slow breath.

Perfect love casts out fear.

Yes, oh, yes. The truth was clear to her now.

She knew what she had to do.

"Goodbye, Father. I have to run."

"Savannah, we aren't finished. You can't—" He cut off his own words. "Where are you going?"

She slung her purse over her shoulder and grabbed her car keys off the counter. "To find Trent."

"*Savannah,* did you not hear a word I said? He'll hurt you, he'll—"

"Yes, yes, I know." She waved a hand over her head, her mind focused on getting to Trent as fast as possible. Before she lost her nerve. "See you later tonight, Father."

Chapter Twenty

Trent started the day groggy from lack of sleep. An occupational hazard he'd experienced many times since he'd joined the Army. The saboteurs were scheduled to land on the beach in twenty-four hours or less. He still had no idea where.

Or when.

He closed his eyes and reviewed his conversation with William Klein once again. Step by step, word by word. The man had revealed himself clearly enough. But Trent sensed he'd missed the key point.

What? What had he missed?

Rubbing the back of his neck, he stretched out his legs, then returned his attention to the papers on the tabletop in his hotel room. He sorted through the ones laid out in front of him. His fingers tingled over a particular sheet of paper.

He pulled it closer, narrowed his eyes over the two words he'd written down the night before. He'd found them handwritten in William Klein's personal copy of *Das Geheimnis der Runen*.

He studied the words again. And came to the same conclusion as before. They weren't words at all, but something else entirely. Two sets of random letters in groupings of six.

Trent ran his finger across each word.

wzyrvv
syxwvw

Not a known language. Perhaps the letters represented something else. They were...

Codes.

Trent's heart dipped in his chest. Could it be this easy?

William Klein's arrogance last night made sense. The man had been hiding the coordinates to the alternate drop zone in plain sight. He'd literally waved them under Trent's nose.

The letters were symbols—*runes*—used to record the location of the alternative landing site.

All things work together for good to them that love God.

A slow smile curved Trent's lips. He needed to crack the code and he would have the location.

"Thank you, Lord," he whispered into the silent room.

Head bent over the paper, he worked the letters around, moving them into different order and various groupings. After several tries he realized there was no way to make discernible words out of the letters themselves.

He straightened in his chair.

What if the letters stood for numbers? And what if the groupings were by twos, not sixes? Latitude and longitude. *Wz...yr... vv...sy...xw...vw.*

He dug in the pile of papers for his charts of the waterways surrounding Jacksonville and the beaches. He checked for the most obvious number first. The degrees of latitude and longitude were identical from the Mayport Naval Base all the way to several miles south of Klein's property. 30 North and 81 West.

If *wz* was 30, and *sy* was 81...

Trent cracked the rudimentary code. A quick calculation and he had the landing site: 30N 19' 55" and 81W 23' 43".

He plotted the points on the chart. The alternative landing site was seven and a half miles north of William Klein's property.

It might as well have been a hundred miles.

Had Trent and his team gone to the empty shed by mistake they would have been chasing their tails all night.

Clever, but not clever enough.

Now all Trent needed was the time of the landing.

If the location had been in von List's book, so was the time.

Trent searched his memory. None of the other notations fit. The page number, perhaps?

The location had been written on page 230. 0230? So simple.

Trent checked his watch. 0820. He had approximately eighteen hours to coordinate his team.

He contacted Kate first. "I have the information we need for tonight."

Her breath caught. "Don't say anything else."

He hadn't planned on it.

"I...I'll meet you at your hotel in fifteen minutes."

"I'll be waiting for you in the lobby," he said.

Fifteen minutes later, down to the second, Kate sauntered into the Roosevelt looking as though she'd materialized from the pages of a fashion magazine.

She was really quite beautiful. Breathtaking. Trent wondered why he'd never been attracted to her. Or why she didn't make his heart twist in his chest like Savannah did.

Savannah. She was a problem. A complication. A—

Shutting off his thoughts, he caught Kate's eye. With a jerk of his head he directed her toward a small alcove off the main lobby.

Neither spoke until they were sitting in two chairs facing one another. Their presence was obscured by a strategically placed rubber plant, some of the leaves as large as Kate's head.

"I found the location of the new landing site." He rattled off the latitude and longitude.

Smiling grimly, Kate closed her eyes. Trent waited while she committed the coordinates to memory.

Once she opened her eyes again, he continued. "I need you to alert the others of the change."

"Consider it done." She looked at her watch. "What time do you want to leave for the beach tonight?"

"2100." They needed the extra time to coordinate their efforts. "We'll want to plan for contingencies."

"Speaking of contingencies, what about Savannah?"

Trent felt his heart constrict in his chest. Thanks to Savannah, he'd changed. He'd tasted hope. And possibly even love.

When this was over...

He pushed the thought away. There was only now. Only the mission. Savannah was a distraction at this point, one that needed to be removed. For her own safety. "I'm going to break it off with her this morning."

"I see." Kate crossed her legs and let out a heavy sigh. "So your conscience has kicked in, after all."

Perhaps it had. But more than that, Trent wanted to protect Savannah. The best way to do that was to take her out of the equation.

"This has nothing to do with my conscience." He made sure his words came out cold and unemotional. "She's served her purpose. I don't need to pursue a relationship with her anymore."

Kate's eyes narrowed. Her foot started swinging, the only sign of her agitation. "Why don't I believe you're being forthright with me—or yourself?"

"Because you have a suspicious mind."

"I'm trained to be suspicious." She angled her head. "And so are you."

"Nevertheless, Savannah is no longer useful."

When spoken so coldly, in that matter-of-fact tone, Trent realized just how duplicitous he'd been. He'd lied to Savannah from the start. Using her to get close to her father had seemed like a good plan. And then he'd met her.

Watching him closely, eyes still narrowed, Kate settled back in her seat. Her foot had stopped swinging. "Are you absolutely certain Savannah is free of guilt?"

"Completely."

"What changed your mind?"

"It hasn't been just one thing, but a combination of factors."

"Trent." Kate took a slow, shuddering breath. "Don't you see? Savannah has possibly led you on a merry chase. First to Peter's office, then straight to that shed on her father's property."

"No." His voice came out harsh, unrelenting. "She was genuinely shocked when Peter arrived at his office unexpectedly, equally so when we found the shed empty. No one is that good an actress."

Kate lifted an eyebrow.

"Not even you."

"If I didn't know better, I'd say you're trying to protect her."

He dropped all pretense of the good guy and let Kate see the man who'd faced down the SS without flinching. "We are not involving Savannah anymore. That's the end of it."

Kate balled her hands into fists. "Remember your training, Trent. You're making a decision emotionally and trying to justify it logically."

Stay on point, he told himself. *Don't let Kate pull you off track.* "We have the coordinates we need. Savannah is no longer necessary to the mission. At this point, she could get hurt."

"Casualties are a part of the equation. You're the one who taught me that."

Yes, he'd taught Kate to expect losses. He'd lost so much making war, he'd convinced himself a few innocent deaths was a necessary evil. All for the greater good.

Somewhere along the way he'd decided he knew God's mind

and had justified sacrificing innocent people in order to save thousands.

He'd been wrong, of course. God didn't want to lose one person. Not even one.

Trent was no longer willing to sacrifice Savannah.

When the war was over maybe he would find her again. Maybe they could have…

Nothing. Trent could have *nothing* with the beautiful Savannah Elliott.

He focused on the conversation once more. "Look, Kate, there's no reason to put Savannah in unnecessary danger. Both times I've spoken with her father he's made it clear she doesn't share his sympathies."

"Thereby revealing *his* sympathies?"

"Not precisely. He's been careful not to say anything that could be used against him."

"The man is beyond arrogant." Kate sounded as sickened as Trent felt.

"Yes," he said. "But with his arrogance comes the seed of his own destruction."

Kate's eyes lit with cunning. "Both he and his assistant think we aren't as competent as they are."

"I say we give them exactly what he expects from us." Trent would send a decoy agent to the shed tonight, ideally pulling Sorensen off point.

While Sorensen was monitoring the decoy, Trent and his team would be at the real drop zone.

"That still doesn't answer the problem of Savannah," Kate said. "What if she won't let you go? What if she keeps dogging you for answers concerning Peter? Even if you try to cut her loose, she could end up in the middle of this, anyway."

Dread filled him. "You're thinking like a woman, worrying about something that hasn't happened yet."

"Oh, but it has, Trent." Kate cocked her head toward the lobby's entrance. "Savannah has come looking for you."

"She's losing patience. She's come for information on Sorensen."

"No. She's come for you."

His heart stopped beating, then revved up to lightning speed.

"Do you really want to get rid of Savannah?" Kate asked.

No! "Of course I do. And once I give her the information she's seeking, she'll gladly walk away." He sorted through possible solutions, came up with several workable ideas that had been in the OSS briefing from the start. One, specifically, would convince Savannah to drop her investigation of Sorensen.

"Trent, darling." Kate gave him a pitying look. "For all your gifts with women, you don't understand them at all. Even if you refuse to help her uncover proof about her father's assistant, Savannah won't *gladly* walk away from you. Not after the way you've courted her."

He gritted his teeth, hating that she was probably right.

"There's a way to get rid of her, if you have the stomach for it." Kate's eyes went soft, dreamy. She reached out and caressed his knee.

Trent shoved her hand away. "Kate, no. I won't hurt Savannah like this." He hardened his gaze. "She's only just recovered from her husband's betrayal."

"Making her think we've been lying to her about our relationship all along..." Kate placed her hand on his knee again. "You know it's the surest way to convince her you don't care and that you're heartless enough to walk away without following through on your promise."

Trent dragged air into his lungs. The spy in him knew Kate was right. Breaking Savannah's heart would be a quick and efficient means to an end.

But Trent could not—he would not—hurt Savannah like that.

If he'd secretly wondered how far he was willing to go to get the job done, now he knew.

Not that far. *Not* that far.

Chapter Twenty-One

Convinced that Trent was worth fighting for, Savannah had set aside her fears, ignored her doubts and stepped out on faith.

Allowing her heart to lead the way, she'd gotten in her car and driven straight over to the Roosevelt Hotel. She'd prepared her arguments during the short drive. Maybe she didn't love him. Maybe she did. She wanted to find out for sure.

Whatever it took, she'd told herself, she would convince Trent to give their relationship a chance.

She'd been so full of confidence, so certain she was making the right decision that she'd strolled into the hotel lobby with her head held high and her heart firmly on her sleeve.

Only to come face-to-face with the shock of her life.

Even now, her mind refused to accept the startling reality that was right in front of her.

Her greatest fear had come to fruition. Again. One word echoed in her mind. *No.*

No. No. No.

This couldn't be happening again. Not again.

There was an explanation. She couldn't have been this wrong about Trent. Or Kate. Kate was her best friend. She would never hurt Savannah like this.

Then why was she at Trent's hotel so early in the morning?

And why were the two of them looking so very cozy together in a hidden alcove off the main lobby?

Savannah's feet remained stuck to the marble tiles. However, her body reacted with a jolt of adrenaline, urging her to turn, to leave. To Run. Run, run, run.

She still had time.

They hadn't noticed her yet. Their heads were bent close together. They were in deep conversation, looking as though they were arguing about something.

Run, Savannah. Run, run, run.

She could still get out with her dignity intact.

She could still pursue her investigation of Peter on her own. It was what she'd planned on doing before she'd met Trent.

Unfortunately, her feet remained frozen to the spot.

She couldn't look away from Trent and Kate. Together. Kate's hand on his knee.

Savannah's body turned hot, then cold, ice-cold. It was the same visceral reaction she'd had when she'd seen Johnny with that other woman.

But, somehow, this hurt so much more.

And then...

Then...

Trent jumped out of his chair and started toward her. His steps were filled with purpose.

At last, she was able to move. She spun around, determined to leave, to avoid the awful, terrible conversation that was sure to come.

"Savannah, wait. Don't go." Trent was by her side before she could take two full steps. His hand took her arm in a firm but gentle grip. "This isn't what you think."

She heard the agony in his voice, the raw emotion that was far more truthful than anything she'd heard from him before. Or was this another well-orchestrated lie?

Had it *all* been a lie?

"Come. And let me explain."

"Why should I believe anything you have to say?"

He moved in front of her, his hand still on her arm. "Because there's a good explanation."

Not wanting him to see the hope she felt flaring in her eyes, she kept her gaze glued to the floor. "I'm sure there is."

"Please."

At the soft plea, she looked up. His gaze had grown fierce, primal and so full of sorrow she knew he was speaking the truth.

"If you walk away now…" He closed his eyes briefly, as though the thought brought him pain. "You'll always wonder. You deserve better than that."

At last, he'd shed his mask, revealing his true self to her. He was no longer sophisticated or charming, but hard, resolute. A dangerous and determined man.

Oddly, she wasn't afraid of him.

She knew he'd been hiding something from her from the moment they'd met. And yet, what she saw in his eyes now was real. All pretense stripped way.

"All right, Trent. I'll give you ten minutes to explain yourself."

He dropped his hand and directed her to the alcove where Kate waited.

Without actually making eye contact, she nodded to her friend. "Kate."

"Savannah. Come, sit here next to me." She patted the chair Trent had occupied earlier.

The moment Savannah did as her friend requested, Kate rose.

"As much as I'd like to stay and watch you two sort this out, this is a private matter that doesn't concern me."

She touched Savannah's arm, then turned to leave. But not before she shot a warning glare in Trent's direction, very much like the one she'd sent him the night they'd met.

Apparently, they'd come full circle.

Savannah's breathing quickened in her lungs, sounding harsh even to her own ears.

It wasn't fair—so not fair—to have found so much and to lose it so quickly. Like sand pouring between her fingers.

Trust only in the Lord.

She should have followed her own advice. Now, another man had broken her heart a mere six months after the last.

Lowering her head, she stared at her hands. "How could you have let this happen?"

She hadn't realized she'd spoken her thoughts aloud until she felt Trent's hand touch her shoulder. "Nothing happened, Savannah. Not between Kate and me."

She paused, letting his words sink in. Closing her eyes, she searched her memories of their short acquaintance.

If Kate and Trent were involved, if they'd been lying to her all this time, there would have been signs. There would have been an obvious closeness in the way they looked at one another, an affection that they couldn't have hidden completely.

No, they weren't in love. In fact, Savannah wasn't sure they even liked one another.

Nevertheless, she deserved to hear the words from Trent himself. A man couldn't kiss her the way Trent had and not owe her honesty.

"Tell me, Trent." She lifted her head and locked gazes with him. "Tell me about your relationship with Kate. And this time, I want the truth."

Trent fought back a fresh wave of guilt. Savannah wanted the truth about his relationship with Kate.

He couldn't give her what she wanted. Not completely.

He stared at her another moment, then came to a painful decision. He had to cut Savannah loose, as gently as possible. "Kate was here to say goodbye."

"Goodbye?" Savannah's eyes widened with shock. "You're leaving?"

His gut rolled with fresh guilt. She was looking at him with that deep, soulful, vulnerable expression that had captured him that first night at the country club.

He wanted to wipe the sorrow from her eyes. Wanted to see her smile at him again, wanted to know he was the one that put the joy in her face.

It was not to be.

The least he could do was send her away with her pride still intact.

"I'm leaving tomorrow morning." Not completely accurate, but close enough. "Kate was here to wish me well."

Savannah continued blinking at him, her body perfectly still but he felt the slight shift in her. "And that's the truth?"

He swallowed, suddenly desperate to make that sadness disappear from her eyes. "The truth is that there is nothing between Kate and me. The truth is that I do have to leave. The *truth* is that what you and I had was real."

"*Had,* as in past tense?"

Trent said nothing. If he told her what was really in his heart, what he couldn't admit even to himself, then he'd have to tell her the rest.

He couldn't take that risk.

"What about your promise to help me?" She didn't need to elaborate. He knew what she meant.

Time had run out for Trent. He could no longer put her off, but he couldn't tell Savannah the full truth about Sorensen, either. The mission was at a critical stage. "You've been mistaken about Sorensen. He is completely loyal to your father. There are no secrets between them."

She frowned. "You have proof of this?"

"I have tapped into every source I know and followed every possible lead. I'm sorry, Savannah, I know this isn't what you want to hear." He touched her hand. "But your father and his assistant are working in tandem toward a common goal."

He was being intentionally evasive. He should have known that wouldn't be good enough for Savannah. "What about the blueprints and shipping charts we found in Peter's office?" She pulled her bottom lip between her teeth. "Surely, those prove Peter is into shady activities."

Now came the lie. "Your father is in the process of buying Anderson Shipyard." Klein himself had left a false paper trail for the OSS to follow, one that would corroborate the story for Savannah as well, if she chose to pursue it further. "What we found in Sorensen's office was the research he'd acquired for the purchase."

She shook her head. "But Peter is so…cold."

Trent didn't contradict her. "He is highly focused, yes."

An endless moment passed while she processed the information he'd just laid on her. "So you're really set on leaving town tomorrow?"

"I must."

"Will you ever return to Jacksonville?"

"No." Not if he did his job properly tonight. Once they stopped the sabotage and had her father and Sorensen in custody, there would be no need for Trent to return to the area. He would be sent on a different mission.

Holding his gaze, Savannah rotated her wrist and then clasped his hand hard enough to press their palms tightly together.

"Come back, Trent. When you're finished with your lecture tour, come back for me."

His lecture tour. In that moment, Trent realized how well he'd kept his cover intact throughout their association. So well, that no matter what he did, no matter *why* he did it, Savannah would suffer another betrayal.

Best to let her think he didn't care for her, that she hadn't changed him and turned him into a better man. Best to let her down now.

"I'm sorry, Savannah. I can't come back for you."

"You *can't* or you *won't?*"

Right. She wasn't going to let him off easily. She wouldn't be the woman he'd fallen for if she did.

He pulled his hand free of hers and focused on a spot just above her eye. "Won't."

"But, Trent, we can make it work." She touched his sleeve tentatively. "Slowly at first, if that's what you want. We can get to know one another through phone calls and letters."

Tension rose to a palpable level inside him. *I want what she's suggesting.*

No, he wanted more. He wanted it all. He wanted Savannah. In his life. Any way he could have her.

Sacrifice one for the multitude. A means to an end. All his rationalizations had backfired on him.

He had to do the right thing now. The moral thing.

"I'm sorry, Savannah." He stood, ran a shaky hand through his hair. "Our flirtation is over. Now if you'll excuse me—"

"No. You don't get to walk away. Not without this tucked in your memory." She pulled him against her, wrapped her arms around his neck and lifted on her toes.

The moment her lips met his, his blood thickened in his veins.

The woman was far braver than he'd given her credit for. Not caring they were in a public place, *she* was kissing *him.*

Completely undone, he roped his arms around her waist and pulled her tightly to him. He kissed her back. With all the pent-up emotions he couldn't express in words.

He longed for what she could offer him. A lifetime of light and peace and love.

Then he remembered how she'd come into his life. *Why* she'd come into his life. Her father was a traitor to the United States, the ringleader of a group of Nazi sympathizers bent on destroying America's industrial might.

And Trent was here, in this moment, kissing the beautiful woman he adored above all others, under false pretenses.

He pushed out of her arms. "Goodbye, Savannah."

"Goodbye? That's it?" She blinked at him with large, round eyes. "Just…goodbye?"

"Try to understand. I don't want to hurt you, but I am leaving tomorrow."

"And never coming back. Yes, I heard you the first time."

"I'm not who you think I am."

"Then tell me who you are, Trent. Make me understand."

"I've already told you all you need to know."

This wasn't about him anymore, or her, or what they could or could not have.

Too much hinged on stopping the saboteurs to give her any more information. He'd already said too much.

"You need to turn around now, Savannah." He reached for her then dropped his hand back to his side. "You have to walk out of this hotel and forget you ever met me."

Her eyes flashed. Blue fire encased in ice. "What aren't you saying? Please, Trent, tell me."

He couldn't.

The mission wasn't complete. And the next eighteen hours were the most critical of all.

"You aren't going to say any more, are you?"

She looked disappointed. Not angry. Not hurt. But disappointed. In him. She might as well have dug a knife in his gut and twisted.

"We're through, Savannah."

"Oh, we are? Because *you* say so? Well, think again, Trent Mueller." She jerked her chin at him. *"Think again."*

He opened his mouth to argue the point, but she didn't give him the chance. With a flick of her wrist, she flipped her hair over her shoulder and then marched out of the hotel without a backward glance.

Head high, shoulders back, heels clicking on the marble tile, she executed what most women would consider the perfect dramatic exit.

One problem. Trent had seen the unshed tears brimming in eyes before she'd turned away. She hadn't let a single one fall, though.

The woman was certainly spirited. And brave.

He'd never met anyone like her. He wanted to go after her and tell her they'd work everything out. He wanted to forget the consequences and take what he wanted.

He resisted the temptation and reset his priorities. Two breaths, three, and by the fourth he was heading toward the bank of elevators.

The Nazis were hours away from landing on American shores.

Time to set a trap.

Chapter Twenty-Two

Later that same night, Savannah refused to shed another tear over Trent Mueller. As of this moment, she was done feeling sorry for herself, done wishing for what might have been.

Lips quivering, she squeezed her eyes shut before more tears escaped.

This was ridiculous. No more crying.

No.

More.

Crying.

Flipping onto her back, she tucked the covers under her chin and blinked up at her bedroom ceiling.

Blessed sleep refused to come. Too many thoughts collided into one another, making it impossible to relax.

Come to me all you who are weary, and I will give you rest.

If only she knew how to turn this confusion and pain over to God.

She'd offered her heart to Trent this morning. He'd tossed it back at her without a good explanation.

What was he hiding from her? Why did she get the sense he was trying to protect her by sending her away? And that Peter was more of a threat than Trent wanted her to believe?

He claimed her father was in the process of buying Anderson

Shipyard, and that was why Peter had had all that information locked in his desk drawer. The scenario was possible.

So why didn't she believe it?

Sighing, she rolled onto her side and blinked out the window. The sky was cloudless tonight, black velvet sprinkled with a million tiny diamonds. The big, round moon spread its light across the river in a wide, golden path.

Shadows cast from the swaying tree branches danced along her walls. Savannah could practically hear the Viennese Waltz accompanying the spooky scene. The music from her first waltz with Trent.

Trent.

Every thought led back to him.

She'd been so sure she'd broken through his façade and had reached the real man beneath the sophisticated outer shell.

I'm not who you think I am.

What if he was more?

Until six months ago, Savannah had led a charmed life. She'd never had to fight very hard for what she wanted.

She would fight now.

She would fight for Trent. And find out once and for all what he was keeping secret from her.

Tossing the covers aside, she sat up and checked the small clock next to her bed. Not yet ten o'clock.

Still early.

She dressed quickly. Feeling like a teenager sneaking out without permission, she tiptoed down the stairs. She skipped the last step—the one that always creaked under her foot.

Moving into the main hall, she wasn't surprised to see a beam of light winking from beneath the door of her father's study. The voices didn't surprise her, either, nor did the hushed tones. This wasn't the first night her father and Peter had worked late. She doubted it would be the last.

She could interrupt them and demand to know if her father really was buying Anderson Shipyard.

She sensed she wouldn't like the outcome.

Besides, if Peter and her father were distracted with business they wouldn't notice her leaving the house. Before she confronted either of them, she wanted to speak with Trent one last time.

She retraced her steps and exited out the back.

Rounding the corner of the house, she smiled despite her nerves. She'd left her car sitting in the middle of the drive, at the crest of a small hill. She would have an easy getaway.

To ensure she didn't alert her father to her nocturnal outing, Savannah placed a blackout cover over each headlight. With the war heating up in Europe, the slotted shields were required when driving anywhere near the beaches.

What she had to discuss with Trent was between the two of them alone.

Thankful for the added cover of night, she slid behind the steering wheel and tapped in to her days as a rebellious teen.

Simultaneously pushing in the clutch and releasing the brake, she allowed the vehicle to roll soundlessly down the driveway. The moment the back wheels hit the road, Savannah jerked the wheel, popped the clutch and headed out before anyone could pinpoint where the noise had originated.

Feeling rather smug, she made the journey to the Roosevelt Hotel in less than ten minutes.

But as soon as the building came into sight, a bout of nerves took hold. Should she go straight up to Trent's room? Or should she call him from the lobby and ask him to meet her down there?

Her lack of planning had her hesitating with indecision.

Once she had Trent's attention, what would she say?

Needing a moment to gather her thoughts, she drove around the block.

As she rounded the back corner of the hotel, three men

dressed in black from head to toe exited the building. They each carried a large canvas bag. The tallest of the bunch took the lead. The other two followed closely behind.

Savannah's pulse quickened. All three men looked single-minded. And dangerous.

Lord, what have I stumbled upon?

She pulled to a stop at the curb. Focusing solely on the man in front, Savannah wondered why he looked so familiar.

That erect posture. The confident gait. Those broad shoulders.

Her breath caught in her throat.

Trent.

The man out in front was Trent. He walked with purpose, not particularly rushing his steps but not dawdling, either.

Where was he going at this late hour?

And where had she seen those other two men?

At the same moment she narrowed her eyes for a closer look, a gasp flew past her lips.

She remembered now.

They were the men from the Carmen Café. The FBI agents who'd come to town to monitor Dr. Klinger's activities.

What was Trent doing in *their* company?

I'm not who you think I am.

A sliver of alarm slipped under skin.

Was Trent a criminal? Had the FBI come to arrest him?

No. The men weren't taking him away. They were following him.

Wishing she hadn't covered her headlights, Savannah squinted into the darkened night. She noted how all three men walked as a single group, matching their steps to one another. Whatever was going on, this was a team effort.

I'm not who you think I am.

Snatches of memories flashed through her mind. That aura of mystery always surrounding Trent. The military bearing he hadn't been able to hide. The way he studied a room with a measured, calculating gaze.

All those questions he'd asked her about her job, her life, her father. And his...*skills*. He'd been so very competent that night he'd helped her sneak into Peter's office unnoticed. Had Trent been using her from the start?

But why?

What had he hoped to gain?

The thought barely registered before the three climbed into a waiting car. Trent took the front seat. The other two sat in the back.

The car's headlights had also been dimmed with blackout covers. Were they headed down to the beach?

At this hour?

And who was driving the car?

Leaning forward, praying for a better look, she received her third shock in as many minutes.

Kate was driving the car.

Savannah's head grew dizzy. For a frightening moment everything around her became a swirl of shadows mixed with light. Her vision grayed, tinged black at the edges.

A small, timid part of her wanted to go home and forget she'd seen any of this. She wanted to forget all about Trent and the FBI and Kate.

But if Savannah retreated now, if she cowered away, she would always wonder about Trent and his motives.

She'd spent six long months wondering if any man could be trusted. No more.

She made a snap decision.

Maintaining a safe distance, she followed Kate's car onto Atlantic Boulevard. They were heading eastbound, straight toward the ocean.

Approximately thirty minutes later, Kate took a right turn on A1A.

Savannah did as well.

They were traveling the exact same route she and Trent had taken two days before.

A horrifying thought occurred to her.

Did this late-night, secretive journey have something to do with the empty shed on her family's property?

No. Too much of a coincidence.

Fifteen minutes later, Kate slowed her car to a crawl just shy of Savannah's beach house.

"Apparently, this is a night for coincidences," she hissed, surprised at the bitterness in her tone.

With the car still rolling, the two FBI agents jumped out, their identical canvas bags in tow. A heartbeat later they melted into the night.

The moment they disappeared, Kate's car sped up.

The drop-off had been so quick, so smooth, Savannah would have missed it if she'd bothered to blink.

A half mile later, Kate slowed once again. Savannah was forced to do the same or risk drawing too close.

This time Trent was the one to exit the car. He turned on his heel and headed straight in Savannah's direction. Before she knew what was happening he yanked the passenger door open and slid inside.

"Trent, what...what are you doing?"

"Drive, Savannah." He spoke in a cold, hard voice that sent shivers down her spine.

She reflexively pulled her foot off the gas. "But—"

"I said drive."

She obeyed, instinctively knowing Trent was not to be challenged on this.

Who was this stranger? And why was he so angry?

I'm not the man you think I am.

Savannah shot a glance in his direction. She could feel the urgency in him, knew he was tapping it down for her sake. She'd just stumbled into something big, something that made her want to recoil into her safe, boring life.

Too late, a voice whispered in her head.

Kate slowed a third time.

Again, Savannah lifted her foot off the gas pedal.

"Go around Kate's car and swing into the second driveway on your left," Trent ordered, his voice emotionless. "Then pull back out and head in the direction you just came."

"But—"

"Do it."

Hands shaking, Savannah did exactly as he instructed.

I'm not who you think I am.

Oh, no. No, he wasn't.

They traveled several long, tense moments in the new direction. Silence hung thick and heavy between them.

Anything, she thought, but this cold, dead silence. "Trent, please. What's going on?"

He kept his gaze focused straight ahead, the unnatural control still evident in his bearing.

"Trent?"

"Why are you following us?" he asked, almost gritting the words.

"I…" She clutched the steering wheel so hard her knuckles started to ache. "I came to the hotel to talk to you…" Her voice quivered so hard she couldn't finish her explanation.

She swallowed and tried a different route. "But then I…I saw you leave out the back alleyway with those…FBI agents and decided to follow you."

Every muscle in his body grew even more rigid than before. "You were planning to enter the hotel from the back alleyway?"

"No, I…" Why was he glaring at her as if she was lying to him? "I was there by accident."

"By *accident.*"

Despite the hot, stifling air in the car, she shivered. "Yes. I needed a moment to think over what I was going to say to you. So I drove around the building to gather my thoughts."

"And that's the truth?" His shoulders remained tightly bunched. "The full truth?"

"Why would I lie?"

"Why, indeed?"

She didn't like the sarcasm in his voice. What had happened to the charming, intelligent, tender man she'd fallen in love with?

"Trent, please." She wasn't sure what she was asking anymore. All she wanted was for him to tell her everything was going to be all right.

He turned his head slowly.

Their gazes melded. Several heartbeats passed, then he looked away and ran an angry hand through his hair. "Do you realize the trouble you've caused?"

"I…" Oh, no. No, no. She wasn't going to let him turn this around on her. "Now wait just a minute. You're the one slinking around in the night, dressed head to toe in black. Why?"

He said nothing.

Not good enough. "*Why* are you and Kate with those two FBI agents? Why are all four of you together so late at night? And why did you drop them off at *my* family's beach house." She knew she was speaking too quickly, her words tumbling over one another.

She pressed on, anyway. "You say you're not who I think you are. Well, then, Trent…*who are you?*"

"Which question do you want me to answer first?"

"You choose."

He seemed to debate with himself.

She let him battle it out in silence. She needed to focus on her driving, anyway, especially now that they were back on A1A. Without the full use of her headlights the road was not easy to negotiate.

Out of the corner of her eye, she saw Trent give one firm nod. She recognized the gesture. He'd come to some sort of a conclusion.

"You aren't going to like what I have to say."

"No," she said. "I already figured that out for myself."

His jaw tightened, but he didn't remark on her response directly. "Your refusal to walk away when you had the chance has changed the rules."

The rules? "What rules?"

"Pull over here." He pointed to a parking space near a main beach access. She looked around, stunned they'd covered so much ground. They were at least seven or eight miles north of her family's property.

Kate parked in the space next to her and cut the engine. She nodded at Savannah, but didn't get out of her car.

"Savannah," Trent said, dragging her attention back to him. "By following us tonight you've given me no choice other than to tell you some hard truths."

A dark foreboding settled in her heart. This cold man was so different from the charming sophisticate she'd met at the yacht club.

But then he touched her hand briefly and a portion of his hard exterior cracked. For a half second she recognized the man she'd fallen for.

Which was the real Trent Mueller?

The charming, attentive college professor? Or the hard-eyed stranger staring at her now?

Neither? Both? Something in between? Perhaps the easy smiles, lazy charm, watchful gaze and dangerous intensity were all parts of the whole.

"I'm not a college professor," he said unnecessarily.

"I realized that back at the hotel."

And yet, his inquisitive nature had fit the job description perfectly, too perfectly to be a complete ruse.

What other career used the same skill set he'd learned in the Army?

Again, he answered before she could voice her question. "I still work for the United States government."

"In what capacity?" she asked, needing him to be clearer.

He trapped her in his gaze like he had that first night across the dance floor. She felt the impact all over again.

The intrigue, the anticipation. The desire to know him better. They were all still there, in her heart.

"Are you with the FBI?"

"No," he said, shaking his head. "I work for the Office of Strategic Services."

"The OSS? You...you're a...spy?" Savannah shot her gaze toward the car parked next to them. "Kate, too?"

His silence neither confirmed nor denied the obvious.

And, yes, it was obvious, now that she let her mind sort through the facts. The truth had been there all along. He'd told her he'd worked as an intelligence officer for the Army.

Feeling dizzy, she leaned her head in her hands.

Other pieces fell together. The way Kate and Trent moved in perfect step with one another, both watchful.

Not romantically involved at all, but working together for the government. As spies.

Spies. A roaring began in her ears, pounding loud and insistent.

Savannah lowered her hands and clung to the seat on either side of her as realization dawned. "You and Kate. You're working tonight."

"Yes."

Stuff like this only happened in the movies.

Trent placed his hand over hers and everything in her relaxed. Angry at her reaction, she fought the urge to shove him away.

"Savannah, you have to understand, I *couldn't* tell you who I was."

She heard the apology in his voice.

Part of her understood what he was saying. The other part wanted to howl at him.

"But, Kate," she whispered past the rawness in her throat. "She's my friend." And yet, Kate had lied to her, too.

So much deception. So much to untangle in her mind.

"Kate couldn't tell you anything, either. We've been working—" he squeezed her hand "—undercover."

A sense of giddy relief tried to take hold. She pulled her hand free from Trent's.

Something wasn't adding up. A piece was missing.

"What could you possibly be doing—*undercover*—in Jacksonville, Florida, of all places?"

"We're here to stop a Nazi plot against the United States."

"What?"

Reeling, she listened in stunned silence as he told her the basic details of the plot and how the Nazis planned to wreck havoc on industrial targets throughout the country.

An image of Peter flashed in her mind. The blueprints. The charts. Research, yes. Not to buy Anderson Shipyard, but to sabotage it.

Peter Sorensen was a Nazi. The enemy in their midst. And her father had trusted him so completely.

Oh, Father.

He would be stunned when he found out the truth. Because, surely, he didn't know about Peter.

No, no. The opposite was too terrible to contemplate.

"If they succeed," Trent concluded, "they will bring the war to American soil."

"But why here?" she asked again, unable to make her brain work out the particulars. "Compared to other cities on the Eastern seaboard, Jacksonville is hardly worth notice."

As soon as the words left her mouth she remembered what she herself had said to Trent that day in her office.

She'd told him about the naval bases in the area, had pointed out the location of the city itself, nestled along a river by the sea. And, of course, the...*shipyards.*

Her heart dipped to her toes.

"Pembroke is one of the other targets besides Anderson Shipyard, isn't it?"

Chapter Twenty-Three

Trent hesitated before answering Savannah's question. Countless emotions tried to rise, to blunt his edge, to pull him off task. But emotions clouded judgment and brought conflicts of interests to a head.

This discussion is not going as planned.

Forced by the twist of circumstances, he had to improvise now, had to think coolly, clearly. No mistakes.

His hands clenched into fists. He forced his fingers to uncoil. By following them, Savannah had become a liability to the mission, one they couldn't afford at this juncture.

Her actions tonight, innocent as they may have been, put them all in jeopardy.

Now Trent had to make a painful choice.

Which was more important, eliminating the threat she posed or keeping her quiet?

"Answer my question, Trent. Is that why you pursued me?" She visibly jerked in her seat. "To gain access to Pembroke?"

He hated the hurt he saw on her face. His gut twisted with regret. And guilt. But the time for lies had come to an end. "Partially, yes."

Breathing raggedly now, she scooted closer to the door, slowly, as if he wouldn't notice her moving away from him.

He noticed.

"So what I thought was between us." Her voice cracked over the words. "It was all a lie."

They didn't have time for this. He answered her, anyway. "No, Savannah. Whatever my original motives might have been, what we had wasn't all a lie."

He silently urged her to look at him so she might know the truth of his feelings, the truth he couldn't utter in this car.

"I don't believe you." She shook her head in disdain.

Her suspicion was like a well-aimed bullet to the chest. Pain twisted in his gut.

He wanted to pull her in his arms and tell her how he felt. That he cared about her—maybe even loved her—with the kind of depth that had staying power.

Her goodness had made him hope for a future free of guilt and pain.

Not that any of that mattered now.

Time had run out for them. He might hate that she was angry and disillusioned and scared. But her feelings couldn't rule the next few hours.

Neither could his.

A shadow of distress flitted across her face. And then she made her break, opening her car door with a swift flick of her wrist.

He clamped a hand on her arm, stopping her exit.

She bucked under his grip. "Let me go."

Her panic hit him at the core. She was afraid of him. Nevertheless, he didn't let her go. He couldn't.

He kept his grip firm but gentle, making sure not to hurt her but giving her no chance to escape him.

"What I don't understand is why bother using me to get a look around Pembroke?" Her angry intake of breath was more eloquent than her words. "There were a hundred other ways to get inside."

Trent didn't respond.

When they'd discovered Savannah following them, he and Kate had discussed how much to reveal to her. Collectively, they'd decided not to tell her about her father's involvement just yet.

Not to spare her feelings, but to protect the mission. Savannah would surely want to confront her father at once, and in the process reveal what the OSS knew.

They couldn't afford William Klein or Sorensen covering their tracks.

What Trent and Kate hadn't planned for was Savannah's intelligent, analytical brain. His silence had given her the opportunity to fit the pieces together on her own. Under the pale moonlight he saw the precise moment she pulled it all together in her mind.

"My father. You used me to get close to my father." Angry tears sprung in her eyes, threatening to spill over. "All that talk about German prophecy, all the questions about the FBI watching him, you think he's part of this…this plot. Just like Peter."

"We have evidence."

"No. *No.*" She yanked on her arm. Hard. For one, precious, half second he lost his grip.

It was enough.

She scrambled out of the car.

Trent was a second behind her. A second too late. And now she was heading—running—toward the beach.

Distress made her steps clumsy. He caught up to her and spun her around to face him. "Get back in the car. Now."

"The empty shed." She sucked in a hard breath. "You think that's where the Nazis will store their explosives. That's why you dropped off those other agents."

It was best for the mission to let her think she'd figured everything out. But he found he couldn't outright lie to her anymore. He could only evade. "Perhaps."

She jerked out of his grip, turned slightly away, but didn't try to run again. "I won't have you accusing my father of this crime. Peter is the Nazi. He's the enemy. Not my father."

Kate joined them. Avoiding direct eye contact with Savannah, she motioned to Trent. "We're out of time."

He nodded. Then hardened his heart. War was deadly. Every battle had to be won. Innocent lives were at stake.

"Savannah. You must return to the car."

Refusing to acknowledge him, she stood with her back to him, her arms crossed over her stomach. She looked lost. Alone.

He'd done that to her.

No. *Her father* had done that to her. With his duplicity and traitorous sympathies.

But like Kate said, they were out of time. "You will either return to the car on your own," Trent said softly so as not to spook her, "or I will...assist you."

She continued staring out over the water. "You might be right about Peter, but you're wrong about my father. I'll prove it to you." The last was spoken in a whisper.

"Savannah," Kate said, her voice equally soft. "Get hold of yourself. Our country is at war. The Nazis plan to attack us on our own soil. *Tonight.*"

Savannah's shoulders hunched forward. "Then you have to stop them."

Trent reached to her, but Kate held up a hand to stop him. She walked around Savannah until they were facing one another.

A silent look passed between them, one that spoke of their shared history. "We need you to return to the car."

"I understand."

Without further argument, Savannah marched back to the car.

Trent followed closely behind her, prepared to stop her if she tried to make another break.

When she slid behind the steering wheel and reached for the key in the ignition, he grabbed her wrist. "No."

When she didn't let go of the keys he pushed his head into the car.

Their faces were inches from one another, so close that their breathing joined in perfect rhythm.

"You can't leave until this is over."

She glared at him. "I won't say anything to my father."

"I can't take your word on that."

She closed her eyes a moment and swallowed. "No." Her voice caught on the word. "I suppose you can't."

Letting go of the keys at last, she sat back and then pressed the inside of her wrists together. "Handcuff me."

"Savannah, I—"

"I said handcuff me." She stared unblinking into his eyes. No emotion. No self-pity. Just ruthless determination. "And then do your job without worrying about me. Stop the Nazis from attacking our country."

Our country. Her patriotism was without question. If he'd accepted that reality sooner she wouldn't be in danger now.

He had many sins to atone for after tonight. But for now he retrieved a pair of metal handcuffs from his canvas bag and clicked them over her wrists. For added security he'd wrapped them around the steering wheel first.

She wasn't going anywhere until he released her.

"Sit tight." Unable to resist, he ran a knuckle down her cheek, and then brushed lightly along her jaw.

She flinched.

He dropped his hand.

"If all goes as planned, Kate and I will be back in a few hours to release you, maybe less."

He turned to go.

The soft whisper of his name stopped him midstride.

"Yes?"

"One day, you will regret lying me."

"I already do, Savannah. I already do."

Trent swept his binoculars across the night-shrouded sea, right to left, left to right, widening the arcs with each subsequent pass. He lowered his hands, checked his wristwatch, frowned: 2335.

The Nazis were late.

"The FBI agents have arrived," Kate said at his elbow. "They know to wait for your signal."

"Good." Their plan wouldn't work if they moved too quickly. All the supplies had to be ashore and the U-boat long gone before they proceeded with the takedown.

"Any word on Sorensen?"

"He was last seen heading toward the Klein beach property. Our boys will keep him occupied long enough for us to complete the takedown here."

Trent allowed Kate's words to sink in. If Sorensen was on his way to the original drop zone, that meant the Nazis still didn't realize Trent had figured out the coordinates to the alternative landing site.

Or...

They'd gone back to their original plan.

Was that why the saboteurs were late?

No matter. Trent and his team had planned for both contingencies, hence the added help from the FBI. They had enough agents positioned at both sites to accomplish a quick and efficient takedown.

Good would prevail over evil, at least for tonight.

But there was still one player unaccounted for.

"What about Klein?" he asked. "Where is he right now?"

"In bed with his wife." Kate let out an unladylike sniff. "The perfect alibi."

"Indeed."

Trent raised the binoculars to his eyes once again. Despite the darkness of the night, the moon illuminated the water for several miles past shore.

Ten endless minutes passed before he caught sight of what he'd been looking for at last.

His muscles hummed with anticipation.

Approximately a mile out, the waters slowly parted into two, identical ripples.

The U-boat surfaced soundlessly, with smooth precision, running parallel to the shoreline.

Trent crouched down, pulling Kate with him. She bristled beside him, her body language speaking volumes. She'd seen the U-boat surface as well.

There was no more talking between them. From this point forward they would use hand signals to communicate.

Trent pointed two fingers straight out toward the horizon.

Following the gesture with her gaze, Kate gave one firm nod. For the benefit of the other agents in the woods, she circled her hand above her head then pointed at the U-boat.

Returning the binoculars to his eyes, Trent watched the activity on the deck of the submarine.

Four men dressed in black wool and stocking caps systematically filled a rubber boat with armloads of supplies. They worked quickly and efficiently, their anxiety palpable even from this distance.

There were no sailors in sight, just the four men. They didn't waste time, focusing all their efforts on loading the boat.

Within minutes, they were shoving the boat into the water. They rowed methodically toward shore, working as a well-oiled machine.

This was no training run.

Once the saboteurs were halfway to shore, the German sub disappeared below the waterline as smoothly as it had surfaced.

Trent gestured for Kate to follow him into the dunes. They

stayed low, sticking to the dark underbrush. They were right on top of the coordinates he'd uncovered in Klein's copy of von List's book.

The real FBI agents were in a position a hundred feet to the north, while Trent's decoys were back at the empty shed on Klein's property.

Everyone was in place.

Now they waited.

Savannah had been born with unnaturally tiny wrists and thin hands. She'd been teased mercilessly about them throughout her youth. But what she'd once thought a curse she now considered a gift from God.

Almost as soon as Trent and Kate had left her alone in her car, Savannah had slipped out of the handcuffs.

Her first instinct was to rush home to her father, to warn him the government thought he was a traitor.

He would assure her of his innocence, of course. He would guarantee that he'd known nothing of Peter's double life.

Savannah would believe him because he never lied to her.

But as much as she wanted to hear the truth out of her father's own lips—right now—she didn't immediately start her car. She couldn't risk jeopardizing Trent's mission for her own selfish end.

Besides, she'd made a promise to stay put.

She would do as she said.

From her vantage point in the car, Savannah could see Trent and Kate clearly. They moved into the sand dunes about a hundred yards north of her.

Not wanting to interfere, but unable to stay in the car and simply *wait,* she wound down the window and leaned her head out.

She counted six other agents beside Kate and Trent. They held their positions like professionals, poised to make their move.

She watched in horror as the small boat rowed closer and closer toward the shore. Their approach proved the Nazi plot was real.

As much as she wanted to shout at Trent for lying to her, she couldn't deny that he'd done so for a good reason. He was a soldier, of sorts, fighting in an ugly war with complicated rules. She could respect that. Admire it, even.

Her father, however, was not a part of this. He was home, asleep in his bed. With her mother by his side. Trent had no right accusing such a good man of treason.

Savannah would prove her father's innocence as soon as she had the chance.

She shifted uncomfortably.

The boat drew closer. Riding atop a large wave, it glided soundlessly onto the wet sand. Oddly out of sync with one another, four men jumped out and wrestled the boat out of the water. A spattering of angry, unintelligible words—German mixed with English—came in bursts, followed by a curt order to work in silence.

Outrage swelled in Savannah's chest.

How dare the Nazis land on American soil? How dare they attempt to sabotage the U.S. war machine?

Savannah wanted to help Trent and Kate. But she knew the best thing she could do was keep out of sight.

And pray.

Oh, Lord, please, put Your hand on this mission tonight.

Feeling helpless, she tried to close off her senses, tried to watch with detachment, as though the events were unfolding on a movie screen.

She didn't have that much imagination.

Heart stuck in her throat, she continued lifting up prayers, pleading with God to bring Trent and his team success.

So much could go wrong. People could die.

Trent could die.

A sick feeling roiled in her stomach. Despite his lies, despite all the reasons to hate him, Savannah couldn't stop caring about Trent Mueller.

The man had breached her defenses. He'd wormed his way into her heart.

He was a hero. A liar. A spy.

And the man she loved.

Savannah blinked away a fresh wave of tears, realizing the saboteurs were unloading their boat. Completely unhindered.

Why wasn't Trent stopping them?

Chapter Twenty-Four

❧

Trent counted off the seconds in his head. The moon was bright. The stars were out. The saboteurs had landed.

On his left, he sensed rather than saw the other agents. Theoretically the Nazis could sense them as well, but he doubted it. They were too focused on getting their booty to shore and out of sight.

None of them had spoken since the quick burst of German mixed with English and the reprimand to stop talking. The only sound other than the crashing surf was the slide of the boat moving across the sand.

These men clearly had a plan and were following it to the letter, but it didn't take Trent long to realize they were not as well-trained as his team.

Either the saboteurs had assumed they were alone or didn't know to check the area properly.

Arrogant Nazis or rank amateurs, either scenario played perfectly into Trent's hands. Their inattention would be their downfall.

Arms full, three of the four saboteurs struck off toward the sand dunes. The third pulled out a knife strapped to his ankle and cut a slit in the rubber dingy. Air whooshed out in a low, menacing hiss.

Without looking to either his left of his right he followed his compatriots, dragging the deflating boat behind him.

Seconds into their mission and these men were already making disastrous mistakes. The Nazis hadn't taken the time to train their men properly.

Somehow, Trent doubted William Klein or Peter Sorensen would have given the go-ahead had they known.

An advantage Trent would use to the fullest, before they could adjust their plan.

The time had come to finish this.

He nodded to Kate. Motioned to the other agents in the woods, then pointed to the saboteurs heading into the dunes. On his mark, they stood.

Trent moved to his left, eyes on his target. The agents and Kate went right.

One heartbeat and two steps later, Trent drew his gun, reversed the weapon in his hand and swung it in a fast, smooth movement.

The man dragging the rubber boat fell to his knees, then flat on his face. By the sound of three consecutive thuds and mumbled cursing he knew the others had gone down just as quickly.

Not a single shot fired. His cleanest takedown yet.

With a knee jammed between his man's shoulder blades, Trent wrestled the guy's wrists behind his back.

"Don't move," he said in English, then repeated the command in German.

After a half-hearted struggle, the Nazi went limp, his face planted in the sand.

Trent raised one hand in the air and caught the pair of handcuffs Kate tossed his way.

Once secure, he yanked the Nazi to his feet.

"You're under arrest," he said. "By order of the United States Government."

Eyes filled with shock and disbelief greeted the statement.

Moments later, the rest of the FBI agents spilled out of the woods. Flashlights beamed wide-arcing bars across the sand. Voices filled the air.

Once gathered together, all four saboteurs adopted the same frightened look in their gazes, as well as the same defeated angle to their shoulders. Trent eyed them closely, gauging their level of training.

These men were no soldiers. They were probably nothing more than former American citizens of German descent, recruited for their knowledge of the United States and command of the English language rather than their abilities.

"Take their weapons, shoelaces, belts, anything they can use to hurt themselves or others," Trent ordered.

These men might not have been soldiers, but they would have been trained for the possibility of capture. General Donovan's orders had been clear. He wanted the saboteurs taken alive. Suicide was not an option.

A few menacing looks from the lead FBI agent, a few threats from Trent, and information flowed out the men's lips like water through a sieve.

Trained in shorthand, Kate took on the duty of transcribing their every word.

Trent felt a grim smile tug at his lips. The Nazis, in their haste to conquer the world, were getting sloppy. They'd chosen incompetent men to make war with the United States.

He doubted the same label could be attached to William Klein. Or his assistant, Peter Sorensen.

Neither man would be pleased when he discovered how easily their plot had unraveled, or how easily the saboteurs had begun relieving themselves of pertinent information.

A nagging concern clawed through Trent. If either Klein or Sorensen found out about this takedown they would begin covering their tracks. Without concrete evidence tying them to the plot, there would be no case against either man. They would walk away free and clear.

Trent couldn't allow that to happen.

But was he already too late?

"I have to get back to town," he told Kate.

She looked up from her pad.

"We need to gather what evidence we can before Klein or Sorensen destroy it."

"Agreed." She looked back at her pad. "You'll find what you're looking for in Klein's private safe at his home."

"You tell me this now?" Kate had kept key information from him?

"I've checked every possible hiding place and have found nothing but legitimate business documents. Klein's home safe is the only one I haven't been able to crack."

Trent studied Kate's bent head. What she said made sense.

"Savannah will know the combination," she added, her hand moving quickly down the page. "She'll get you in."

"You overestimate her loyalty to me."

"No, Trent, you misunderstand. She won't open the safe to help you." Kate kept her focus on her work. "She'll do it to prove you wrong."

As if to punctuate that last statement the sound of a car engine turning over split through the air, rising above the commotion on the beach.

"And now she has a head start."

"Not for long."

Trent took off at a dead run.

Savannah pushed her foot to the floorboard, sending her car hurtling at a breakneck speed. She'd never driven this fast before. She'd never had a reason to.

Blood pounded through her veins. Was this how Johnny had

felt, this intense need to cover ground as fast as humanly possible?

Perhaps.

But Savannah wasn't running away from anyone or anything.

She was running *to* someone. Her father. With the hope of proving him innocent of Trent's accusations.

She ignored the doubts trying to make their way through her mind, ignored the snatches of thoughts and memories trying to wiggle into her consciousness.

William Klein was not a traitor to his country. But what of his assistant?

What role did Peter play in all this? What unholy influence had the Nazi had on her father?

She thought of Peter's cold eyes and hard demeanor. She'd always wondered why her father had kept him in his employ.

Was Peter the key?

Was he holding something over her father? Threatening him, perhaps?

It was possible. More than possible, especially when she remembered the impromptu conferences they'd held behind closed doors. The easy access Peter had into her father's world, the way he showed up at odd times of the day. And night.

He'd been at the house this very evening.

Covering ground fast and effectively, commandeering the curves with less finesse, Savannah still arrived home in record time.

She slowed her speed to a crawl, then swung into the drive.

Peter's car was gone. And all the lights in the house were off.

Mere hours before, Savannah had left under the protection of night. Her goal had been to find Trent and convince him they stood a chance. She'd wanted to fight to save what they'd shared.

She was still fighting. But now it was to save a life. If found guilty of treason her father would be put to death.

Savannah's mouth went dry at the thought.

Please, Lord. Please, let Trent be wrong.

With her prayer echoing in her head, she cut the engine and slammed out of the car. Making a mad dash around the back of the house she entered through the kitchen.

She skidded to a stop, suddenly frozen in fear.

A tremor of unease whipped through her.

What if Trent was right about her father? How would she ever bear the betrayal?

A clock chimed from a distant room, echoing off the walls. One chime. Two. Three. Four.

A cold, dead silence followed.

It was four o'clock in the morning.

Surely her father was still in bed.

Tiptoeing silently through the house, Savannah made her way toward his private study. If there was evidence for or against her father it would be in there. Most likely hidden in his safe.

She fumbled along the corridor, relief nearly buckling her knees. Her father's study was cast in pitch-blackness. If he was part of the Nazi plot taking place tonight he would be awake, waiting for news of the beach landing.

Hope quickened her steps. She slipped into the study and clicked the door shut behind her.

It was darker than usual, probably due to the fact that her father had drawn the curtains earlier tonight. Waiting for her eyes to adjust, Savannah pressed her back against the closed door.

Once she could see better she paced toward her father's desk. Not sure what she was looking for, she rounded the massive piece of furniture and sat in the cushioned chair. The springs creaked softly beneath her weight.

She flattened her hands on the edge of the desk, pushed backward and eyed the drawers on her right. She tugged gently on the top one. The drawer slid open. Unable to see the contents she clicked on the small lamp nearby.

The drawer was empty. As was the one below. And the one below that.

In fact, all the drawers were empty.

Just like the tool shed at the beach house.

Too many coincidences.

Savannah's hand gripped the desk for support. Was her father working with Peter, as Trent claimed? She forced herself to think objectively and considered her father's personality. William Klein was not a man to be misled easily.

All along, Savannah had thought her father had fallen prey to Peter's influence. But if that were so, if Peter was the enemy, her father would have figured it out. He would have fired Peter on the spot. Unless he shared his sympathies.

Dear God, please, no.

Where would she find her proof, one way or the other?

The safe.

No other explanation made sense.

She swung around and eyed the dreadful painting above her head. It was a landscape by an obscure German artist. Savannah tried to shrug off her misgivings. So William Klein had terrible taste in art. That didn't make him a traitor.

And yet, Savannah wondered.

Why had her father purchased only paintings by German artists? Why had he read only literature by German authors? Or touted the superiority of German engineering?

Why, why, why.

Hands shaking, she rose and eyed the painting closer. It really was rather awful.

Teeth sunk into her bottom lip, she pulled on the lower right-hand corner of the frame. The painting swung on its hinges with an eerie squeak.

One tug and she discovered the safe was locked. Expected, of course.

She blinked at the large metal box, wondering what the combination would be.

Closing her eyes, she prayed for guidance.

Lord, help me. How do I proceed?

The answer came immediately. Innocent or guilty, one thing she could always count on was her father's love for her.

Could it be that easy?

She spun the dial to the right several times, clearing it, eventually stopping at the number ten. Next, she twisted the dial back to the left, one full turn and then stopped at eleven. Back to the right. Number seventeen. And then...

Click.

The combination was her birthday. October 11, 1917.

Hands shaking harder now, she pushed down on the handle and yanked open the door. Still unsure what she was looking for, she rummaged through the papers.

Five minutes later, her eyes filled with blinding tears. In her trembling hands was the evidence Trent had spoken of. Bank drafts. Ledgers. Numbers to secret accounts.

Charts. Blueprints. Grainy photographs of various buildings.

She'd found an undeniable paper trail that proved her father was not only working with the Nazis, he was funding the regime as well.

No. *No.*

She fell back a step and the papers dropped from her fingers.

There must be an explanation.

She sank to her knees and buried her face in her hands. Breathing became a monumental challenge. She wanted to roll up in a tiny ball and beg God to take her home. Now. End this horrible, burning pain in her chest.

Rocking back and forth, she knew she was going to be sick. But a cold sense of providence anchored her rising stomach. One thought emerged: she had to find out if any of this was true.

Only one person could answer her questions definitively. Her father himself.

She lowered her hands. But then a hard piece of round metal dug into the base of her skull.

"Don't move, Savannah." The flat American accent sent chills down her spine. "Or I'll shoot."

Peter. The ruthless voice belonged to Peter Sorensen. They'd been in this situation before, in this very office. Only this time, Peter had all the power.

"Get on your feet. Slowly."

There was something in the way he put his words together she'd never heard before. Not even the last time he'd found her snooping. Raw hate. He *hated* her.

Knowing not to argue, she stood.

"Turn around."

The reflex to disobey came fast, too fast. But any bold move would play right into his hands.

Savannah pivoted around and confronted ice-cold disdain.

"You've been nothing but a problem from the start." Peter's lips curled with contempt. "Now you will pay."

Chapter Twenty-Five

Fused with the shadows, Trent moved soundlessly through the darkened house, his footsteps fast and light on the hardwood floor. Weapon drawn, its muzzle pointed to the floor, he turned down the main hallway.

Muffled sounds came from the study.

He recognized Savannah's voice, raised to an octave higher than usual. She was upset, maybe even afraid.

His chest heaved.

Someone was with her. A man. His words brusque and angry. Menace dripped from his flat, Midwestern tone.

Sorensen.

Even in anger he held to his American accent. The man was truly ruthless.

Trent increased his pace. No time to lose.

Five feet out, he heard papers flutter through the air. A woman's sharp gasp of pain followed.

His muscles trembled with rage.

Don't think, he warned himself. *Act.*

Covering the last few feet with a single step, Trent peered into the room.

A small one-bulb lamp cast the interior in flickering shadows. He ran his gaze along the perimeter, caught sight of Savannah.

Sorensen had a gun pressed to her head.

Terror like he'd never known before swarmed through his mind, thundered inside his chest. A surge of adrenaline urged him to storm the room and take out the immediate threat.

But then his training kicked in and Trent held steady. For Savannah's sake, he needed to take in the situation as a soldier, *not* a man afraid for the woman he loved. Yes, *loved*.

Grabbing a fistful of hair, Sorensen yanked Savannah's head back. "How did you get in the safe?"

A moan of pain slipped past her lips.

He pulled harder. "Tell me."

"I figured out the combination."

"How?"

"It…it is my birthday."

"Fool," Sorensen spat.

Trent forced down every ounce of emotion, his fury the hardest to control.

What he did next would determine Savannah's fate. He knew the risks and was prepared to die. But he couldn't do anything rash. Or stupid. A life hung in the balance.

Not just any life.

The life of the woman he loved.

Sacrifice one for the multitude.

That had been his motto ever since becoming a spy. He'd rationalized the loss of innocent lives for the greater good. For God and country.

He'd been wrong. So very wrong.

God didn't want innocent bloodshed, no matter the circumstance.

There was still a chance for restitution. Trent would save Savannah. At all costs.

He released a soundless breath, considered possible scenarios, gauged the best and worst of every resulting outcome.

Savannah still stood with her back to him, hands in the air, her body rigid.

Sorensen held his weapon with an unflinching hand.

The man was cold and ruthless. Trent needed to be colder, more ruthless.

And quick.

He raised his weapon.

With cool precision, he entered the room and pressed the gun to Sorensen's head.

"Let the woman go."

Sorensen gave no visible sign he'd heard the command.

"Ah, Mueller, you've arrived at last." Releasing a short, frigid laugh, he yanked Savannah against him and then spun them both around to face Trent. "But you have come too late."

Hand steady, gaze locked with his enemy, Trent drew back the hammer of his gun. "You think I won't shoot you?"

Sorensen regarded him with contempt. "We both know you would never risk the life of an innocent. That's the problem with you Americans. You let your consciences get in the way."

Trent made the mistake of glancing at Savannah. Her eyes were large and round, but she didn't look ready to buckle. She looked prepared to fight for her life.

Not fragile or vulnerable, but brave.

Everything he'd ever wanted—had never planned for or dreamed possible—was wrapped up in this woman. And he could lose it all with a single bullet.

He broke eye contact. Panic was his greatest enemy. He focused only on what he could control. One step at a time.

Keep the Nazi talking. A distracted man equaled a careless one.

"Peter Sorensen is not your real name. Who are you?"

It was the right question to ask. Pride filled the other man's eyes, revealing his greatest weakness. "I am SS Sturmbannfueh-rer Hans-Peter von Heinberg." His American accent disappeared inside a thick German one. "And you, *Captain* Mueller, are a spy for the Americans."

"Correct." Trent gave him a coldblooded grin. "But more to the point, I am part of the team that just foiled your plot to sab-otage our country."

Other than his gaze turning dark with fury, von Heinberg didn't react to the news.

"Which, I see by your lack of surprise, you already knew."

"There will be other chances to make war on your country." The man's sculpted features filled with demented glee. "This is a mere setback. In the end, we will succeed."

"No," Trent said. "We will stop you every time."

"Your overconfidence will be your downfall."

"I might say the same to you."

"Aryans are the most advanced people alive." His voice held the obsessive fanaticism Trent had witnessed in other SS offi-cers. "The Master Race is smarter, faster and more efficient than the rest of you. Russia, Great Britain, America, you will all submit in time."

Savannah chose that moment to struggle in von Heinberg's grip. "You're despicable."

He tightened his hold on her hair and then yanked. Hard. She choked back a sob, but her gaze filled with furious determina-tion.

She might be scared, but she wasn't going to give in to the emotion.

Trent felt a dangerous tenderness, followed by a bone-deep urgency to protect her from harm. The force of his emotions could endanger her.

Clearing his expression, he focused on von Heinberg. *Only* on von Heinberg. If he looked at Savannah again he might do something stupid.

Like try to be a hero.

"Let the woman go. She's of no use to you now."

"There you are wrong." The Nazi spoke in typical German succinctness. Hate flowed from him in waves. He wasn't going to release Savannah. He had too much to lose and she was his only way out alive.

Trent realized what he had to do.

He had to sacrifice himself. His life for hers. It was his only chance to save her.

There is no greater sacrifice than a man laying down his life for another.

Trent risked a glance at Savannah, letting his true feelings show in his gaze.

"Take me in her place," he said.

"Trent, no. He'll kill you." She looked at him with panicked understanding. And…love. Desperate, unmistakable love.

Another time, another place, a different situation, they could have had a future together.

"Jesus made the ultimate sacrifice for mankind." He was compelled to declare his faith out loud. "I'm not afraid to do the same for you."

Savannah's smile warmed her face and went deep into her eyes. "And I for you."

"You are both fools," von Heinberg growled. "You put your hope in a nameless, faceless deity. Hitler is the one, true god. And we, the SS, are his avenging angels."

Now or never. Trent lowered his gun.

Unprepared for the easy surrender, von Heinberg hesitated a fatal half second. His weapon moved a fraction of an inch away from Savannah's head. It was enough.

Trent dove.

A shot rang out.

The hot jolt of pain slicing up his shoulder told him he'd been hit. Not Savannah, him.

A blast of light split across his vision.

He kept moving, dragging her to the ground then covering her with his body.

Someone had entered the room. For her protection, Trent kept Savannah under him.

Angry, rapid-fire German filled the air. He recognized the newcomer's voice. William Klein.

Trent couldn't decipher the man's words before another shot rang out. And then another, this one lower-pitched. Two separate weapons discharged at one time. The ensuing howl of pain was animalistic and furious.

There came a second round of shots, one on top of the other.

A loud thud.

A second, heavier one.

Despite the blinding light in the room, Trent's vision grayed. The smell of gunpowder filled his nose.

"Savannah. *Savannah.*" He could feel her struggling beneath him. "Are you hurt?"

"No," came the breathy response. "I…I'm all right."

Relief was overcome by the mind-numbing pain in his arm. His thoughts grew hazy, swimming over one another. And then…

His world went black.

Savannah couldn't breathe, couldn't lift her head, couldn't move at all. She was trapped under Trent.

And he wasn't moving.

Panic clawed through her.

Before he'd asked her if she'd been hurt, she'd counted at least five gunshots. But there might have been more.

It had all happened so quickly.

Her breathing grew ragged, every breath painful to take.

The world had grown dark.

No, her eyes were closed.

Open your eyes.

She struggled to obey the silent command in her head. The effort made her nauseous.

There was so much noise. High-pitched, female shrieking. Her mother? Was that her mother screaming?

Savannah's heart lodged in her throat.

Had that been her father's voice she'd heard arguing with Peter? In German?

She didn't realize her father spoke fluent German. Why hadn't she known that?

Despite the confusion swirling around in her head, one bold truth threaded through all the others. Trent had jumped in front of a bullet. For her. He'd been willing to sacrifice his life. *For hers.*

He'd been right all along. About the saboteurs. About her father.

Her father. How had she been so wrong about a man she'd trusted without question all her life?

The female screaming continued, growing louder and more frantic.

At last, Savannah forced open her eyes. Trent was laid out on top of her. His breathing was dangerously shallow, his eyes closed tight.

His face was pale as death.

She croaked his name past parched lips. "Trent."

No response.

She nudged him gently. "Trent."

Still no response.

Oh, Lord, please let him be all right.

"Trent!" She prodded him harder. "Wake up."

He moaned then shifted slightly, enough to give Savannah hope.

"That's right." She wiggled her hand free and touched his cheek. "Come on, Trent, come back to me."

His eyes blinked open. Then slammed shut again.

Afraid to take her focus off him, but needing to know the danger had passed, she twisted her head to the left.

Her gaze connected with Peter's cold, lifeless eyes staring at her without ceasing. A red stream of blood trickled out of a hole just above his right eye.

Bile rose in her throat. She'd never seen death this close up before.

"Savannah," Trent whispered in a voice raw with pain. "I'm…am I hurting you?"

"No, I'm fine."

She lied, of course. She wasn't fine. She doubted she would ever be fine again. Her father was a traitor to the country she loved. Trent was a spy.

And Peter was dead.

She squeezed her eyes shut against an onslaught of helpless tears.

How would she ever recover from all the shocks and betrayals?

She wouldn't. Not alone. Not without God's help.

All things are possible through Christ who strengthens me.

Yes. She would turn to her heavenly Father instead of the earthly one who'd betrayed her trust.

She would rely on the Lord's strength. As she hadn't done before.

Trent took a slow, deep breath, groaned and then rolled off of her. With what appeared to be great effort, he lifted his head but collapsed back again.

"I just need—" he drew in a shuddering hiss "—a moment."

He didn't sound quite right. Savannah shoved to her knees.

"Breathe, Trent. That's it," she encouraged. "Just breathe. In. Out."

Advice she needed to take herself. In. Out. In. Out.

She couldn't think over all that noise. Where was that blood-curdling screaming coming from?

She pushed the question out of her mind.

Trent was hurt.

Cradling his head in her lap, Savannah ran her gaze over him. Head to foot and back again. He had one injury. Just one. His right arm was bleeding through his shirt, saturating the dark material.

"You've been shot," she said, hoping the panic she felt didn't sound in her voice.

His eyes flickered open. He winced at the harsh light, but kept his gaze on her. "I'm sorry, Savannah. For…everything."

She saw the truth in his eyes. The sorrow. The regret. The sliver of hope that all was not lost between them.

Of course there was still hope. In the ultimate show of love, he'd risked his life for hers.

She touched her lips to his forehead.

He gave her a crooked smile in return.

Unable to look away, Savannah allowed her other senses to take in the activity around them.

The screams had finally stopped. Soft, soulful sobs had taken their place.

"Ma'am, you need to move aside." Savannah lifted her gaze and found a kind-faced man staring back at her. "He needs medical attention." She didn't miss the urgency in his eyes.

She looked down at Trent. He was still so pale. "I…yes. Yes, of course."

She shifted out of the way, careful to avoid Peter's motionless body.

Only after ensuring Trent was in good hands did Savannah take in the rest of the room. She counted eight men milling around, including the two FBI agents who had shown up in the Carmen Café days ago. All eight were dressed in black, some more formally than others.

They were investigating the contents of the room in pairs. One lone man, a white-haired, craggy-looking gentleman sorted through the papers she'd found in the safe.

A sick feeling rose in her stomach. There could be no denying her father's treason now.

He would have to pay for his crime. If only she could reconcile the reality of what he'd done with the man she'd thought she'd known.

The hair on the back of her neck rose on end.

"Father." He was sprawled out on the floor just inside the doorway. Blood poured out of a spot a few inches below his ribs.

Her mother was bent over him, sobbing uncontrollably.

Savannah rushed across the room and fell to her knees. When her eyes met her father's she didn't see a Nazi or a traitor or a man who had plotted to bring war to the United States.

Blinking through her tears, she saw the man who had taught her how to tie her shoes. The man who had welcomed her home when her husband had betrayed her. The man who had called her daughter all her life.

Her heart twisted painfully in her chest. "Oh, Father."

"Savannah." He lifted his hand. She took it without question.

"I never meant to hurt you," he rasped.

Oh, but he had. He'd hurt her beyond reason. With his lies. His treasonous loyalties. His betrayal that was so much worse than what Johnny had done. Johnny's lies had only hurt her. Her father's could have cost hundreds—thousands—of lives.

"Forgive me," he whispered, his eyes blinking slowly.

Forgiveness. He wanted her to forgive him.

Savannah didn't know if she was capable. There were so many things she wanted to say to the man she'd thought was her father, so many questions that needed asking. She caught sight of her mother's face twisted in pain and horror and sorrow.

What would happen to Alma Klein now? Her whole world had been dedicated to her husband. Her husband the traitor.

Forgiveness. He asked so much of her, too much. And yet, even after all he'd done, the man was still her father. Could she offer him mercy over judgment?

It was the Christian way.

"How could you have betrayed your country?" she whispered past her shock and pain. She had to drop his hand to wipe at the tears on her cheek.

"I did it for us, Savannah. For our family's future and for... the Fatherland." The words wheezed out of his mouth. "*Always* for the Fatherland."

Savannah thought she might be sick. Her father had given his allegiance to the enemy for a reason that made no sense to her.

Did he truly believe Germany would win the war? Was that why he'd turned against his own country?

Before she could ask her father to explain, his eyes closed for the last time. In the next moment, he drew his last breath.

He would never hear her words of forgiveness. And Savannah would never know if she'd have been able to say them.

Chapter Twenty-Six

By the time the last of the FBI agents left the premises, the sun had broken free of the horizon and had turned the low-riding, frothy clouds bloodred.

Trent leaned his head back against the wall.

He had a long, painful day ahead of him.

At least the bullet from Sorensen's gun had left only a small flesh wound in Trent's bicep. He'd suffered worse. And now that the bleeding was under control, he didn't need a trip to the hospital.

His place was near Savannah, regardless of her anger and disillusionment with him.

She was talking quietly with Kate now, their heads bent together over their joined hands. He felt the urge to go to her, to pull her into his arms and offer what comfort he could.

Even if she allowed him that honor, this wasn't the time. Or the place. The coroner had barely taken away the dead bodies. Alma Klein had only just been given a sedative an hour ago and sent to her room to rest. It would take a long time, perhaps days, for her to recover her strength.

There were a lot of hard questions that needed answering, by both Savannah and her mother. But not now. Not today.

An older, heavyset man with intelligent, inquisitive eyes

stopped beside Trent, a hint of sadness evident on his lined face. "I predict a lot of fallout from this one."

"Treason is always messy, General."

Donovan nodded. "True enough. At least we have the saboteurs in custody and they're talking." He turned his attention to where Savannah sat speaking with Kate. "The woman and her mother will have to be debriefed."

The woman and her mother. Not Savannah. Not Alma or Mrs. Klein. In the eyes of the government, they were related to a proven traitor with heavy suspicion still hanging over their heads.

"I'd like to conduct the interviews myself," Trent requested. He would get the information the government needed without hurting either woman more than absolutely necessary.

He couldn't say the same of any other operative.

Donovan paused before responding to the request. "Can I trust you to be impartial?"

"You can trust me to uncover the truth," Trent answered honestly. "But it'll take time."

"Something we don't have."

"Sir, I—"

Before he could finish, Donovan batted his objection away with an impatient wave of his hand. "You have two days to wrap things up here. Then I want you back in Washington for your next assignment."

Two days. More than Trent had expected. Less than he needed. "Thank you, sir."

Donovan rewarded him with a craggy smile, nodded at Kate then left the room.

Kate waited until General Donovan was gone before she worked her hands free from Savannah's and rose to her feet.

Head still bent, Savannah remained where she was. Her hair curtained her face. But from the set of her shoulders Trent could tell she was worn out and weary.

What if she wasn't able to handle all the betrayals? What if she—

No. Savannah was brave and strong. She would get through this.

Trent would help her.

"How is she?" he asked the moment Kate stopped beside him, uncaring that he wasn't doing a very good job of pretending he didn't have feelings for Savannah.

Giving him an understanding smile, Kate squeezed his shoulder. "She's devastated but not broken, stronger than any of us realized. Still." Kate sighed heavily. "Go easy on her, Trent. At least at first."

"That's the plan." He pushed away from the wall.

Seeing him, Savannah stood abruptly and hurried toward the bay of windows overlooking the river. She turned her back to the room, the gesture effectively shutting him out.

He moved in her direction, anyway.

When Kate matched him step for step, he felt the warrior rise up in him. "I want to speak with her alone."

Kate shook her head but didn't fight him on the matter. "Remember what I said."

"Go easy." He cleared his throat, impatience welling inside him. "Got it."

"I'll be just outside if you need me," Kate said.

Trent waited for her to leave the room before completing the short trek to Savannah.

He kept his steps slow. But his breathing had turned harsh, even to his own ears.

And then he was by her side, standing next to her, feeling her agony as if it were his own.

"Savannah, I know you've suffered a terrible shock, but it might comfort you to know your father was the one who shot Peter."

She didn't respond.

He reached out to her but then thought better of it. Not yet. He shouldn't touch her yet. "His love for you was stronger than his loyalty to the Fatherland."

She wrapped her arms around her waist and drew in a ragged breath. "It's supposed to be cloudy outside. Where's the rain?" A tear slid down her cheek. "The sky should be crying for all the loss here today."

He didn't know what to say to that.

Sighing, she turned her head toward his. More tears swam in her eyes, those deep, expressive eyes that had grabbed him the second he'd seen her across the dance floor.

He couldn't lose her now, not when he'd only just found her. He'd always scoffed at the idea of wartime romances, how the danger supposedly heightened emotions to a fever pitch.

Now he understood.

No matter how this had all started, he loved her now, beyond reason, beyond his best efforts to remain impartial to her feminine charms. That, he realized, was the nature of love.

"Savannah, I'm sorry."

She didn't acknowledge his words.

"I'm sorry for lying to you. For betraying your trust. For... everything."

Her bottom lip quivered and then...

The rest of her tears broke free, sliding unfettered down her cheeks.

Feeling powerless, so utterly helpless, he pulled her into his arms and held her tightly against his chest.

His grandfather had once said that a man had to feel the loss before he could experience the gain. Trent now knew what the older man had meant. He'd nearly lost Savannah this morning. And now that he had her in his arms, he wasn't going to let her go.

He buried his face in her hair. "I love you."

* * *

Savannah let Trent's words settle over her, slowly, poignantly. He was so careful with her, holding her tightly and yet oh-so-gently against his powerful chest.

The realization that she loved him in return came at a cost. Love required trust. She'd once put her trust in Johnny Elliott. He'd betrayed her.

She'd put her trust in her father.

He, too, had betrayed her.

Could she trust Trent now?

She'd sensed from the moment they'd met that he wasn't what he seemed. Her instincts had been right. But now she knew the real man beneath the carefully orchestrated façade.

Trent Mueller was a man of courage and conviction, a man willing to sacrifice everything, including his own life for his country. And for her.

The truth shall set you free.

"I love you, too," she whispered into his shirt, not quite brave enough to look in his eyes. "But what about…my father? How can you look at me and not think of him?"

"Because you're not him, you're you. From the start I was unable to put the two of you in the same category in my mind." He pulled back and placed his finger under her chin. "I shouldn't ask this of you, but can you forgive me for coming to you under false pretenses?"

Forgiveness. It always came back to that.

"I understand why you lied," she said, not quite answering his question.

Was the act of understanding his motives the same as forgiving him?

Three men had betrayed her. Two were dead. One was staring into her eyes with rough honesty in his gaze.

With his jaw darkened by stubble, his intensity focused solely on her, Trent was no longer a mystery to her. She was fully aware of the warrior beneath the handsome exterior. She'd seen him in action this morning, knew how deadly he could be if the situation warranted. His *skills* were extensive.

But she wasn't afraid of him. On the contrary, she recognized the deep code of ethics he lived by.

"Savannah, you didn't answer my question." His words were a cross between a demand and a plea. "I need to know if you forgive me."

Could she forgive him?

Saying the words was only the first step. The hard work would come later. One day at a time. But in order to forgive Trent she would have to forgive Johnny and her father first.

Jesus had suffered betrayal as well. The worst possible kind. And yet, he'd asked His Father to forgive his betrayers. *For they know not what they do.*

If Jesus could forgive like that, then Savannah needed to find it in her heart to do so as well.

Lord, help me say the words and mean them.

"Yes, Trent. I forgive you."

Her heart instantly lifted, as if a tight band had been removed from around her chest.

Smiling the lazy smile she'd grown to love, Trent pulled her back into his arms and lowered his head slowly, giving her a chance to turn away.

She held steady.

"I won't let you down," he promised, his face inches from hers.

"I know."

The moment their lips met, a sense of peace fell over her.

This was where she belonged. In Trent's arms.

He eventually drew his head away. "Let me take care of you, Savannah, as no man has ever done before."

"You really think I need to be taken care of?"

"I think you are a strong, independent, capable woman who can take care of herself." He pressed a finger to her lips when she tried to speak over him. "But that doesn't mean I don't want to love and protect you for the rest of my life."

Such pretty words. "But we've only known each other for such a short amount of time and you'll have to leave for another assignment soon."

Savannah hesitated. She had her mother to think of now. She feared Alma Klein would never be the same after her husband's betrayal. Savannah understood that sort of pain. She would have to be strong for her mother in the coming weeks.

Trent's voice broke through her musings. "I seem to remember a very smart woman once telling me that we could start slow, with letters and phone calls at first."

"Is that what you want?" she asked. "A slow courtship?"

"I want you to be certain of your feelings for me." His smile disappeared. "As long as the war continues, I can't promise anything but sporadic communication and short visits."

"I…understand." And she did, more than she would have thought possible a few days ago. The role that Trent performed for the war effort was important. Too important to expect him to put her ahead of his duties.

In war everyone had to make sacrifices.

"What do you say, Savannah?" He traced his fingertip along her jaw. "Will you take a chance on me? On us? Will you let me prove I'm a man worthy of both your trust and your love?"

The idea of giving her heart to this man was exhilarating. And terrifying. But she'd discovered that love wasn't always easy. It required hard work.

Savannah had never been afraid of hard work.

"Yes, Trent." She stared at him and saw kindness, patience, compassion. The character traits that had always been a part of him. "Let's give it a try."

Epilogue

Two years later

Savannah spun in a slow circle, the fluorescent lights causing her head to ache. She didn't care. Today was the happiest day of her life to date. "Well, Kate, how do I look?"

"Oh, Savannah, you look like a bride." Her friend sighed.

Smiling despite the depressing surroundings, Savannah pivoted to face the row of mirrors in the woman's bathroom of the General Hospital in Washington D.C.

"I *do* look like a bride," she said, her smile broadening. "Even in my uniform."

At the last minute, she'd decided against the customary wedding gown and had chosen to wear her WACs uniform instead. She was, after all, getting married in an Army hospital. Considering the unique venue, a wedding dress hadn't seemed appropriate.

It hardly matter what she wore. What mattered was the ceremony itself.

"I'm really going to marry him," she whispered, her fingertips fluttering across her lips.

If it had been up to Savannah, she'd have married Trent long ago. Right after the debriefing that hadn't been nearly as painful as she'd expected.

Probably because Trent had been gentle in his questioning.

When the idea of marriage had come up, he'd insisted on waiting, declaring she had to be absolutely certain of her decision. He didn't want to start their life together with a single doubt in her mind.

So, they'd taken a slower, more traditional route for their courtship.

The sporadic letters and crackling phone calls had lasted a total of three months. Trent had been the one to grow impatient first. Savannah hadn't been far behind. He'd moved both her and her mother to Washington right after that. They'd been able to spend more time together, whenever he was stateside.

Savannah couldn't say that she liked their time apart. The worry often brought her to her knees. Quite *literally* to her knees. Where she'd promptly handed over her fears to God.

Even now, with the war still going on, some days proved harder than others.

She'd joined the Army recently, determined to do her part for the war effort, just like the man she loved.

The situation hadn't been ideal, but bearable.

Then Trent had come home two weeks ago, injured badly enough to warrant an extended stay at this Army hospital. Savannah had put an end to the nonsense. No more waiting.

She'd proposed to Trent herself.

He'd been absolutely powerless to refuse her. A faint smile curved her lips at the memory.

"What's put that happy look on your face?" Kate asked, propping her chin on Savannah's shoulder from behind.

"I'm remembering my marriage proposal." She laughed. "I finally had Trent right where I wanted him."

Kate lifted a single eyebrow. "A man in traction can hardly

run away, Savannah. Not that Trent would have done any running had he been able. He loves you."

"And I love him."

"A happy ending." Kate stepped back. "And now all your favorite people are here to witness the blessed occasion of your wedding."

As if hitting her cue perfectly, Savannah's mother swept into the bathroom. Savannah turned and studied her. Alma Klein was still painfully thin, but the haunted, grief-stricken look was no longer in her eyes.

Savannah had to believe she would eventually recover from the loss of her husband and the events that had surrounded his death.

"Oh, my darling." She rushed forward and kissed Savannah's cheek. "You're positively glowing."

"I'm happy, Mother, so very happy." The war was still going on, but Trent was alive. He was home. And they were about to become husband and wife.

"Then let's get you married," Kate said, all but shoving her toward the exit.

Her steps light, Savannah practically glided down the hall toward the private room where Trent and an Army chaplain waited.

Upon entering the room, her eyes went straight to her future husband. He was looking back at her—staring, actually. The bruising and contusions on his face were still evident, but they'd lessened considerably over the past week.

She would not think about how they got there. She would only think about right now. Trent was safe. And he was hers. All hers.

Whether or not they had one day together or countless years, she would consider every moment a gift from God.

He smiled. And her breath caught in her throat.

Even in a hospital bed, wearing simple pajamas and a robe, he was the most handsome man she knew.

And she couldn't stop staring at him.

Seconds ticked by, pounding in perfect rhythm with her heartbeat, and yet, Savannah remained where she was, actually captivated into immobility by the man she was about to marry.

The chaplain cleared his throat.

Slowly becoming aware of the other people in the room, Savannah took several more swallows of air.

Trent lifted his hand to her. She was by his side at once.

He placed a kiss on her knuckles. "Hello, beautiful."

His familiar, rich baritone washed over her like liquid silver, sending a pleasant anticipation through her.

"Hello, Trent."

He smiled again and her heart skipped a beat. He really was quite handsome, tawny and golden, with his strong jaw and sculpted cheekbones. Even with shadows under his eyes and bruises on his face, he took her breath away.

"I love you, Savannah."

"I love you, too."

He pulled her on the bed with him. Not wanting to hurt him, she perched gingerly on the edge.

He tugged her closer. "Ready to start our life together as husband and wife at last?"

Overwhelmed by emotion, she gave him a shaky smile. A lifetime with this man wouldn't be enough. Not nearly enough. But it was a good start. "Oh, yes."

"Well, then, let's begin." The chaplain stepped forward and opened his Bible. "Dearly beloved…"

* * * * *

Dear Reader,

Thank you for taking a trip back to 1943 with me. I so loved exploring this time period, when patriotism was at its zenith in this country. As my father often says, it was a great time to be an American. I believe that's still true. God Bless America!

Although Trent and Savannah's story is completely fictional, Hitler's terrorist attack on the United States was real. Operation Pastorius was a well-thought-out, well-planned attempt to sabotage key targets in America. Hitler knew the only way to win the war was to stop the U.S. industrial might. He failed, of course. But the story of his attempt is a fascinating one. I believe more so because of its lack of success.

I also want to take a moment to give my father a quick shout-out. He was invaluable in the research of this book. He lived through the war and was a proud member of the U.S. Navy. Although not an eyewitness to the Nazis' attempt to sabotage America, he lived mere miles away from where the saboteurs landed in Ponte Vedra Beach, Florida. I grew up near the spot as well. I can no longer walk along the beach or look up at the sand dunes without thinking about what might have happened had the Germans succeeded. I'm glad we'll never know.

I always love to hear from readers. You can contact me at www.reneeryan.com.

In Him,
Renee Ryan

Questions for Discussion

1. In the opening scenes, Savannah is struggling with her grief over her husband's death and the resulting gossip. Do you think the scandalous circumstances surrounding the night he died have made it harder for her to grieve him? Why or why not?

2. What is Trent's main goal when we first meet him at Savannah's party? How does he plan to accomplish the task? What is his rationale for what he's planning to do? Do you believe, like Trent, that the end justifies the means in times of war? Why or why not?

3. What did the Nazis have planned for the United States? If they had been successful in bringing the war to American soil, what would that have looked like? Do you think it's harder to be moved by a war that isn't fought on your own soil? If so, why?

4. Early in the story the reader discovers that Savannah distrusts her father's assistant, Peter Sorensen. Do you think she has a genuine reason to distrust him, or is her suspicion based on leftover feelings regarding her husband? Have you ever had a past event color your opinions? Explain.

5. Why did Savannah take a job as a bookkeeper at a local shipyard? What has happened in her life as a result? Have you ever found healing in your own life through a similar means? When was the turning point for you?

6. Why did Trent agree to help Savannah search Peter's office? What did he hope to gain? He utilizes "skills" he

claims he learned in the Army, but where did he really get those skills? Do you think clandestine warfare is a viable option in some cases? Why or why not?

7. Savannah's father is a connoisseur of all things German. What are the dangers of such a passion? When does a passion become an obsession? How can a person keep from stepping over the line?

8. Why do you think wartime romances occurred so often during World War II? Do you think people can fall in love that quickly? Why or why not?

9. Savannah's mother focused her entire life around her husband's. Do you think this was a wise move on her part? What else could she have done? Have you ever sacrificed your own dream for someone else's? What was the result?

10. Throughout the book Savannah struggles with the issue of forgiveness. What are her specific challenges, especially in terms of betrayal? What conclusion does she come to about forgiveness in the end? Have you held on to a hurt for too long? What would be required for you to release the offending party?

11. Trent rationalizes his behavior as a spy with the notion that it's often necessary to sacrifice one in order to save the multitude. Do you think this is true? Why or why not? What conclusion does Trent come to in the end? What does he do to show that he's changed his mind about the sacrifice of an innocent?

INSPIRATIONAL

Inspirational romances to warm your heart & soul.

H I S T O R I C A L

TITLES AVAILABLE NEXT MONTH

Available October 11, 2011

MARRYING THE MAJOR
Victoria Bylin

FAMILY BLESSINGS
Amish Brides of Celery Fields
Anna Schmidt

ONCE UPON A THANKSGIVING
Linda Ford & Winnie Griggs

UNLAWFULLY WEDDED BRIDE
Noelle Marchand

REQUEST YOUR FREE BOOKS!

2 FREE INSPIRATIONAL NOVELS
PLUS 2
FREE
MYSTERY GIFTS

Love Inspired

HISTORICAL
INSPIRATIONAL HISTORICAL ROMANCE

YES! Please send me 2 FREE Love Inspired® Historical novels and my 2 FREE mystery gifts (gifts are worth about $10). After receiving them, if I don't wish to receive any more books, I can return the shipping statement marked "cancel". If I don't cancel, I will receive 4 brand-new novels every month and be billed just $4.49 per book in the U.S. or $4.99 per book in Canada. That's a saving of at least 22% off the cover price. It's quite a bargain! Shipping and handling is just 50¢ per book in the U.S. and 75¢ per book in Canada.* I understand that accepting the 2 free books and gifts places me under no obligation to buy anything. I can always return a shipment and cancel at any time. Even if I never buy another book, the two free books and gifts are mine to keep forever.

102/302 IDN FEHF

Name	(PLEASE PRINT)	
Address		Apt. #
City	State/Prov.	Zip/Postal Code

Signature (if under 18, a parent or guardian must sign)

Mail to the Reader Service:
IN U.S.A.: P.O. Box 1867, Buffalo, NY 14240-1867
IN CANADA: P.O. Box 609, Fort Erie, Ontario L2A 5X3

Not valid for current subscribers to Love Inspired Historical books.

Want to try two free books from another series?
Call 1-800-873-8635 or visit www.ReaderService.com.

* Terms and prices subject to change without notice. Prices do not include applicable taxes. Sales tax applicable in N.Y. Canadian residents will be charged applicable taxes. Offer not valid in Quebec. This offer is limited to one order per household. All orders subject to credit approval. Credit or debit balances in a customer's account(s) may be offset by any other outstanding balance owed by or to the customer. Please allow 4 to 6 weeks for delivery. Offer available while quantities last.

Your Privacy—The Reader Service is committed to protecting your privacy. Our Privacy Policy is available online at www.ReaderService.com or upon request from the Reader Service.

We make a portion of our mailing list available to reputable third parties that offer products we believe may interest you. If you prefer that we not exchange your name with third parties, or if you wish to clarify or modify your communication preferences, please visit us at www.ReaderService.com/consumerschoice or write to us at Reader Service Preference Service, P.O. Box 9062, Buffalo, NY 14269. Include your complete name and address.

LIH11B